PRISONERS OF CULTURE

George A. Pettitt

PRISONERS
OF CULTURE

CHARLES SCRIBNER'S SONS · New York

Printed in the United States of America

Library of Congress Catalog Card Number 68–57070

CONTENTS

FOREWORD

This book grows out of more than two decades of study and discussion of the ways in which human societies, primitive and civilized, throughout the world, have approached the problem of transmitting knowledge from one generation to the next and of socializing children for reasonably satisfactory participation in the culture to which they are born.

The more one learns about the unexpected and often curious similarities and differences between culture patterns and the peoples who carry them—and sometimes would rather die than allow them to be changed—the more one is impelled to try to explain the culture-creating process and its tendency to elaborate and become more complex even while its owners are apparently struggling to protect it against change and voicing nostalgic regret over changes which have already occurred.

If one yields to this temptation to know and hunts diligently for the scattered and fragmentary evidence which seems relevant, he finds himself engaged not only in study of hominid culture growth over the last million years or so, but in a farther-reaching inquiry into the culture-creating propensity which blossomed on the branch of the primate order to which human beings belong but which has roots as old as the first centralized nervous systems in the multicelled organisms which built the animal kingdom.

This book tries to summarize the results of such a study and to discuss a few of the conclusions to which it must inevitably lead. More specifically, it seeks to formulate some of the disconcerting questions roused by such cultural dinosaurs as American civilization. Is man walking the dog or is his pet walking him? Does contemporary man really want to go in the direction he is moving, and at a constantly accelerating pace? Obviously a single volume can do no more than lay a foundation for so vast a subject, but enforced brevity may be an advantage, since many problems of modern civilization go unanswered because the key to the situation is lost in a welter of details. One glance from the top of a mountain can often yield better orientation than a month of walking in canyon bottoms. To those who object to exploring without a transit and a chain one might reply, with the nineteenth-century English biologist, Thomas H. Huxley: "If a little knowledge is dangerous, where is the man who has so much as to be out of danger?"

Scholars in the atmospheric sciences point out that until the weather forecaster has electronic computers capable of handling the countless variables involved in meteorological phenomena, he should confine himself to probabilities and not confuse the issue by seeking detailed accuracy. Hopefully, this book proceeds in that way as it considers the problem of man in relation to culture. Just as a meteorologist tries to establish the magnitude of a weather movement by working out isobars, or lines of equal barometric pressure over considerable areas of the earth's surface, I shall try, in all humility, to establish the isobars which instinct and custom create and to indicate possible relationships between these parameters and the personality storms which lead to truancy from educational opportunity, delinquent and criminal rebellion against cultural rules, retreat from reality into mental illness, and the anomie of job fragmentation in industry, unemployment, and compulsory leisure.

Many writers have already analyzed American civilization in great detail.[1] This book does not take issue with these observers, or any others. For it intends to add perspective to their opinions, stepping completely out of modern civilization and taking a good look at basic assumptions which escape consideration because they share a kind of diplomatic immunity called, in this case, *a priori.*

Of course, I know no more than any other commentator about the exact goal of man on earth, or whether the trend of civilization represents progress toward that goal, whatever it may be. What is of concern here is whether man can assimilate all the ingenious benefits of civilization, at the accelerating rate now viewed with such pride. There is much evidence that not all individuals can survive childhood unscarred or can live out the rest of their lives in a satisfactory way, when confronted by the demands and tensions of highly complex, industrialized, and urbanized civilization. On this, one need only examine the case history files of psychiatrists and general practitioners. There, in each individual case, the clinician tries to identify particular early experiences or current situations which directly precipitated the trouble. One may do the same with truants from school, juvenile delinquents in general, and criminals. But this book intends to emphasize the over-all differences between the demands imposed by simple cultures and by complex cultures on the tolerance of the central nervous system.

As far as available tests show, the average infant born to face civilization is not essentially different from the infant born in any of the major primitive societies which persisted down to modern times. Indeed, it has been said that infants the world over are so much alike that any group of healthy specimens could be switched with any other group of healthy specimens and neither would meet any insurmountable difficulty in achieving the cultural expectations of the society into which they were adopted, provided that they were not handicapped by the prejudices of their foster parents or their new community neighbors regarding such superficial matters as skin color, hair texture, eye shape, and the like. This cannot be proved, of course, but neither can one produce scientific evidence to disprove it. To carry this point further, nothing about the size of brain cavities, or details of skeletal structure, indicates that modern infants are substantially different from those born to Cro-Magnon parents in the Old Stone Age, perhaps twenty-five to thirty thousand years ago.

This is not said to disparage the current heirs of American or any other civilization, but to illustrate the kind of fact which anthropological evidence injects into a study of civilization. One species within the order primate, known scientifically as *Homo sapiens,* has proved to be so flexible and adaptable that, for tens of thousands of years, it has survived every problem with which nature and hominid ingenuity have confronted it, with no observable major change in body design, fuel system, wiring, or electrical supply. Small wonder that men go on elaborating civilization with the tacit assumption that the average infant has a potential for adaptation to the products of culture-changing minds which is, like the vast reaches of outer space, without any limit which, presently, can be either perceived or conceived. Yet one may question whether this tacit assumption is justified.

When one turns to man's relation to his own culture, whatever it may be, he recognizes that loyalty to that culture is essential to the survival of the society which supports it. But loyalty to an idea does not necessarily prove that the customs built around it are normatively right or good. Rather, when considering one's own culture, one tends to ignore the possibility that it may be wrong. One is satisfied to note errors in other cultures and even try to correct them, in the case of Adolf Hitler's culture, for example, or that maintained by the Communist Party.

Alertness to the normal distribution of ocular motes and beams would promote objective examination of man as a culture-producing primate and lead one to understand that customs have tended to develop accidentally rather than by group plan. The course of a road may have been set by a cow seeking a short-cut to her barn. As will appear later, some such process has influenced the development of America's awe-inspiring faith in universal, compulsory education and its crusading ardor to have machines take the place of man in industry, and it should be added, of women in the household. One cannot study the normal antipathy of man to culture change without concluding that America's almost religious faith in change is an acquired abnormality. Contemporary Americans have come to look forward to change and to live in expectation of it, much as Muslims, in the past at least, have dreamed of entering Heaven on a white horse.

American attitudes toward culture change have fostered an environment which is highly satisfactory only to the most adaptable of adults. It is least satisfactory to juveniles who arrive on earth with certain instinctive expectancies developed over a million years of selection for survival under Stone Age conditions. Children are the guinea pigs of civilization. They are brought into the world by parents themselves often raised in the isolation of the nuclear family and therefore rather uncertain about the correct behavior for parents. Civilization makes it difficult for parents to welcome unplanned children. Until very recently intelligent planning of families has been discouraged. The burden of surviving an unplanned or openly opposed arrival has fallen upon the infant. When these child guinea pigs are old enough, adults try to condition them for adult life by caging them in school for many hours a day. Perhaps the object of this is to make adult life seem good by contrast. Those who do not weather the process may end in hospitals, or in prisons, or in their graves.

So far, adults have not studied their guinea pigs to determine what was best for them but have hoped that those who survived the treatment would eventually produce a race of more highly civilized little pigs. This book proposes to inquire into the possibility that observing the reaction of the guinea pigs might give better guidance for improving civilization.

George A. Pettitt

PRISONERS OF CULTURE

CHAPTER I

Man in Perspective

There are on record a number of cases of persistent amnesia in which the afflicted individual loses memory of his own identity and of all past experiences that might help him to recover it, yet retains enough factual knowledge and patterned personality to function as an approximately normal human being, able to deal with the problem of survival and to plan his future life without reference to the identity he has lost. To a limited extent, everyone has this same kind of experience; his memory of childhood picks up at some varying number of years after birth, and the earlier part of life drifts beyond reach of the conscious mind.

Human societies suffer from a similar affliction. They have no conscious memory of their birth and early development. Except for the fragments it may pick up from recorded history, every society suffers from what one might label *sociocultural amnesia*. At any given moment in time, it finds itself equipped with a body of knowledge and patterns of beliefs and behavior accumulated over the course of years under circumstances lost to the collective memory. An individual victim of amnesia may be helped to bear his affliction by hope that some day, somewhere, he will find his lost identity. Society, however, needs a background for its self-pride. It also needs to justify what it does and thinks in the eyes and minds of oncoming generations. So it fabricates a past out of myths and legends which can be woven into a tapestry large enough to account for everything of societal concern in the observable universe and sufficiently intricate to explain new discoveries as they are made.

Although one primary object of a manufactured past is always to rationalize the social *status quo*, it also attempts to establish societal goals and ideals of behavior for the future. But it is also necessary to account for cultural changes imposed by force, or given irresistible popularity by respected leaders. Either the tapestried backdrop which adds grace to the past must be reworked, or supplementary tapestries must be woven. The latter is the case with rapidly changing cultures such as those making up Western civilization. The tapestry covering cracks in the oldest wall of the cultural palace is gradually overlaid with new designs; but in addition, as new walls are built, other tapestries are prepared to supplement the first one. Expanding technology and new knowledge are picked up, thus providing a different past, present, and future, and inconsistencies with the original are courteously ignored. True, the weavers of new tapestries exercise personal curiosity by delving into the truth or falsity of the master tapestry. But they do so as antiquarians commenting on a treasured museum piece rather than as reformers. Their activities are tolerated because the dead past is believed to have little bearing on the present in any event, and bizarre discoveries may be accepted as a subject for amused conversation rather than serious discussion.

Yet factual knowledge about man's past has been accumu-

4

lating so rapidly in recent years that naïveté about human history is no longer universally accepted as sophistication. What anthropology has to offer by way of fossil evidence and extrapolations from world-wide crosscultural studies of primitive societies often gives a new perspective on otherwise obscure problems of the present and future.

Not much more than three hundred years ago, a brilliant Irish theologian, James Ussher—who earned an appointment as Regius Professor of Divinity in the University of Dublin at the early age of twenty-six—believed that he could prove from internal evidence in the Bible that man was created in 4004 B.C. Although his logic was later questioned, it had wide acceptance for a time, appeared as a marginal note in the King James version of the Bible, and probably contributed to Ussher's eventual appointment as Archbishop of Armagh. His experience indicates that embellishments on an existing belief, even though the incidental confirmations they offer are false, will be avidly accepted; the originator continues to be respected as one whose intentions were good even though he was mistaken. On the other hand, a contemporary young French theological scholar, Isaac de la Peyrère, concluded from internal evidence in the Bible that man must have existed before Adam. This tore a hole in the tapestry of the Christian past rather than embellished it, and Peyrère received short shrift. He was forced to recant this heresy and his books were burned by the public hangman— evidence of the seventeenth-century treatment of those who put holes in tapestries.

When Charles Darwin wrote *On the Origin of Species by Natural Selection,* about one hundred and ten years ago, the great English naturalist was sufficiently aware of popular sentiment to avoid specific application of his theory of evolution to the development of man, but this did not save him from verbal castigation for his obvious implications. Benjamin Disraeli, later Prime Minister of Great Britain, remarked in a speech at

Oxford: "What is the question now placed before society with the glib assurance which to me is most astonishing? That question is this: Is man an ape or an angel? I, my lord, I am on the side of the angels. I repudiate with indignation and abhorrence those new-fangled theories."

Despite this reluctance to alter accepted explanations concerning the origin of man and the past history of the earth, evidence calling for a change continued to accumulate. Stone tools, and skulls so different from those of modern man as to be characterized as pathological, began to turn up in increasing numbers as a result of construction excavations and cave explorations in England, Belgium, Gibraltar, Germany, and France. Deliberate search for evidence eventually brought finds of Stone Age tools to the tens of thousands and skeletal remains of their makers and users to several hundreds. Recently, largely as a result of advances in nuclear physics, it has become possible to date these finds with reasonable accuracy, using as a time clock the unvarying rate of decay of carbon 14 to carbon 12, and that of potassium 40 to argon 40. The former method can be used on organic structures which ceased to live up to thirty thousand or perhaps as long as fifty thousand years ago; the latter method provides a time scale for dating archeological deposits which are a million or more years old. Equally important for determining the relative age of isolated fossil finds has been the discovery of a number of actual living sites of ancient man. From these, by meticulous study of the remains of what he discarded as garbage, one can glean at least rough conclusions about his ways of life and levels of culture.

Although much is yet to be learned about the history of man—and there is every hope of learning more in the future—enough is known to permit drawing a few general, tentative conclusions about those factors which made early hominids unique among even closely related forms of life on earth, and about the probable motivations which led them up the ladder of culture, from making tools by breaking pebbles to planning spaceships for a trip to the moon. The available material evidence about the time elapsed since the first primate identifiable as a true hominid appeared on earth is still sparse and widely scattered, perhaps because relatively little of the surface of the earth has been intensively searched. Further, organic matter eventually decays or disintegrates unless it chances to be left in a spot favorable for preservation. Stone tools, of course, do last, and skeletal bones, teeth, tusk ivory, and horn resist the ravages of time quite well under circumstances which lead to petrification or protection from the elements. Only rarely do softer tissues of animals or plants survive, as a result of freezing in glaciers, immersion in the chemically strong dampness of bogs, or desiccation in extremely dry caves. Long-used living sites are often identifiable by foot-packed earth and accumulations of detritus, organic or inorganic. After the domestication of fire, lenses of carbon occur, and on occasion bits of heat-hardened clay used to build up hearths offer their testimony about the uses to which the fire was put.

Despite limitations, the bulk of evidence has steadily grown, and together with obvious implications concerning the behavior of early men, as contrasted with that of other animals and of modern primitive groups, such evidence offers an improved perspective on the nature of man, on his relationship to modern cultural practices, and on the direction in which so-called progress appears to be moving.

The best place to begin a search for such a perspective is with the earliest known hominids on earth and with the essential question of why they began the accelerating process of culture accumulation. That process started and proceeded too slowly to be regarded as a miracle; yet it is a mystery because closely related lines of primates have demonstrated that it was possible to survive without bothering about culture. The only serious threat to the continued successful existence of the great apes, to be specific, is their distant cousin, man, his cultural weapons, and his ideas about how the surface of the earth should best be used.

The earliest tool-using hominid for whom there exists the kind of record that a living site provides was active in the Olduvai Gorge, in Tanzania (formerly Tanganyika), East Africa, at least 1,750,000 years ago by potassium-argon dating. There is some question about which of two somewhat different varieties of hominid actually occupied and owned the living site. The skull of an *Australopithecus* was found on the site, but one of the discoverers, Dr. L. S. B. Leakey, has questioned whether the Australopithecine was an actual tenant or just the remains of a dinner left by another early hominid that Leakey calls *Homo habilis*, living in the same area at the same time. For this discussion, it makes little difference. A number of Australopithecine remains have been found in southern and eastern Africa and the gross characteristics pertinent to this inquiry can best be taken from these remains.

The Australopithecines were not much larger than a modern ape, such as the chimpanzee, but they differed from any known ape in a number of crucial respects. Their brain cavities were somewhat larger, their jaws less massive, and their teeth more human than simian in size and configuration. Moreover, the *foramen magnum*, the aperture in the base of the skull through which the brain connects to the post-cranial nervous system, was more appropriate for an animal that locomoted on his hind feet, with his head balanced on top of a spinal column, than for a quadruped with his head cantilevered on the end of a horizontal spinal girder. This evidence for bipedal locomotion is confirmed by the structure of the pelvis and the shape of the femur bone. *Australopithecus* clearly ran on his hind legs, even though he may not yet have developed the free-swinging leg movement required for continuous walking.

Probably the differences which distinguished early hominids from other primates were involved in the concatenation of circumstances which led to regular and extensive use and manufacture of stone tools. But this is only part of the story. The living site in Olduvai Gorge showed that the occupants differed from apes in the degree of dependence they placed on meat as a dietary staple. Along with numerous fractured stone pebbles which can be identified as having been gathered and brought to the spot from distant places, there were numerous bones of game animals. That these first hominids were relatively inefficient and not overly confident of themselves as hunters appears from the debris, which was made up of the bones of small game animals or the young of larger game animals. This fact implies not only caution about the size and strength of the game being tackled, but a lack of acquired ability to hunt cooperatively, in groups. The early hominids lacked the physical strength, speed, jaw configuration, and teeth of the selectively evolved pack-hunting carnivores. Apparently they also lacked weapons of sufficient range and effectiveness to compensate for their physical handicaps, not to mention the want of a communication system adequate for strategic planning in advance and tactical maneuvering in action. Besides almost certain lack of a spoken language, there is no evidence that early hominids knew the use of fire.

The epoch-opening achievements of this early hominid, whether *Australopithecus* or *Homo habilis*, cannot be accounted for by citing his differences from other contemporary animals. That he *was* a mammal and basically like other primates laid the foundation for both his ability and his desire to approach the problem of survival in a new way. The great apes and hominids share so many similarities that it would be exhausting to enumerate them. Skeletally they are, bone for bone, variants of one basic structural design. Even when modern men are compared with living apes, their anatomy and physiology are

9

strongly reminiscent one of the other. Female apes, like female hominids, have relatively short estrous cycles, are more or less receptive to male attentions throughout the year, have relatively long gestation periods, and usually give birth to single infants who are completely dependent on the mother for a long period and require many years to mature fully. Apes can walk on their hind legs and will do so on occasion, particularly if they want to look impressive or grasp or carry something in their hands. Despite the shortness of their thumbs, apes can oppose them to other fingers and can perform delicate manipulations with more success, sometimes, than their human observers. Their eyesight is binocular, stereoscopic, color-sensitive, and closely comparable to that of the hominids. They exhibit outward manifestations of emotion comparable to those shown by man. Under pressure, in captivity, apes reveal far greater learning and problem-solving capacity than they would normally need, or have been observed to use in the wild. Their relationship to the hominids is further confirmed by blood groups, by susceptibility to many diseases common among human beings, and even by sharing with man a family of body lice not encountered elsewhere. Hominids and other primates may differ widely in outward appearance, but under the skin, if a louse's sense of taste can be trusted, they are not so different after all.

Modern apes and monkeys offer at least auxiliary information on what the ancestors of modern man might have been like two million years ago. They are not lineally related; that is, man is not an ape that has succeeded, nor is the ape a man fallen on hard times. The two happen to occupy separate branches of the same evolutionary tree; no one knows what their common ancestor was like or how long ago he lived. Wild primates are extremely difficult to study in the field but valuable work has been done on chimpanzees and gorillas, as well as on baboons, howler monkeys, and macaques.

10

The higher primates are gregarious, just as man is. Their habit of grooming one another's fur stimulates continued association among adults and so furthers social integration. Primate groups also exhibit a simple kind of social organization, based on a dominance hierarchy among males. Primate bands appear to be held together by something more than erotic attraction of one sex for the other. Males and their female consorts continue to exhibit a kind of connubial relationship even during periods when the female is pregnant or in lactation as a result of the birth of an infant. Bachelor males congregate in temporarily separate groups for no apparent reasons other than companionship and a greater sense of security. Juveniles maintain their attachment to their mothers for years after birth and form persistent groups for play. Although adult males do not show great concern for the youngsters they have sired, they will tolerate their bumptious behavior, come to their rescue in moments of danger, and admonish them with threatening grunts when play degenerates into open fighting. Group interest in the birth of young is evidenced by the curiosity of other females who gather around to observe and touch the newborn.

Stereotyped postures, gestures, and sounds are widely prevalent in simian bands for communicating emotional reactions to situations and events. A dominant male advertises his status by staring down his subordinates and by a certain dignified incisiveness in his movements. Subordinates stare only at those lower in the hierarchy, make obeisance to superiors by turning their rumps toward them, and acknowledge this obeisance from those lower in rank by a touch on the shoulder. This particular exchange is obviously a symbolic use of female-male behavior, a mock presentation and mounting generalized to express and acknowledge any obsequious relationship. A subordinate male may indicate his awareness of an admonitory stare from a superior by contorting his face into what might be called a grimace. He may also lower his tail between his legs and contract his testes. Among macaque monkeys, the strictness of the dominance hierarchy varies not only from species to species, but from band to band within a species, apparently reflecting the personalities of the leaders. In very rigidly organized hierarchies among macaques, females may be more circumspect about sexual activities, and the entire band may be noticeably more conservative in its attitude toward the adoption of new foods. But regardless of strictness or laxness in the dominance hierarchy, all ape and monkey bands are alike in having a repertoire of emotive sounds which are used in specific situations to convey particular information.

The essential problem of hominid culture development might be restated: How did the evolutionary preadaption of the higher primates for culture development come to be exploited so effectively by the particular branch which produced *Homo sapiens*? Many theories have been suggested, all involving the early appearance of bipedal locomotion, an increase in brain size, and a shift from an almost exclusively vegetarian diet to one in which animal flesh was a staple. The omnivorousness of primates in captivity is attested by countless reports. Chimpanzees have a taste for ants, or the formic acid flavor they offer. Field studies show that they will devote considerable time and energy to gathering such dietary supplements as termites, ants, the grubs of the gall-fly, and the young of several species of mammals. Comparable activities by baboons have been reported.[1]

The hominoids were once supposed to have been arboreal animals forced to abandon life in the forest by some climatic catastrophe which eliminated all conveniently available forest habitats. This dramatic change in the ecological picture, it was further suggested, led to evolutionary selection for ability to locomote in an upright position, both because it freed the hands and arms for carrying, throwing, and carrying on new kinds of survival activity and because it raised the eyes above the level

12

of tall grasses and low brush and extended the food-gathering range, which made hunting more practical. All these changes in turn, presumably, would put a higher premium on brain size and intellectual potential in the struggle for survival.

This simplistic explanation raises a number of questions. If a major change in climate and a shift in forest belts did occur, why did it affect only the hominoid line? Almost all other primate lines continued to live in heavily forested areas and still do. But granted that some dramatic change forced the hominoid line to give up a forest existence and adopt a terrestrial life, where is evidence to prove that bipedal locomotion was an advantage that would be selectively perpetuated? Evolutionary processes have not shown any selective advantage in bipedal locomotion at the hunting-gathering level. Aside from human beings, the marsupial kangaroos, and a few saltatorial rodents, nature seems to have concluded that bipedal locomotion was "for the birds."

Support for the opinion that a forced shift from quadrupedal to bipedal locomotion was a real disadvantage does not depend solely on the obvious, that it made tree-climbing more awkward. It entailed a shift in posture and weight distribution to which even the modern human body is not completely adjusted. The cushionlike disks of cartilage between the vertebrae of the spinal column were not designed to work under continuous compression and frequently give trouble. Without the support of a tail, such as a kangaroo possesses, falling backward or sitting down too hard frequently damages the vestigial end of the spine. A vertical stance throws all the weight on two feet, which consequently suffer from broken arches, and it increases the workload on the heart and vascular system. Both sexes suffer from varicose veins. Pregnant women may develop milk-leg as a result of carrying a foetus in a position that interferes with blood circulation in the lower abdominal region. If these difficulties still persist after some two million years of bipedal locomotion, one can assume that they caused even more trouble to the early hominoids.[2]

Furthermore, other primates, notably the baboons, have successfully survived a terrestrial existence with quadrupedal locomotion. Essentially bipedal animals other than man show no tendency to develop phenomenally large brains as a result of their dominantly upright posture. Common sense requires one to consider the possibilities other than a drastic change in ecology as an incentive for terrestrial living. It would be more reasonable to assume that the change began by chance mutation and genetic drift toward a skeletal structure which made living in trees more awkward and walking upright on the ground less awkward, and therefore the path of least resistance. The original shift, perhaps, from the semiquadrupedal locomotion seen among modern chimpanzees and gorillas to a dominantly bipedal form, may have been merely the best available solution of a real problem resulting from a quirk in genetics. That the shift eventually became an advantage was most likely a change resulting from the existing broad potentials of primate anatomy, including, in the hominoid line, a slightly larger and probably more complex brain.

That man can still climb trees—and that some primitive peoples are adroit climbers—does not weaken the assumption that changes in anatomy, accompanied, perhaps, by increased size and weight, made an arboreal life less desirable than one which utilized *terra firma* as a home base. Studies make clear that climbing or swinging by the arms from limb to limb is a hazardous way of life, even for primates superbly adapted to it. The gibbons, unquestionably the most adept and graceful brachiators among the great apes, have frequent falls. Of 233 specimens collected in the wild, 58 percent of the adults who had survived beyond middle age exhibited healed bone fractures, in one case seven different fractures. Among orangs, markedly heavier but also slower, 34 percent of the adults had survived

14

bone fractures. Undoubtedly, if one knew how many fracture cases had not recovered, the percentages would be higher. On the other hand, among chimpanzees and gorillas, both of which build nests in trees for sleeping, but spend a large part of the day on the ground, fractures are relatively less frequent. Nevertheless, the incidence of fractures among these semiterrestrial apes is still higher than that reported for hominids. In 1910 a check of fractures in the skeletal bones of some three thousand Nubians excavated from ancient African graves showed fewer than 1 percent to have suffered such accidents.[3]

In the light of these statistics, it seems preposterous to suggest that an evolutionary development of skeletal structures better adapted to bipedal locomotion was promoted because it increased ability to survive an arboreal life. One may more cogently assume that the change resulted from genetic mutation and that its immediate disadvantages were overcome, at least partly, by some simultaneously occurring, equally fortuitous change—specifically an increase in brain size—which opened compensatory opportunities for survival. For, one basic motivation for culture elaboration seems always to be a search for ways to overcome an existing problem, natural or artificially created. It is logical to assume that this motivation existed from the beginning. Living on the edge of a forest, or in open country, was attractive, in part, at least, because it solved a problem by lessening the danger of bone-fracturing falls. It accords well with what is known about the operation of the primate brain to assume, also, that such a change in an ecological niche would require some shifting in diet habits, and that closer proximity to a greater variety of potential game animals would lead to increased experimentation in capturing and utilizing this more concentrated source of nutritives. The amount of food that must be poured into a hominid infant before it becomes fully mature, relative to adult body weight, is markedly greater than for any other mammal. But also the primate brain, working for a body

15

that can utilize a wide variety of both plant and animal foods, seems to get peculiar satisfaction from matching wits with food that must be captured and that frequently raises enough objection to the process to introduce competition, chanciness, and even some degree of danger. Both the capture and preparation of animal foods present problems which would promote the use of weapons and cutting tools.

A full appreciation of this explanation of the beginning of hominid culture—starting with chance mutations and the continued development of a bodily structure and brain mass that offered no immediate advantage to a forest-dwelling, fruit- or root- and leaf-eating primate—depends on some acquaintance with the evolving character of nervous systems, and the central clearing houses which are called *brains*, in the animal world. Every multicelled organism, if it is to survive, needs to have its parts able to communicate about movement toward food and away from danger. Even a headless worm, if it is to avoid energy-consuming, and perhaps disastrous, taffy pulls, must get agreement between both ends about the direction in which movement should take place. As larger and more complex animal bodies evolved, more extensive, complex, and effective nervous systems had to develop to keep the bodies alive. Specialized nerve endings came into existence to deal with different categories of phenomena: internal discomforts, body balance, position of body parts; surface discomforts arising from changes in temperature, pressure, or pain- or itch-causing events; and such attributes of the environment as could be identified by their emission or reflection of light, sound waves, or odors, by their chemical nature, as indicated by taste, or by their physical texture, hardness, shape, and size, as indicated by touch.

Operational speed of the nervous system also tended to increase, through the development of warm-bloodedness, the lengthening of nerve fibers between nerve cells, proliferation of booster stations, and extension of insulation or sheathing around nerve fibers. Functional efficiency was also increased by routing messages involving decisions concerning action through some kind of clearing center and by progressively concentrating these centers into the head end of the organism. All this happened, not by planning in advance, but by mutations of many kinds and by perpetuation of those changes which better assured survival and reproduction of the individual genetic pattern in which the changes occurred.

It is essential to remember that, either by parallel development or selective convergence, all nervous systems so far studied operate in accord with the same basic electrochemical principle. The receptor ends of nerves have an excitation threshold. When the exciting stimulus floods over this threshold, the receptor initiates an electrolytic impulse which travels inward on the nerve fiber somewhat as does the spark in a powder fuse, at speeds up to 400 feet per second. If the stimulus continues at the same level, other impulses follow. The receptor cannot alter the amplitude of its dotlike impulse messages, but their frequency tends to vary with the strength of the exciting impulse up to the limit of the receptor's recharging or refractory rate, augmented by impulses from nearby receptors which may be sympathetically aroused by the excitement. The tremendous number of receptors capable of sending messages to the brain, some two billion in the case of hominids, poses quite a problem. The brain is apprised of the origin and meaning of a message by the fiber over which it arrives. Memory records help the brain determine the significance of the message. Precipitate action before a decision is reached is usually prevented by a latency governor on effector nerves, which cannot initiate muscular action until the "go" signal is repeated, perhaps over several different circuits.

The central nervous system, therefore, if it is to operate with any efficiency at all, must call on past experience for advice. When action is not appropriate, the central nervous system must be able to put the quietus on receptor nerves which are excited by a relatively insignificant event, or which are unnecessarily repetitive. The brain must, therefore, be able to hang up on overly excited receptors by inhibitory feedback to the gaps or synapses in a nerve fiber, and perhaps, to the booster stations along the route. A commonly experienced example is the decline in pain messages from an injury, say, a smashed thumb, with passing time. The efficient brain must deal rather autocratically with the demands or pleas for specific action sent by its receptors. The weakness of the system is that the brain is not always a fully informed, impartial judge. Its ten billion or more neurons store memories of which the brain is no longer consciously aware. It develops emotional reactions which it cannot itself explain. Moreover, it is pressured into actions which the normal intelligence system has neither initiated nor fully analyzed, merely because some countless number of neurons are temporarily unemployed and restlessly waiting for something to do, preferably something with novel arousal potentials. The brain has a dual mission: to minimize disturbing messages about the body and the environment and to maximize its own activity satisfactions.

In order to account for the origin of culture and explain its subsequent development, one must be concerned with this remarkable organ, a messenger boy risen to the exalted post of chairman of the board, after millions of years of evolutionary history. Scholars have confused themselves by attempts to set the brain of man on a pedestal dedicated to rationality and to dismiss the brains of other animals, including other primates, as occupants of a corral fenced by instinct. Only within the past few decades have scholars begun to recognize that all brains fit somewhere on a continuum: with instinctive reaction patterns dominant at one end and, on the other, progressively greater reliance on conditioned instincts, accumulated experience, deliberately sought knowledge, and logical or creative thought.

The ability of an organism to learn from experience depends, basically, upon its potential for memory storage and recovery. Its ability to meet novel situations and the problems they pose is equally dependent upon use of these memories in association. To a degree, at least, such abilities are demonstrated by brains far less complex than those of humans and some even handicapped by infinitely less flexible and adaptable bodily machinery. The flatworm *Planaria Dugesia trigina,* one of the simplest forms of life in which a nervous system and rudimentary brain can be defined, seems to be able to learn by conditioning. After being subjected to a mild electric shock preceded by a flash of light, it comes to react to the light in anticipation of the electric shock. More interesting, however, not only do organisms at this low level learn to respond to a flashing light just as they instinctively responded to an electric shock, but also, what they learn seems to be recorded in the cells of the nervous system by structural changes replicated in cells subsequently formed by fission. The flatworm can regenerate lost parts by some "do it yourself" process; when a worm is cut in half, each half grows a replacement, whether head or tail. When an educated worm was cut in half and allowed time for regeneration of the lost parts, the newly built halves participated in the conditioned response to light even though they had not existed when the conditioning took place. Apparently, the learned response to light was replicated in newly formed cells along with the genetically established cringing pattern.[4]

Although such experiments require further confirmation, transfer of a conditioned response from one rat to another by extracting and injecting RNA (ribonucleic-acid molecules) has recently been reported.[5] What needs emphasis here is that an observer of the educated flatworms who was unaware of their earlier conditioning might well conclude that cringing when a light was flashed represented a normal part of the genetically established instinct pattern. Many specialists in natural history think that human beings tend to overemphasize the role of instincts in the lower animals and to underestimate it in themselves. Not only are men prone to ignore both the degree to which generalized instincts may be specialized by experience and the difficulty of distinguishing learned responses from genetically determined reactions, but they tend to ˜egard instincts as mere built-in reactions which best assure the biological survival of species unprepared to consider problems on their merits and to make an intelligent decision concerning them. Psychologists, it is said, have concentrated on the relations between instincts and visceral needs because those are easiest to establish; hence they have missed some of the higher animals' subtler goals which are comparable to man's. It is difficult to account for man's stubborn striving toward irrational goals without acknowledging the continued existence of instinctive patterns of acting. A human infant's readiness to suck at its mother's breast is clearly instinctive. Yet it involves discrimination; the infant rejects sharp, cold objects with an immediate and intuitive sort of appraisal which is just as innate as the sucking instinct. Some naturalists go further, maintaining that any animal which can perceive its environment also has an elementary form of insight, a kind of primary learning ability which provides the core for its central drive.[6]

Instinct could be regarded as a phylogenetically accumulated and genetically coded combination of species wisdom and idiosyncrasy, providing behavior patterns which give the possessors either a better than average chance of survival or a more interesting mode of existence without substantially lowering their ability to survive. Further, since instincts tend to be quite general and often accommodate a wide range of later developing, specifically detailed behavior, it is not necessary to postulate a new kind of mind in early hominoids to account for the beginning of culture proliferation and elaboration. All the existing evidence tends to indicate that one criterion for survival of species is a surplus brain potential which will enable the organism to adapt to changes in ecology. Far less complex minds than those to which the hominoids fell heir, some operating almost exclusively on instinct, have, nevertheless, developed amazingly complicated behavior patterns, often not clearly related to survival. In cases where, for sake of argument, one tries to demonstrate how the instinctual behavior contributed to survival, one may be brought up short by observing that other varieties of the same, or closely related, species, living in the same kind of environment, survive without this particular pattern and present a markedly different picture of what is essential to life.

The use and manufacture of tools has long been regarded as the identifying criterion of true hominids, yet it is now known that various other forms of life, not only among closely related primates, but other mammals and birds and insects, use tools and occasionally manufacture them. One might mention how chimpanzees and baboons use sticks for recovering honey from otherwise unreachable hives in hollow trees. Particularly noteworthy are the persistent efforts of chimpanzees to add a tidbit to their diet by collecting and trimming straws or twigs with which to fish for termites. Young chimpanzees have been observed awkwardly trying to imitate their elders in termite fishing, either by picking up abandoned twigs and poking them into fished-out holes in termite nests, or inefficiently fashioning their own.[7] They will, on occasion, throw objects with some appearance of aiming them rather than just tossing them in the air. They also use crushed leaves as a sponge to soak up water or to wipe dirt from their bodies. Observations indicate, moreover, that these are, in major part, examples of learned behavior.

The historically famous Galapagos Islands finch was cited by Charles Darwin as a user of thorns and twigs to harry grubs out of crevices which its blunt bill could not plumb. The Darwin Centennial Expedition of a few years ago found that this finch was not only still operating, but actually *manufactured* appropriate probes, as necessary, by holding a twig down with one foot and trimming it with its bill. An equally famous tool-user is the greater spotted woodpecker of Great Britain, which hacks a V-shaped crevice in the bark of trees to keep pine cones from bouncing as it pecks seeds out of them. Other reports describe mammals using stones as hammers (the Javanese crab monkey) and as anvils on which to crack bivalves (the southern Pacific Coast sea otter). Although beaver dams are rather large to be classed as tools, nevertheless, they are manufactured devices; the same holds true for beehives, and the nests of wasps, birds, chimpanzees, and gorillas. A comparable difficulty in definition occurs in the common use of gravel as a filler for the gizzard in certain varieties of birds. A particularly interesting example in the same category is that of the ten-legged crustaceans (the decapods), which come into the world equipped with a balancing organ, the statocyst, but no statolith to operate it. In order to tell up from down, decapods must provide themselves with a statolith by picking up a grain of sand in a claw and inserting it in the statocyst, through an exterior slit. Technically speaking, they are the earliest known users of a prosthetic device, antedating false teeth, artificial arms and legs, and the like, probably by many millions of years.

An outstanding example of the importance of learning in forms of life dominated by instinct is *imprinting*, seen among certain species of geese and ducks, but also observed in a mild form in a variety of birds, fish, and mammals. Young of the species involved come into the world with an instinct to follow their parents, but no instinctive sense of discrimination about how to identify a parent. Graylag goslings will follow the first slowly moving object which their eyes light upon after hatching, whether it be their mother, a pillow tied to a string, or just a human being. At first they blindly follow any object resembling that which triggered their instinctive response, but observation and learning appear to be equally instinctive, and in a remarkably short time goslings are able to differentiate their own mother, pillow, or human being from all others they meet. Baby chicks are faced with the same need to augment instinct with learning; they peck and make swallowing movements instinctively, but do not know what is worth pecking and what is worth swallowing until they have had a chance to observe others and go through a trial-and-error apprenticeship.

The point here is not that the mind of the first hominid was on a plane with those of subhuman animals, but rather that, if simple brain structures so far down the evolutionary scale are capable of amazing achievements, at least sporadically, then it is reasonable to suppose, without assuming some miraculous change in the quality of the central nervous system, that a brain slightly above the average for primates, stimulated by the problems that faced the hominoids, could use and manufacture tools regularly, shift from a vegetarian diet, and find surplus potential to cope with the problems raised by that change.

Even minds still guided primarily by instinct have a tendency to elaborate on behavior in connection with the primary problems of life: acquiring food, finding a mate, and caring for the young that may be born. It is also pertinent to observe that the degree of elaboration rises to its highest peak in group-living insects, birds, or mammals. It is logical to assume that these problem areas gave the hominoids stimulus for their earliest essays in culture and that their gregariousness aided them in this enterprise. They could benefit not from the preadaptive potential of this or that mind alone, but from the highest potentials occurring in the group. In discussing the relationship between what the earliest men did, and what lesser brains did still earlier, one may quote Konrad Lorenz: "You think I humanize the animal? . . . Believe me, I am not mistakenly assigning human properties to animals; on the contrary, I am showing you what an enormous animal inheritance remains in man to this day." [8]

There is no better illustration of the complex and abstruse matters which can be dealt with by even miniature and primitive brains when held in close association, than that provided by various social insects of the order *Hymenoptera* and *Isoptera*. These orders are evolutionarily very old and have undoubtedly been held down in body and brain size by using their skeletons for exterior armor plate and by too great dependence on osmosis for oxygen distribution. But they demonstrate that, given time enough, a tremendous amount of information can be transmitted from generation to generation by genetic coding, including a certain amount of insight, and by instincts which can be fully exercised only after practice. The common Old World honey bee, *Apis mellifera,* can use either terrestrial or solar navigation in flying to newly discovered sources of nectar or pollen. The scout who makes the find indicates its direction by performing a "waggle dance" up the side of the hive. The angle by which he departs from the vertical is the angle of flight relative to the sun's direction. And because the apparent direction of the sun changes from hour to hour, the guide bee must make appropriate changes in the angle at which he dances up the hive. He does this, apparently, with the aid of some internal, physiological clock. It is also apparent that young bees cannot use this instinctive system of navigation until they have made hundreds of trial flights and also joined in waggle-dancing on an apprentice basis. Judgment of a kind is involved in this and other hive operations. Those working in the hive move from task to task of their own volition, as need for one task exceeds the need for others. A nectar-gathering field worker is confronted with two situations in which hive workers refuse to accept his burden of nectar or pollen. In one case it is because of a need for water to keep down the temperature of the brood combs, and the field workers promptly leave to find water. In the other case, the hive is filled to capacity and the time has arrived to find an additional hive site. Field workers then leave to investigate every nook and cranny, keeping in mind that the new hive cannot be too close to the old hive; it must be large enough for the purpose, but not so large that it would be impractical to maintain the temperature within the required small range of 94 degrees to 96 degrees Fahrenheit. Bees quite clearly have many judgments to make based on insightful perception and experience. Yet one cannot conclude that these complex practices became instinctive because they were essential to survival. Many species of bees do not follow all these practices. The New World honey bees, *Meliponini,* follow an entirely different system of guiding nectar gatherers to a new food source. They use a pilot bee and blaze the trail with odor marks. But one cannot say that a tropical jungle made this different system essential to survival, for not all the *Meliponini* use it. One can only fall back on the fact that each variety instinctively feels that the way it navigates is "the only way to fly." In this, too, they adumbrate the hominids.[9]

An even greater variety of instinctive practices is followed by the six thousand or more known species of ants. They, as well as the bees and termites, were constructing their own shelters, with temperature and humidity control, long before the hominids got around to it. One could say that nurseries for young are essential to survival in species where the longevity of adults is so limited. But this scarcely accounts for the variety of ways in which they do it, by using ready-made cracks, crevices, and holes, digging underground burrows, constructing mounds, or even gluing leaves together with the viscous fluid emitted by their own larvae, which they hold aloft like portable staplers. The ants might well claim that they antedated hominids in agriculture and animal husbandry, for some grow fungi in underground gardens or herd aphids both for the honey dew they excrete and the protein they supply. A typical ant burrow

25

contains many other kinds of organisms; some pay for their keep by labor or honey dew, but others serve no discernible purpose other than offering the kind of companionship which superior hominid minds achieve by keeping a dog or cat around the house.[10]

All this emphasizes that elaboration of behavior by some species of a given order of genetically controlled organisms, far beyond the minimum which other species of the same order find necessary for survival, is a characteristic of even limited brains in relatively complex bodies. In many cases, conditioning, learning, practice, experience, or whatever it may be called, seems to be just as instinctively pursued as the simplest of reflexes. Quite frequently one finds a kind of perceptive insight. Caddis fly grubs—which build pupation cases of an instinctively standard pattern in an instinctively standard way—when driven out of these cases and presented with a case made by another grub, direct their activities toward repair of the particular damage and changing the size of the case. They meet this emergency situation not with a standardized, instinctive solution, but with a practical approach apparently involving a conception of what the final housing should look like. A somewhat similar kind of judgment is used by cell-building hornets whose nests have been punctured. They examine the damage, round out the puncture hole, and construct a patch to fit it, working from inside the cell on a concave surface rather than from outside on a convex surface as in the original, instinctive construction. Finally, they collect pitch and use it as a glue to hold the patch in place.

It seems reasonable to conclude that instinctively operating brains with long survival have a potential for meeting emergency situations which is commensurate with the complexity and versatility of the physical equipment of the body. The fossil evolutionary record of the horse, which is known in great detail, shows clearly that changes in body size and configuration precede increases in the size and complexity of the brain and that survival during the interval depends primarily on a preadaptive potential in the central nervous system.

A great many birds and animals, besides primates, under experimental laboratory conditions, reveal potentialities for what humans call *intelligence*, which animals normally have no occasion to use in the wild. The presence of this potential in other highly evolved mammals is perhaps less clearly indicated by what they can be forced to do under experimental conditions than by what they do voluntarily under natural conditions when freed from all pressure, particularly that created by hunger pangs. For want of a better name, because of insufficient study, this is labeled *play potential*.

The play potential is most frequently exhibited by the young of various species of mammals and of some birds, though it also occurs among adults when they are enjoying relatively hunger-free leisure. It is promoted by group living, whether in temporary groups, such as those represented by the litters of carnivores, or in permanent groups, such as those formed by gregarious birds and mammals. Adult domesticated cats and dogs play more than their wild progenitors, perhaps because this propensity has been selectively cultivated, but only when they are not hungry and preferably when they have a play-minded human as a foil. When food is no longer a continuing cause of anxiety, domesticated cats play with captured mice.

It is quite likely that the play potential was responsible for many of the otherwise unexplainable elaborations of sub-human life. No bird or animal wastes time or motion in the process of capturing food. But the wide prevalence of intricate courting procedures seems to be a clear proof that finding a suitable and amenable mate has always been primarily a leisure, after-dinner pursuit. It is reported that among certain carnivorous flies, the *Empididae* and the *Hilara*, as well as among certain varieties of spiders, the female puts food so much higher than love on her scale of values that, if hungry, she will kill and eat her suitors. Male flies of those species try to overcome this difficulty by bringing the female a dinner wrapped in silk of their own manufacture. Taking advantage of the time required to unwrap it, males sometimes substitute a bit of flower anther or some other plant fragment, hoping to do their bit for the perpetuation of the race before the female discovers she has been hoodwinked.

There are many less gruesome examples of the attitude of the brain toward the sometimes conflicting demands of the body for food and for release of sexual tensions. The latter clearly can be put off longer than the former, and the play potential has a freer hand. The bower birds of Australia, New Guinea, and adjacent islands illustrate the point as well as any. All the nineteen known species have developed the idea that whistling, singing, strutting, preening, or aerial gymnastics are uncultured ways of attracting the attention of a female and that building a nuptial bower of grass or straw is the only proper way to approach the problem. The females apparently agree. Bower birds go to no end of effort to elaborate courtship in a way that all the rest of the bird world proves is not really essential for survival. Moreover, each of the nineteen species appears to have its own conception of what a bower should be like. Some go so far as to paint the bower with fruit juices, or plant a lawn of moss decorated with cut flowers, or bejewel the path to it with shells, pebbles, and even coins if they can get them. Other studies show that symbolic courtship behavior is quite common. Man, with a far more ambitious brain operating on the same principle, and with a far greater development of the play potential, should be conceded the privilege of elaborating behavior without having to prove that the elaboration is a practical necessity or even a rational improvement on that which it elaborates. Early hominids probably exercised this privilege, just as their modern descendants do. One should also remember that there is an ancient and fundamental connection between erotic impulses and aesthetic achievement.[11]

In my opinion, the magnitude of this play potential, accompanying an extremely drastic loss of quadrupedal efficiency in an otherwise highly versatile physical body, precipitated the hominoids' interest in culture and converted them into hominids. Various facets of the play potential stimulated the development of activities regarded as the criteria of early hominid culture. Strangely enough, the play potential has not aroused much serious interest among anthropologists or psychologists until quite recently, even though naturalists have tried to explain it in the lower animals. Half a century ago, a noted American zoologist, after studying the mimicry of sounds by certain species of birds, concluded that this phenomenon could not be explained as anything other than an agreeable mental experience, and he added that probably most imitation of one animal by another was similarly motivated.[12] Early in the present century it was customary to dismiss play as something in which juveniles participated because of a surplus of physical energy; probably, too, it served the useful purpose of assuring exercise and a certain accumulation of social practice. Yet the surplus energy theory requires one to explain how the energy expended by a cat in chasing a rubber ball came to be more "surplus" than energy expended in chasing a mouse.[13]

The first scholar who fully appreciated the significance of the play potential in man, the dominant influence it had on the course of culture development and its detailed elaboration, seems to have been the twentieth-century Dutch historian, Jan Huizinga. He reached his rather startling conclusions after a long and unsuccessful effort to explain human customs and history on rational grounds. He wrote:

". . . The spirit of playful competition is, as a social impulse, older than culture itself and pervades all life like a veritable ferment. Ritual grew up in sacred play; poetry was

29

born in play and nourished on play; music and dancing were pure play. Wisdom and philosophy found expression in words and forms derived from religious contests. The rules of warfare, the conventions of noble living, were built up on play patterns. We have to conclude, therefore, that civilization is, in its earliest phases, played. It does not come from play like a babe detaching itself from the womb; it arises in and as play and never leaves it." [14]

Play, as Huizinga defines it, is any activity entered upon voluntarily without material interest or benefit and deferable at the whim of those participating. It concerns matters outside ordinary life, yet is subject to rules which must be observed: willingness to suspend disbelief, to accept a pretense, or to keep a secret. Such activity, furthermore, must recognize the appropriateness of time and place, and welcome rather than avoid an element of tension, uncertainty, or chanciness.

The meaning of the term *play*, and the nature of activities involved, have been further analyzed and classified under four headings: *agôn*, in which competition is the attraction; *alea*, in which chance dominates; *mimicry*, in which simulation or pretense dominates; and *ilinx*, in which vertigo or dizziness is sought as an uncommon, and therefore desirable, objective. Each of these categories includes activities ranging from *paidia*, or spontaneous exuberance, at one end to *ludus*, or calculated, contrived behavior under rigidly observed rules, at the other.[15] Mechanical rides in amusement parks have been cited as an example of the attractiveness of vertigo as an escape from the routine normality of brain functioning. Vertigo and mimicry combine in the efforts of the whirling dervish or Maulawiyah Muslim to equate dizziness with the achievement of a higher spiritual level. So far, apparently, no student of the subject has considered this cerebral penchant for abnormality as a factor promoting use of neurotropic drugs as a shortcut to intoxica-

tion, hallucination, or anesthesia. Neither has there been any
effort to connect up neuroses, psychoses, or suicide with a
built-in need for escape from reality, and a willingness to seek
it in a private world while living, or in some unknown world
beyond death.

Play potential, considered simply as an attribute of complex brains which calls upon a healthy imagination to create
interesting fictional situations when ordinary life grows bore-
some, undoubtedly affected the development of early culture.
That potential includes curiosity and exploration of the new and
strange, as well as manipulation of familiar objects in new
ways, all in search of another reality or some exciting nuance
of the old reality. Again, this is an attribute which the early
hominids undoubtedly shared with other mammals, but which
was more characteristic of their larger, more complex brains
and was promoted by their anatomical versatility and dexterity.

When F. Fraser Darling made his classical study of the
red deer of Great Britain in the second quarter of the twentieth
century, he found that fawns and even adult hinds engaged in
play which approached the level of an organized game. Particular hillocks were so frequently used for a kind of "run-chief-
run" and for butting contests that they were nearly denuded of
grass. It seemed clear to the British naturalist that the deer
were participating because of the pleasure they got out of it;
neither superabundance of energy nor instinctive practice for
later life was an adequate explanation. Play was a means of
heightening the satisfaction which individuals derived from a
social situation.[16]

Even aggressive fighting between animals of the same
species frequently has certain play characteristics. Unless an
aggressor has a resisting opponent, the activity loses its charm
and fizzles out like a wet firecracker. An aggressive mouse, for
example, appears to be one that had a successful experience in

31

combat early in life and came to regard it as a most pleasurable kind of excitement. But if a potential opponent refuses to fight back, there can be no game, and the aggressor turns his attention elsewhere. This appears to be true, also, in encounters between far more dangerous fighters than mice.[17]

The problem of distinguishing hominids from other animals by some simple but elegant definition is rendered difficult by the fact that they all have relatively complex central nervous systems with a built-in play potential, and they all, sporadically at least, will develop patterns of behavior which have to be recognized as culture-like. Hominids walk upright on two feet, but so do birds and a number of mammals. Primates, quite generally, can and do locomote bipedally when they have a reason to abandon the more efficient, semiquadrupedal locomotion. Hominids live in socially organized groups and utilize an elaborate system of communication. But many other animals exhibit the same proclivities on a considerably less sophisticated level. There was a time when man was roughly defined as a tool-using and tool-manufacturing primate. Then attention was turned to distinguishing hominids on the basis of culture transmission. They were cultured primates with regularities in social behavior transmitted from generation to generation by some means other than genetic inheritance. They supported a culture made up of many separate but related customs which were acquired habits of behavior rather than instinctive reactions.

More recently it has become clear that there is no sharp demarcation between instinctive and acquired or learned behavior. Animals largely guided by instinct do amend and alter their genetically coded responses in accord with individual or group observation, experience, and learning. Teaching of the young often seems to be an essential part of the instinct to feed and care for them. As a result of accumulating knowledge it becomes necessary to circumscribe the area within which hu-

32

man beings may proudly declare themselves unique. So now it is proposed that we recognize two levels of culture: proto-culture, which hominids share with other animals, and true culture, which involves the proliferated use and manufacture of tools, the utilization of sources of energy outside of the body (fire, for example), and a language which is independent of emotional reflexes and infinitely expansible.[18]

In other words, the hominids of Australopithecine times cannot be regarded as the sole originators of culture. They were, rather, more talented elaborators of an already existent proto-culture, depending on a larger brain and more highly developed play potential.

This chapter has tried to lay a foundation for better understanding of man and his problems by inquiring into the sequence of evolutionary events and the circumstances leading up to, and surrounding, the start of his career as a problem solver and problem creator. For millions of years, probably, man was just one of many members of the order Primates in the class Mammalia. As such he was already one of the lucky winners in the evolutionary sweepstakes, avoiding the genetic combinations which might have narrowed his adaptability to some specific ecological niche and participating fully in the greatest prize in the biological lottery: a directorial brain larger and more complex than necessary for continued existence in a routine way, and therefore preadapted for any evolutionary change requiring something more than a routine response.

This evolutionary change, when it did come, might well have led to disaster. It appeared to be a disadvantageous mutation which continued on by linkage to some other advantageous combination of genes or by blind genetic drift. It involved skeletal changes that could hardly be perpetuated by selection of the fittest for non-tool-using life either in the trees or on the ground. Eventually this gradually acquired awk-

33

wardness made an exclusively terrestrial existence and bipedal locomotion the least of the evils. Moreover, it helped to add practical advantages to the always more exciting pastime of capturing game animals. It freed the hands and arms for transportation, for throwing weapons, and for carrying home the bag.

Culture in Perspective

‖‖

The history of man and his experiments with culture after the age of the Australopithecines and the Olduvai Gorge living site of Africa cannot be documented with fossil evidence step by step, but must be pieced together by post-mortem deductions which take into account the peculiar nature of man's expanding brain, the problems and opportunities created by environment and accumulating cultural innovations, and the inevitable pressures of increasing population density.

A million years or more may have elapsed between the picture presented by the living site in Olduvai Gorge and the view obtained from excavation of the Choukoutien caves, some thirty-seven miles southwest of Peking. It has not been possible to date this living site exactly, but it seems to have been occupied during the first of three major glacial retreats during the Pleistocene Ice Age, perhaps half a million years ago.

Here one meets a new variety of hominid: taller, more

stoutly built, and having a considerably larger brain cavity than the Australopithecines. He was still far from handsome by modern standards. Both his chin and his forehead receded; his profile was further marred by a supraorbital ridge of bone, a straight bar torus, more reminiscent of a gorilla than the Adonis over whom Aphrodite grieved. But comely or not, evidence shows that his intellectual achievement surpassed that of the much earlier inhabitants of the Olduvai Gorge. Carbon lenses and hardened chunks of clay indicate not only that he used fire regularly but that he built up hearths and probably cooked some of his food rather than eating it all raw. Mastery of fire may also account for his living in caves. It has been suggested that use of fire preceded the advance of hominids into higher latitudes during the Ice Age and made it possible to hold at bay any larger carnivores who were already accustomed to taking refuge in convenient caverns.

Tool proliferation is indicated by the greater number of worked stone pieces (two thousand of them being found in a single cave) and by the presence of worked bone implements. The significance of the fractured pieces of stone, mostly quartz, is again heightened because they were not of local provenance but had to be collected elsewhere, often at a considerable distance, and brought to the cave. The number and types of game animals whose bones formed a large part of the cave debris indicate not merely long residence and a relatively sizable population, but a heightened ability to hunt large animals, which in turn implies more effective weapons, skill in their use, and cooperative hunting. Some 75 percent of the game animals represented were mid-Pleistocene varieties of deer, but the cave dwellers also took boar, bison, ostrich, water buffalo, otter, and several other species of animals now extinct.

A cursory review of these tangible evidences of improvement in material living conditions might still lead one to wonder whether *Pithecanthropus pekinensis*, or Peking Man, was making full use of his brain potential. The average brain capacity of four reasonably intact skulls was 1046 cubic centimeters, as compared with an average of 576 cubic centimeters for five comparably preserved Australopithecine skulls. Even if one compares the smallest of the measured skulls of Peking Man with the largest of the measured skulls of the Australopithecines, 915 cubic centimeters against 750 cubic centimeters, the difference is still marked. There is no overlap between the two groups, as there is between the Australopithecines and modern great apes.

Cooperative hunting, which seems to be implied, and use of fire, which is documented, are a greater achievement for an essentially self-serving brain than appears at first glance. For one brain to cooperate with another, some sort of communication appears to be essential. Emotive cries can and do arouse group action to meet imminent events, but hunting large game with the aid of manufactured weapons, or even keeping a fire alive, requires planning for a future contingency hours if not days in advance. Both demand recognition of personal responsibility for a group enterprise and persistent concentration on a certain sequence of actions in discharge of that responsibility.

The Choukoutien cave debris allows one to draw an additional deduction which is indicative of abstract thinking and highly illuminating as to the line of development that culture was to take. When Peking Man brought a dead game animal home, he brought the entire carcass. Bone fragments are representative of all parts of complete skeletons. But when Peking Man disposed of his own dead, he kept only the heads. If they died inside the cave, he must have carried the bodies out. If they died outside, he brought home only the severed head. For of the fossil remains of Peking Man found in the Choukoutien caves, there were skulls or skull fragments for forty-odd individuals, but only seven thighbones and one armbone to represent their forty skeletons.[1]

It has been asserted that this occurred because Peking Man had a special craving for human brains, but this is a most implausible explanation for many reasons. First, almost all the Choukoutien skulls give evidence that their owners died by violence. The skulls were already fractured; very little more bashing would have been required to open up the brain case. Yet in every instance where the base of the skull was available for examination, it was clear that the *foramen magnum* had been rather carefully enlarged and that the brain, if extracted, had been removed by this laborious method. This procedure has a formal, rather ritualistic aura. Indeed, identical methods of extracting brains were used by certain primitive peoples down to historic times for avowedly ritualistic reasons, one of which was to salvage the spirit or power of the dead person and to pass it on to those still living, in a kind of brain-tasting communion service. On the other hand there are very few instances of hominids developing a hunger for flesh of their own kind.[2] For the most part, human beings regard cannibalism with abhorrence, even under extreme famine conditions. Other mammals also show a reluctance to eating anything identifiable as one of their own kind, and more often than not display curiosity tempered by apprehension in the presence of death.

In view of the later concern of the hominid mind with the question: "After death, what?" it seems entirely reasonable to attribute the evidence left by Peking Man to early attempts to wrestle with the mystery and irreversible finality of physical death and to find some magical way of ameliorating its effects. This, one might say, is the beginning of a basically religious approach to life and death.

The Choukoutien skulls characteristically carried marks of death by violence, either the kind of wounds that a knife or lance would have made or wounds made by an ax or a club. This evidence of death by violence continues in the fossil record throughout the Stone Age. It could well help to explain why

the hominid brain continued to increase in size at an evolution-
ally phenomenal rate over such a long period of time. Without
question, an increase in brain size was advantageous in the
struggle for survival, but there is no clear proof that the struggle with nature for food and against subhuman competitors
would have been so sharply selective of those with large brains.
Common sense favors the supposition that the size and the ef-
ficacy of brains were crucially tested in contests between groups
of hominids over territory and other matters in dispute.

A struggle, involving both weapons and communication-
aided strategy and tactics between rival social groups and their
gene pools, would more quickly alter reproduction rates. Several of the ancient cave tableaux upon which modern man has
stumbled strongly suggest that one group slaughtered another
more than occasionally. It may be that without wars of annihilation for many hundreds of thousands of years hominid brains
would never have developed to their present size, and para-
doxically, might never have been able to recognize the futility
of wars, or rather, never developed a knowledge of nuclear
physics which forces modern men to recognize that war can
lead only to destruction. War, in other words, seems to be a
culturally stimulated form of competition, biologically valuable
in its early days, but, like many other aspects of culture, now
so elaborated that it creates more problems than it solves. War
is now leading to an end that would be absurd if it were not so
catastrophic. Organized fighting by teams of warriors can probably not be accounted for without reference to Huizinga's play
potential and the category of play in which tense competition
and chance are attractive goals. War has been cited as an example of extremely serious play involving costumes, codes of
individual behavior, and rules of group conduct. Tangled in play
is the tendency of a complex brain to move on from mastery of
its own sensory receptors to control of the stimuli which the
environment provides, including activities initiated by other

brains. Even lowly deer mice, *Peromyscus crinitus,* exhibit laboratory behavior which can best be described as a compulsion to control their environment. They do not particularly like electric lights or power-driven running wheels and quickly learn to turn off the power when the switch is made available to them. But they will also voluntarily turn on the switches in an exploratory way, and when this happens, they object to having anyone else turn them off; that is, they promptly turn the switches back on again.[3] Self-willed stubbornness is widely characteristic of complex brains, including the most complex of all, that belonging to *Homo sapiens.* The independence of apes and monkeys in deciding what they will do and when has been stressed by researchers.[4] One cannot call this recalcitrance. It is rather the exercise of cerebral authority in opposition to the recalcitrance of other minds. It should be remembered that the brain of a mouse, while small in an absolute sense, is relatively larger in ratio to body weight than the brain of a human being.

Roughly speaking, the history of man and culture went into obscurity again for two or three hundred thousand years after Peking Man is known to have occupied his condominium at Choukoutien. At the point where evidence from later living sites allows one to pick up the story, hominids had further evolved into Neanderthal Man, a polyglot population in which some isolated groups developed genetic factors for a more modern type of smooth-surfaced skull, although the great majority continued to exhibit cranial characteristics reminiscent of the much earlier pithecanthropoids rather than foreshadowing the later-appearing and modern Cro-Magnons. In one major respect, however, the Neanderthalers anticipated what was to follow. They set a record for brain size which matches or exceeds the average for modern societies. As contrasted with Peking Man's average of 1046 cubic centimeters and range of 915 to 1225, the brain cavity for six classic Neanderthal skulls had an average capacity of 1438 cubic centimeters and a range of from 1300 to 1610. For comparison, the mean racial capacities for modern man range from 1195 to 1520 cubic centimeters, although the modern skull has a relatively greater development of the frontal lobes or neo-cortex area, and Neanderthal skulls gained greater capacity by expansion of the posterior sections.

One can scarcely account for the anomalous size of Neanderthal brains with the time-honored supposition that an increased complexity of technological culture was the agent which selectively promoted genetic lines capable of producing more capacious central nervous systems. For that assumption scarcely explains why relatively simple cultures at the Stone Age level had such a marked effect, whereas the infinitely more complex culture of subsequent ages has failed to continue the process. One might better assume first, that under very primitive conditions with populations expanding and territorial and ideological conflicts increasing, the mentally most competent groups had a greater chance of survival. Secondly, this process ended when the size of babies' heads at birth began to outstrip the separately evolving enlargement of pelvic arches in the female, when increasing size of living groups made annihilation less probable, when capture of women reduced the genetic differences between groups, and when cultural borrowing eliminated many gross disparities in the effectiveness of weaponry and the efficiency of fighting strategy and tactics. One might add that indecisive conflicts over extended periods of time would be more likely to reduce the number of highly competent males on both sides than to increase them.

The record left by the Neanderthalers further emphasizes that increased brain capacity preceded the development of more complex cultures. It was not until after the hominid brain reached its maximum gross size to date that most of the great cultural achievements of man occurred and that the foundations were laid for that supercomplexity called civilization. It is illogical to assume that some sequence different from this was in-

41

volved in the earlier appearance of proto-culture and the transition from proto-culture to a uniquely human culture.

The achievements of the Neanderthalers tend to confirm another generally accepted conclusion, namely, what a brain of given capacity can achieve is more or less directed and limited by what earlier brains have already achieved. Hence, the worn aphorism that culture begets culture; and the pessimistic philosophy that culture is a juggernaut which man may push, or on which he may nip a ride, but which he cannot direct or stop. Certainly the material culture of Neanderthal Man, and even some of the non-material aspects which one can only infer, do seem to connect with cultural developments that occurred as much as a quarter of a million years earlier, when pithecanthropoids were enjoying their heyday. They were still fracturing and chipping stone tools and weapons rather crudely, still making use of caves for shelter, and still, presumably, borrowing rather than producing fire.

Two noteworthy basic changes did appear, nevertheless: a tendency to standardize the form of tools and the methods of producing them, and a tendency to develop local preferences for one type of tool or production procedure over others without any clear relationship to utility or efficiency. Apparently, the complex brain, dependent for efficiency on standardized message-handling procedures and on accumulation of correct and incorrect responses for recurring situations and events, tries to order the natural environment and establish rules of behavior, primarily in order to bring reality into conformance with expectancy, and incidentally, adding the attribute of "rightness" to habitual behavior. This theme can be illustrated by handedness: the simian primates are ambidextrous, but human beings, almost universally, use one hand preferentially over the other. Whether this is a specific quirk in the genetic information pattern or an incidental effect of differential development rates in the two halves of the foetus, is not known. But it is generally true that the right hand is preferred by about 80 per-cent of a modern population. The human brain, traditionally, has tried to insist, therefore, that the right hand is the correct hand, and the left hand, the incorrect hand, without regard for the idiosyncrasies of the individual. The earliest evidence for preferential handedness is provided by the greater stoutness of the right clavicle in the skeleton of a noted Neanderthaler, the Old Man of La Chapelle, whose 1610-cubic-centimeter brain cavity evoked the remark that he must have been brainier than an average modern Parisian.[5]

Neanderthal Man, at different times and localities, pro-duced a variety of so-called hand axes, some pointed, some with a cleaver-like blade, and even some with an S-shaped curve to the cutting edge. He used the flakes knocked from boulders in the manufacture of axes as scraping and cutting tools. There is no certain proof that he ever hafted a stone point or blade, although later Neanderthal tool assemblages from Africa con-tain triangular flakes, with tangs chipped out, which imply lash-ing to some kind of handle. On the other hand, in an early Neanderthal assemblage excavated at Clacton-on-Sea, England, chance preserved one wooden spear whose point had been hardened by being held in a fire. Despite their surprisingly large brains, these late Ice Age hunters produced only one real innovation in weaponry: some groups made and used a throw-ing weapon known as the *bolas*, consisting usually of three stone spheres tethered together by thongs. This missile offered an ad-vantage over a single stone, even one thrown with the aid of a sling, in that the bolas had some of the qualities of a shotgun: if only the tether thong struck the target, the kinetic energy and inertia of the stone spheres would wrap the thong around the body or legs of the quarry and bring it down.

Outside the field of technology there appears a close rela-tion in spirit between Neanderthal Man and Peking Man, al-though here, too, elaboration produced different results. Evi-

43

dence of death by violence continued during Neanderthal times, as did the practice of saving skulls, enlarging the *foramen magnum,* and extracting the brain, presumably for ritualistic transmission of spirit and power. But Neanderthal thought about death and what might be salvaged went on, logically, to the question of what happened to the potential or demonstrated spiritual power of individuals if one failed to get complete salvage. Neanderthalers were the first hominids on earth to leave clear evidence of placating, respectful homage to the dead by entombment or burial of part or all of their remains—at least the head, and on occasion the complete body. Neanderthal Man may have fallen short of his successor, Cro-Magnon Man, as an artist, but he clearly arranged the first human funerals; the disposal of Skull No. 1 at the Mount Circeo cave site in Italy is an example. The owner of the skull, typically, left plausible evidence that he died by violence. Typically, also, the *foramen magnum* had been neatly enlarged, presumably for extraction of the brain; in addition, the skull was carefully deposited in a litter-free chamber of the cave, and its importance was emphasized by a ring of stones around it on the cave floor. There were three heaps of bones, too, which can best be interpreted as the remains of a sacrificial offering of parts of the carcasses of three important game animals, a Bos, a boar, and a deer. Further, other cave-entombed Neanderthal skulls remind one strongly of the skull altars that hominids of contemporaneous primitive societies continued to build in isolated corners of the world.[6]

This conclusion is confirmed and extended by pointing out that, at Ferrassie, near Les Eyzies in France, a cave complex dating back to the Mousterian period, the apogee of Neanderthal culture, contains an entombment of skulls in which the remains of a child of six years are distinctively honored by a triangular covering of stone, in which a cryptic series of depressions had been laboriously chiseled. The cave chamber was further distinguished by an equally cryptic series of earth mounds, and by scattered flint points. Indicative of the wide dispersal of Neanderthal peoples, and of their commonly shared concerns and anxieties, is a report on a cave burial site in Teshik-Tash, Uzbekistan, containing the remains of a youth whose grave is lined with the long bones of mountain goats and decorated by a half-dozen pairs of horns from the same animal standing vertically on the ground.

The disappearance of the Neanderthalers and the rise of modern man's immediate and almost identical predecessor, Cro-Magnon Man, mark the end of leisurely culture growth and the beginning of a period of more rapid and still accelerating invention. This transition can be dated only by its climax, about thirty thousand years ago. Scholars do not know to what extent it represented an invasion by Cro-Magnon Man followed by annihilation of Neanderthalers, but one suspects some Cro-Magnon assimilation of Neanderthal genetic lines along with Neanderthal culture. There is suggestive evidence of cross-breeding in skeletal remains found on Mount Carmel in Palestine, but in any event the shift in dominance took place with unprecedented rapidity. One cannot avoid the suspicion that one factor in the change might have been that Cro-Magnon Man discovered the bow and arrow. Today the bow and arrow is a children's toy or an adult archer's hobby. But the bow, and its improvement by subsequent inventions, once constituted a weapon that revolutionized man's capacity for bringing down game, including enemy human beings. Even the first firearms were not intrinsically competitive with weapons like the crossbow, but they gained popularity because teaching a military recruit to handle a gun was far easier than training him to use a bow.

With the advent of Cro-Magnon Man, so similar to modern man that he would scarcely do more than arouse admiration if one met him on Main Street, the proliferation of culture really began. There are a few scattered evidences that Neanderthalers made beads or pendants, but with Cro-Magnon Man ornamentation of the body advanced rapidly. He also developed clothing for cold weather, semisubterranean houses, and houses perhaps raised on piles over water, oil lamps, cave art, awls, bodkins, needles, buttons, safety pins, fishhooks, the spearthrower, spear and arrow points of flint or obsidian, communal drives in hunting, and, finally, the domestication of animals and plants for producing rather than hunting or harvesting food. Village and city development followed, and the invention of writing and thus of modern civilization. To accomplish all this, Cro-Magnon Man had available a brain already maximized in total mass tens of thousands of years earlier, although somewhat changed in configuration, and undoubtedly improved internally by additions to the neo-cortex and a more intricate system of connections between neurons.

A number of different types of evidence point to a continuing and more highly elaborated belief in the existence of supernatural influences on natural events, and the development of a conviction that those influences could be controlled to some extent by mortals. Cro-Magnon Man, judging by the craniums which have been preserved, continued to die by violence more often than not, and he also continued to mitigate the loss by enlarging the *foramen magnum,* and passing to survivors bits of the brain for such residues of spirit and power as they might retain. But he also elaborated significantly on the practice of showing respect for the dead, and perhaps laying their ghosts by entombment or burial, as introduced by the earlier Neanderthalers. Graves and tombs begin to appear which contain the personal possessions of the deceased—tools, weapons, utensils, ornaments—and possibly, supplies of food. Such practices developed along with a new concept of a life after death in a world inhabited by spirits; the purpose of grave furnishings was to victual the dead for this trip and to equip them for a second life. Equally important, Cro-Magnon Man began to offer this respectful and precautionary treatment to women as well as to men and juveniles. Color was also added by smearing bodies or bones with red ocher, a practice which continued down to contemporary times.

This same general concern for supernatural influences and their control apparently led hominids to artistic endeavors, for Cro-Magnon Man was the first of the line to create lasting and ambitious works of art, and there is every reason to believe that he produced them for magico-religious ends. His earliest efforts were devoted to ceramic figurines of women with highly exaggerated sexual identification, most plausibly aimed at insuring the fertility of women and maintaining or increasing population. This supports the implication of bower bird courting procedures, that in the complex brain the erotic and the aesthetic tend to complement each other. But Cro-Magnon Men also used art for the magical control of the game they hunted, by capturing the spirit of the game animal in a lifelike representation and wounding it in advance with painted arrows or, in the case of clay models, with miniature darts. The best proof of the magic purpose of this art lies in its having been placed in the deepest and most inaccessible chambers of underground caverns, and from repeated use of particular wall spaces, even though equally good adjoining wall surfaces remained blank.[7]

This art allows one to deduce something more which is important in understanding the motivation for culture growth and the incentive for accepting change. Its quality, whether static or dynamic, is so high that it could have been produced only by specialists, part-time or full-time, and after long practice. Direct evidence of Cro-Magnon specialization, at least in producing ceramic figurines and statuettes, comes from an area quite distant from the centers of cave art in France and Spain— the semipermanent settlements of house-building mammoth hunters in the Pollau Mountains of southern Moravia. The excavator reports that one structure was obviously not an ordinary dwelling place, for it contained the remains of a crude kiln and so many fragments of molded ceramics that one could hardly avoid classifying it as a domestic factory operated by a family of specialists.

Incidentally, some of the art of this settlement suggests a relationship to religion which goes far beyond magic control of supernatural influences. At one of the lowest levels there was found the skeleton of a woman, clearly a personage of more than ordinary importance, who exhibited a pathological condition of the left maxillary joint that is often associated with facial paralysis. At a higher level there was uncovered a ceramic representation of a woman's head with the typical lines of paralysis on the left side of the face. And still higher was found a piece of mammoth ivory decorated by an engraving of a woman's face with the same lines of facial paralysis on the left side. This engraving, moreover, was clearly representative of a mask worn by someone assuming the ceremonial role of the facially deformed woman. It is admitted that the meaning of this evidence is a matter for conjecture, but it is suggested that engraving and ceramic may record the deification of a mortal woman, an apotheosis, twenty-five thousand years ago, before the end of the Old Stone Age.[8]

One might characterize the history of human culture as the progressive accumulation of new activities originated by the play potential of complex brains, and promoted by persons who believe they find in the new activities a means, compatible with individual talents and interests, for advancing social standing or economic security in society. To illustrate the applicability of this statement to known cultural changes, one can do no better than choose the first of which there is a clear record, the adoption of meat as a dietary staple. Before that time, one may assume, on the basis of the prevailing social organization of other primates, that the only way for a male to advance himself from the periphery to the center of the social group was by fighting his way up the hierarchical dominance ladder. When meat began to attract increasing attention, a new and different role was created, that of hunter. It offered an alternative route to prestige for those who were dissatisfied with their place in the dominance hierarchy and possessed hunting talent and diligence. It may be taken for granted that they would emphasize the importance of hunting by their proud demeanor and by their missionary zeal.

One may guess that the dominant males found this competition difficult to eliminate, for they had no language and could not even say with a sneer: "Those who can, do—those who can't, hunt." In this instance, the hunters were certain to improve their status. This still occurs among contemporary primitive tribes. One classic study of the primitive Arunta of Australia comments that when the evening fire was lighted, the successful hunters of the day bustled about the center of the group, giving orders and laughing. The unsuccessful ones sat quietly and morosely on the group's periphery.[9] Not all new specialties, of course, were so obviously related to the welfare of the group, and accounting for their development requires closer study.

The Stone Age of culture history is customarily divided into an Old Stone Age and a New Stone Age because, about ten thousand years ago, stone weapons and tools began to appear which were finished by laborious grinding and polishing of the surface. One cannot account for this change on the grounds of technological improvement and efficiency alone. In some cases, the method led to superior products; in others, it did not. One may doubt that a search for greater efficiency had much to do with the change. It is in better keeping with modern knowledge of brain reactions to conclude that some experimentally inclined Cro-Magnon individual with time to spare tried

49

the process, and that it took hold because of the fine appearance and pleasant feel of the resulting pieces. Probably polishing stones also offered a new avenue of accomplishment for individuals who liked to substitute patient labor leading to predictable results for the chancy skill involved in stone chipping and flaking.

Actually, to designate the period after 10,000 B.C. the New Stone Age is about as misleading as designating modern times The Age of Glass, Gas, and Cosmetics. Far more important achievements were developing, including domestication of plants and animals, the brilliant discovery that pots and jars could be made out of the same material that had been going into figurines, statuettes, and ornaments for a score of thousands of years; the development of farming villages; the production of copper, bronze, and finally iron by forging, smelting, and casting processes; the growth of temple estates and of city states; and the invention of graphic symbols for spoken languages. The most significant of the early developments was the domestication of animals and plants, for that made possible great population growth and proliferation of the specialized occupations other than food gathering, collecting, producing, and distributing, which structured civilization.

Scholars still tend to explain the origin of herding and agriculture in terms of the practical advantages that they subsequently demonstrated, without sufficient attention to the psychology of the inventor and the situation in which these inventions actually took place. First, it is doubtful that either herding or agriculture arose as a sudden inspiration, or even as a result of prolonged experimentation, with more dependable food production in mind. Field studies in South America, particularly, show that neither agriculture nor animal husbandry holds an irresistible attraction for successful hunters and gatherers. The Chamacoco in southwestern Brazil, even though related to agricultural tribes, preferred to avoid the dull labor involved in agriculture, except for the support of ceremonies requiring gourd rattles, which they had to grow to get. Other nomadic tribes apparently felt it was both more dignified and more exciting to extort what they needed from the agricultural tribes at harvest time with the threat of bloodshed.[10]

In North America, several Great Plains tribes which were engaged in agriculture when Columbus arrived got horses from the Spaniards, and found that both riding furiously after buffalo and engaging in new kinds of war games were more rewarding than cultivating corn with stone hoes. Farther north—among the Ojibwa, where nomadic hunting groups carried on desultory agriculture by planting on one visit to a site and collecting what chanced to grow and survive until they got back on the next visit—the practice could be accounted for as an extension of an already traditional practice, that of harvesting and caching wild rice.

The oldest known agricultural communities, of course, were in the Old World, and more specifically, distributed along the so-called Fertile Crescent that ran eastward from Asia Minor. In this general area there is evidence of the early presence of the wild grasses and game animals from which many basic cereals and domesticated meat animals have developed. It is usually taken for granted that the hominids who lived in the area took up herding and agriculture when faced by a shortage of game animals and wild plant foods. This seems extremely improbable. In periods of drought when food shortage might become a very pressing problem, it obviously would be necessary to consume all the food that one could gather or collect in order to stay alive. To put part of it in the ground, or to try to tame and domesticate animals at such a time, would have been the height of folly. It might have hastened immediate starvation and brought no later reward to the survivors, because the same conditions that made wild foods scarce would have operated to prevent the success of propagation experiments. From

51

what is known of the complex mind, it does not turn to new ideas under the stress of hunger. If it knows a way to get food that has worked in the past it meets hunger by continuing known methods more diligently. Hominids typically have kept their old customs and either extended the ground they covered, or migrated to new territory.

From what is known of human behavior, it is far more plausible to assume that domestication of animals and plants began in a period of plenty when both means and time were available for experimentation and when nothing depended on the results achieved.

One can assume, secondly, that the probability of individual family experiments with domestication, and of their spread to other families, would depend on the existence of customs which gave domestication experiments some supplementary *raison d'être* during their early relatively unproductive stages.

For domesticating animals, the recognized and widespread custom of keeping pets may well have played a greater role than many writers on the subject have indicated. All authorities are quite ready to accept as fact that the earliest known domesticate, the dog, may have been primarily a pet. Some primitive peoples did fatten dogs and eat them on occasion. They have also been used as watchdogs, as hunting assistants, as draft animals, as beasts of burden, as garbage disposal units, and even as a source of fur fiber for blanket weaving. But the dog's most universal role was and is that of friend and boon companion. It is frequently pointed out that certain species of the genus *Canis* (wolves or jackals, for example) may have been attracted to man before man recognized them as anything other than a nuisance: Man was a hunter; his camps were often a source of rich garbage, which made it profitable to hang around.

The later domestication of *game* animals has confused our thinking. Jumping from the known—man lived by hunting these animals—to a conviction that food must have been on his mind when he first essayed to domesticate them is not really warranted. Primitive hunters brought home the young of many animals as pets. After all, even ants tolerate the continuing presence of other insects in their nests for no discernible reason other than the company they provide. As the English biologist Francis Galton pointed out about a century ago, not all animals can be domesticated, but primitive man managed to find out which could be, and he did not miss any major ones that civilized man subsequently found. This can mean only that he knew the available animals and their behavior in captivity; and he would have had to start this acquaintance with animals at the pet stage, when they were still too young to be dangerous, and primarily a source of entertainment, particularly for children. It is even a good bet that the idea of reproducing while still hanging around the house, and thus accidentally demonstrating a potential economic usefulness, occurred to the pets before it occurred to their hominid owners. Moreover, their progeny would have tended to remain in the pet classification rather than the food classification as long as juvenile opinion, adult tolerance, and favorable economic circumstances prevailed. Kids and lambs, both in size and playfulness, would be preferable to calves as pets; and it is noteworthy that domestication of goats and sheep preceded that of cattle, perhaps by several thousand years, as far as one can tell from archeological evidence from the Near East, notably at Shanidar and Jarmo in the upper Tigris River drainage system.[11] It is not always possible to distinguish a goat from a sheep in the fossil record. The earliest record of a domesticated Equus appears to be a picture of one being ridden which was excavated from a deposit at the Elamite city of Susa dating to the fourth millennium B.C. It is not clear whether it is a true horse or an onager (donkey-ass), but in any event logic suggests that the idea of riding came out of play with a young pet, for the Equus was not a major game

53

animal in this area, and riding is an activity that would have to come from play experience rather than as an idea out of the blue.

The domestication of plants, involving more real labor for a long-delayed and uncertain reward, shows an even more acute need for predisposing cultural habits. There is evidence that such predisposing factors did exist, but the nature and extent of their relationship to agriculture are not very clear. Nevertheless, the following factors are particularly significant: a sufficiently luxuriant supply of edible wild plant products which could retain their nutritive properties for a year or longer, to encourage at least semisedentary living cycles; construction of housing spacious enough, and weather-resistant enough, to provide dry storage for plant products; the invention of stone tools (notably the blade sickle) efficient enough to make possible harvesting and storing a year's supply of wild plant products; a cultural awareness that stored food was a tangible measure of security and future happiness.

Some such combination of cultural traits—keeping in mind the characteristics of a complex brain—would provide an incentive both for developing agriculture independently and for borrowing it from others. A particularly provocative situation would develop when one year ended with an unused surplus of wild grass cereals which had to be cleaned out of storage facilities to make way for a new harvest. What to do with the surplus would be the kind of culturally developed problem that the human brain finds most stimulating for creative play. The surplus could not be lightly discarded because of the labor that had gone into collecting it and the security that it symbolized. Yet constructing more storage pits for the surplus did not seem worth additional labor since the surplus was old and the new supply was bulky. The surplus was venture capital, usable for experimentation without peril to the group welfare. Putting it somewhere for watching, and even scratching it into the soil,

54

would add a new interest to life unsullied by anxiety over the outcome. With curiosity at work and the prospect of a kind of game in sight, the hominid involved would inevitably pick over the surplus for the most attractive seeds and plant them close by. Settlement soil was rich in elements that promote plant growth. Under such conditions, even casual experimentation could well yield a product superior to that obtained on the open range and thus reveal a new occupational specialty for hominids interested in raising their status within the group. The hominids involved might well, of course, have been the women who gathered the seeds in the first place. They would have the added advantage of a staff of juvenile assistants too young to participate in hunting and therefore constituting an additional labor force.

To substantiate this conjectural account, one may emphasize that many hominid groups did adopt a sedentary existence, with substantially built houses containing storage pits dug into the floor, and that they did have stone-bladed, handle-hafted sickles with the sheen of long use on their blades, long before the period when agriculture was adopted.[12] There were substantial settlements at or before the time of incipient land cultivation at Jericho in the Jordan Valley, at Jarmo and Shanidar in the upper Tigris River drainage, and probably elsewhere. Part of the reluctance to consider this as a forerunner of agriculture derives from awareness that the intensified use of wild grasses had begun perhaps 25,000 B.C. in such places as the Pollau Mountains of southern Moravia, but agriculture is not certain until after 8000 B.C. This long interval may be attributed to the Ice Age which was probably unfavorable to agriculture, even though appreciation of the potentialities of the cereal grasses was great enough to lead artists to engrave seed heads on mastodon ivory.

Whether agriculture or animal husbandry came first, seems a question which leads nowhere. At sites where both occurred, the bones of early domesticated animals are better preserved than evidences of early cereal grains. But if one looks more closely at the problem, it is plausible to assume that a given settlement concentrated first on one or the other, and that, normally, agriculture could not prosper in competition with grazing and browsing animals until the latter became important enough to warrant herdsmen in constant attendance, or fencing around either the animals or the planted areas. One might assume that if women had already started cultivation, they would have objected strenuously to haphazard experimentation with animal husbandry by the men. On the other hand, the presence of experimental animals, before the development of cultivation, would have had a less spectacular and more gradual effect on the work of women in gathering plant food. And the women's point of view was something with which primitive men had to reckon.

In any event, women quite generally adopted the care of gardens and cultivated areas as long as the digging stick, their time-honored tool and weapon, was the primary implement. Men took over only when newfangled contraptions, such as hoes or plows drawn by oxen or horses, came into use. Before that, men were purely auxiliary to the women, clearing land, breaking the ground, building terraces where necessary, and constructing roads or paths from settlements to land under cultivation. In some cases, men would not even touch the harvest unless an emergency existed. Producing plant foods was, for some thousands of years, a female specialty, just as hunting major game animals was a male specialty. The satisfaction that members of each sex achieved as essential contributors to group economy undoubtedly played a part in promoting these specialties and in maintaining group solidarity.

Although the development of agriculture and animal husbandry had to start in those areas where wild plants and game animals were relatively abundant, when dependable methods of cultivation had been worked out through trial and error, and the productivity of labor had been expanded both by increasing the number of varieties of plants domesticated, and by improving yields through use of seed from the most productive plants, a new geographical and economic dimension was created. Hominids could expand into areas where scarcity of natural food resources had previously prevented settlement, by taking their food-production processes with them. They were also able to free a greater percentage of the population from the time- and energy-consuming labor of hunting and food gathering. People, along with seed and animal breeding stock, moved southward from the Fertile Crescent to broader, flatter valley lands and began to develop walled cities and temples, wheeled vehicles for transport of goods, and graphic symbols for better recording and communication of numbers, words, and the concepts they symbolized. Culture began to elaborate at a faster pace because the play potential of the hominid brain was given greater opportunity for voluntary expression and was increasingly stimulated by interplay with other brains in larger population centers within broader communication areas.

Understanding the relationships of man to culture in modern times requires more intimate acquaintance with specific cultural trends in the past as illuminated by individual and group situational problems. But before approaching those problems, it is necessary to discuss incentives for developing culture.

CHAPTER 3

The Sexual Dialectic

When explorers and traders began accumulating information about the world and its inhabitants during the last four centuries, the most impressive facts were the number of different human societies that existed and the diversity of the cultures they supported. Anthropology grew out of interest in studying and analyzing this vast array of sociocultural systems as they came to the attention of the provincial populations of Europe. It was early believed that the key to human history would be found in the origin and development of these cultural and physical differences among newly discovered societies. It was even suggested that a number of strange-looking populations with bizarre patterns of behavior could best be accounted for as remnants of an earlier creation than that which brought the obviously more civilized and therefore superior peoples of the Old World into existence.

Even after it became apparent that all peoples of the world

were brothers under the skin, belonging to a single species of primate identified as *Homo sapiens,* their physical and cultural differences continued to excite more interest than their similarities. It was taken for granted that they should display such physical similarities because of the demonstrated superiority of human anatomy and physiology over the design and functional efficiency of other genera and orders of animals and show cultural likeness because of some vague but unique attribute called human nature.

Only recently has enough knowledge of the evolution of man and his culture-creating propensity become available to suggest that cultural similarities widely occurring among societies of all races, without regard to environment, or history of cultural contacts with other societies, do have heuristic significance. Human nature, however defined, or however cavalierly ignored, is a vital element in culture change and culture stability, in culture diversification, parallelism, or convergence. None of these can be explained without reference to human nature, and there is sufficient need for an explanation to warrant a closer look at human nature in any and all its manifestations.

Ascribing human behavior to human nature may, on the face of it, appear pointless, an attempt to understand something which can be observed and described by giving it a name which cannot be defined. But science once gave point to research by ascribing fire and flammability to a nonexistent substance called *phlogiston.* Why then withdraw from contemplation of human nature because it is just a probability principle? It does exist, and it does maintain a certain equilibrium through time, as can be demonstrated by the continued, universal occurrence of equivalent patterns of behavior within equivalent categories of culture.

A contemporary scholar has listed seventy-three elements of culture common to every human society still existing or known to history. These elements range from languages resolvable into identical components, cosmologies, religious rituals, ethical-moral codes, and marriage-initiated families, to such details as eating at mealtimes, rules of etiquette, and attempts to control the weather. Every society differs from all others in some details of behavior within these categories, but every society recognizes the importance of the purpose served and develops a system to meet it. The American goal of cultural change as a criterion of social progress does not stand among these universals.[1]

In order to show how such universals might develop, marriage and the family may be taken as good examples of universal social institutions. One may then inquire into their origins in the light of what is known about the early history of man, and what is beginning to be learned about the human brain as controlling organ in human nature. First—and with apologies to Sigmund Freud and his studies of central Europeans—field observation of the higher primates offers no evidence to support the argument that sex is an all-pervasive and constantly dominant factor in primate group life. Sex conflicts are not found to be a potent cause of group dissension and disintegration. One should remember that modern man, like the bower birds of New Guinea, has tended to elaborate sex beyond its original expression.

Secondly, among hominids, as among many other bisexual forms of life, the male is larger, stronger, and more active than the female. This has undoubtedly come about because of biological advantages. Security against attack is augmented by half the population having greater size and fighting ability while the other half remains smaller, so that the total food needs of the group are held within bounds. On a year-round average, the larger males need more food for optimal efficiency than the smaller females. Security would be better achieved by giving added strength and size to the males since they are not periodically incapacitated as the hominoid female is. Even apart from these practical considerations, there appears to be no advantage in making the sex that is responsible for child-bearing also responsible for group defense. Greater size and strength in women might be incompatible with group survival. In some species of carnivorous flies and spiders, where the female is the stronger, she is as likely to kill and eat the male as mate with him. Such behavior has, perhaps, tended to elimi-nate group-living species in which larger females developed.

Whether this be true or not, the hominoid line started with sexual dimorphism favoring larger size in the males. Later, as brains increased in size, it seems likely that the female of the species became aware that she, the smaller and weaker of the sexes, was burdened with the pain and labor of procreation. As long as hominoids were largely vegetarians, this probably did not matter too much, for females could provide for them-selves and their young just about as easily as the heavier males could satisfy their greater appetites. Nevertheless, judging from the way female simians scream at their lazy male consorts when young are in danger, one may conclude that, with a major increase in brain size, there would be some latent, subconscious resentment about the unequal division of biological burdens.

The shift from dependence on plant foods to an omniv-orous diet—with meat regarded as a symbol of social status even if not an essential for survival—would tend to bring this latent resentment to the surface. The larger, stronger males took over the new occupation of hunting, and presumably whether they brought any game back to camp was at first a matter of accident. Traditionally, one may assume, they had not contributed to the sustenance of either female consorts or offspring. Consequently, the females found themselves really underprivileged. They did not have the long canine teeth and jutting jaws and claws of specially evolved carnivore females, and they were more handicapped by their young.

When this situation developed, as it would, the hominoid

line encountered its first major social problem, as a by-product of the delightful new idea of playing a competitive game with one's food before dinner. The game would appeal to that aspect of the play potential of complex male brains which responds to a chancy outcome, involving tension and even danger. But the female, as a non-participant in the exhilarating chase, would be chiefly concerned over her share of the spoils. Although her brain, like her body, was about 10 percent smaller than that of the male, she never lacked ability to recognize her personal problems and try to solve them. Males, who for one reason or another, perhaps mere pride in their prowess, brought meat back to the group, would find themselves the center of female attention. In this effort, again, one female could find herself handicapped *vis-à-vis* other females, when she was suckling an infant and most needed additional food.

Early hominoids left no record of their effort to meet such problems, but one can guess what would happen next: female avoidance of non-cooperative males, with a possible decline in pregnancy rates; and then infanticide and abortion. Of course, the timing of such reactions is uncertain but from their wide occurrence among primitive peoples one knows that these female reactions were not recently acquired. Twenty-four hundred years ago, Aristophanes used the theme of a female sit-down strike in his comedy *Lysistrata*, and he knew that his earthy humor would not be alien to his audience. More pertinently, the spacing of children, and infanticide and abortion, are common reactions of women in primitive societies, either when infants cannot be welcomed and properly cared for or when there is no other way to express spite against a husband or his family.[2] Students of Indian life observed many conflicts between the women's desire to be free from the burdens of motherhood and the tribe's interest in having enough boys to make up for losses suffered in war.[3]

Antagonism deriving from the adoption of meat in the

62

diet without reasonably fair distribution between males and gravid females would have raised serious apprehension in small groups of hominoids. Low longevity averages for adults, and high mortality rates for infants and children, made the competitive position of the group and its continued survival dependent on a relatively continuous supply of births. The male hunters would learn by experience that they had to bring game home in order to keep their consorts happy. Slow learners would find themselves on the periphery of the circle of eligible mates. The most successful groups would be those which made mating a publicly witnessed contract—with the male acknowledging responsibility as provider of meat for his consort and her offspring, and the females tacitly accepting gathering plant foods close to camp as their field of specialization. Judging by the wide distribution of status rewards for women who contribute to the strength of the group by successfully bearing and rearing children, and the lack of respect or overt contempt for barren women, among contemporary primitive societies, one may assume that this kind of public pressure also was of early origin. The time when marriage developed cannot be exactly known, but develop it did; marriage as a social institution dedicated to the nurturing of children is universal. And marriage is still, primarily, this kind of social institution, however it may be embellished and elaborated by human ingenuity.

Some scholars have maintained that marriage came into existence as a means of publicly acknowledging the proprietary rights of a given male over a particular female, and that this was the only means of preventing disruption of the group by fighting. But observation of simian primate bands gives no evidence that squabbling over sex was serious enough to outweigh the attractions of security and group companionship. An attitude of proprietorship may well have been an incidental *effect* rather than an *object* of marriage; violent jealousy may be as much a response to cultural expectancy among dominant males who have assumed the marriage responsibility as it is a sexually stimulated response. Such jealousy rather smacks of the righteous anger of an instinctively dominant male who suspects that he has been defrauded by a subordinate contractual partner and who believes that he is demonstrating his manhood in a socially approved way by violent reprisal.

Men accept the idea of sharing a wife, just as women accept the idea of sharing a husband, provided that this is a socially sanctioned form of marriage contract. Polyandrous marriages, with multiple husbands, or polygynous marriages with multiple wives, are found in many parts of the world. In fact, one study discovered that, among 475 different societies, 378 were basically polygynous, 31 approved of polyandry, and only 66 were basically monogamous. The most populous countries are monogamous, and this form of marriage is therefore accepted by far the greatest number of people.[4]

One of the first conclusions to be drawn from this conjectural history of a basic institution is that human nature cannot be regarded as a single packet of reactions to circumstances and events, which every individual receives as a genetic heritage. The packaging has at least two different mixes: one for males, the other for females, reflecting a size difference, a different functional design, proportional changes in hormones and other body chemicals, and a difference in emotional lability. The additional degree of differential in size, strength, and physical and mental maturity in children requires one to consider the natures of the undeveloped male and female which function, temporarily, as if they were different kinds of human nature. If basic culture changes are chiefly initiated by male human nature, as they often are, then compensating changes must occur to keep the feminine plurality of adult society happy.

As an example of how this adult competition works, take the technological improvements converting agriculture from a specialty for women which gave them an integral part in the economic system, into an occupation largely if not entirely dominated by men. Out of this, especially in the upper strata of society, came such compensations, from the early Middle Ages on, as church weddings, a social pedestal for women, a code of chivalric behavior on the part of men, love sonnets, emphasis on romantic love, and beauty as a goal which could be achieved by using cosmetics. More practically, motherhood was glorified, and women were praised for skill in household tasks and even such leisure specialties as knitting, crocheting, and embroidery. One should mention, too, that in the early cities of Mesopotamia, women had moved into the professions of scribe and teacher by the second millennium B.C., if not earlier. In Babylon under Hammurabi, women were operating so many houses of hospitality for the weary wayfarer, selling home-brewed beer among other things, that they had to be regulated by law.

None of these compensations and new opportunities completely solved the problem. The compensations were accepted and in part retained permanently, but further technological advances took much of the glory out of operating a household and eliminated the need for home handicrafts to such an extent that many women found themselves idling along like a fifth wheel on the economic bandwagon. Further concessions had to be made to them, such as a more equitable share in inheritances, the invention of community property laws, and formalized alimony. On their own, women won the right to vote and run for public office, greater equality of job opportunities, equal pay for equal work, public acceptance of the respectability of performing in public, a place in professional sports, and even participation in male vices, such as smoking and drinking in public. To the best of their ability women have insisted that there be a meaningful place in civilization for female human nature as well as male. In the heat of their struggle, however, male and female adults both continued to disregard the increasing frustration of the human nature of children. Technology has shoved them out of the economic system. Only now, as adults become painfully aware of young people in protest, are they beginning to realize how exile from the world of work thwarts juvenile human nature.

At this point marriage may appear to be only an armistice in the perpetual war between the sexes. That would be subornation of calumny. Marriage provided the close and continuing social bond necessary for the development of proto-culture into culture. As a publicly witnessed oral contract between men and women for cooperative care of young, it formalized division of labor between the sexes and required a complete reorganization of society with specific reference to these contracting couples. Individuals directly concerned with the prime contract had to be explicitly identified. Further, society as a whole needed rules to determine degree of affiliation with the contractors in order to protect the contractors from unjust exploitation and to establish a basis for reciprocity and integration among active contractors, or between them and other members of society temporarily or permanently out of the contracting business.

Marriage made subgrouping of society into the nuclear family, the extended family, and the sib or clan a functional necessity. The advent of these subgroupings would require members to be identified by appearance, by recognized gesture, or by specific sound symbols. In fact, organizing families may be listed as one of the most important stimuli toward use of sound for something more than expression of a situational emotion, or a call for immediate physical action or reaction. Such intimately bound and cooperatively operating groups would, furthermore, create the close association and shared interest in routinely repetitive situations, which would challenge complex brains to establish means of communication. Inter-family contacts and temporary groupings for hunting or gathering would lead to mutual agreement on the meaning of these special combinations of phonemes and thereby promote the development of organized language.

Scholars have tried to estimate what stage of culture would absolutely require language. It has even been suggested that the presence of a language in some early society known only through its fossil remains might be assumed if the left sides of the skulls, housing the major speech areas of the brain, were larger than the right. A similar connection has been hopefully assumed between asymmetrical skulls and preferential handedness. Unfortunately, no connection has been found in living peoples between the location of speech centers or the asymmetry of skulls and right-hand or left-hand preference.[5] The only dependable skeletal determination of handedness is based on comparison of the relative size of the clavicle and limb bones on the two sides of the body. Determining when a true language evolved is, for the present, akin to fixing the geographical location of the end of a rainbow. One can say only that using crude stone tools may have created a need for some expression denoting "Drop it, that's mine." The family brought in the need for identifying individuals by specific subgroup and for developing those systems of kinship terminology which occur in all human societies no matter how simple their culture.

Another universal trait which seems to attest to the age and importance of the family as a culture-promoting institution is the prohibition of marriage between close kin. This trait, identified as an "incest tabu," varies in application from society to society but is universally most specific in regard to members of the nuclear family: father and daughters, mother and sons, and brothers and sisters. Throughout the world, folklore explains the incest tabu with the statement that sexual relations between close kin are unhuman and therefore immoral. Prac-

67

tical reasons are also offered at the folklore level. The Arapesh of New Guinea, when pressed for comment, declared that it would be sheer stupidity for a young man to marry his sister and miss the chance of establishing the right to call on another family, particularly on brothers-in-law, for help in time of need.[6]

Early pseudo-scientific explanations were equally practical. It was pointed out that marriage between close kin would tend to bring into dominance the deleterious recessive genes in the blood line; a tabu against this practice was universal simply because societies which did not observe such a tabu were genetically weaker and eventually died out. Inbreeding among European royalty, it was asserted as evidence, sporadically produced haemophilia and other undesirable afflictions. It is now known that doubling recessive genes by inbreeding can also improve the stock and that a number of royal families—including those of ancient Egypt, Peru, and the Hawaiian Islands—followed the practice of brother-sister marriages to keep their azure blood pure. It is reported that Cleopatra was a descendant of fourteen generations of brother-sister marriages. Evolution clearly has been dominated by procreation among closely related animals; if inbreeding were invariably deleterious, the hominoid line, among many others, would probably have perished long before it advanced far enough to think of the incest tabu.

Many well-known anthropologists have emphasized that incest tabus aided small societies to survive by promoting marriages outside the family group and so establishing bases for potential alliances with other groups. Obtaining women from outside by capture or ostentatious negotiation added prestige to their acquisition and became the sporting, and therefore desirable, way to proceed. A tabu against any other kind of marriage would merely acknowledge the "rightness" of the admired procedure. It has also been suggested that the incest tabu formalized a widespread necessity. Since longevity was so low and infant mortality so high in ancient times, a parent rarely lived long enough to mate with a child, nor were two children of the same family likely to reach mating age in close sequence. In other words, the incest tabu again emphasized the rightness of a custom based on necessity.[7]

Scientific parsimony apparently requires one to recognize the antecedent importance of the family and the possible role of the incest tabu in preserving and protecting it as a successful socioeconomic institution. Incest tabus grow out of the family and a system of differentiated kinship; their universal occurrence together certainly implies a reciprocative relationship.[8] Unregulated father-daughter matings would negate the primary purpose of the family by increasing offspring without providing additional adult manpower to see the resulting progeny through infancy and childhood. Even more dangerous to the economy would be informal matings between brothers and sisters before they were physically, mentally, or socially mature enough to give proper care to offspring.[9] This last contingency probably had the greatest influence on the development of the incest tabu. The hominid, like other primates, produces very slowly maturing young who may be precociously active sexually. Possibly the development of the family as a social institution served to promote opportunities for clandestine sexual experimentation among its younger members. The early shift to meat as a staple food made the maturity of parents a still more important criterion of economic adequacy. That concerns of this type were dominant in promoting the incest tabu is further evidenced by the generally high regard that primitive societies have for marriages between young blood relatives living in separate family groups. Every existing incest tabu forbids brothers and sisters to marry but they are widely encouraged to arrange marriages between their respective children, and particularly cross-cousin marriages, that is, marriages between the sister's son and the brother's daughter. This system divides and so tends to equalize authority between the sexes, with each specializing on marriage arrangements for children of the opposite sex.

In both hand-preferences and incest tabus, biological and cultural amnesia are quite obviously at work. The reason for hand preference defies complete explanation at present; yet, until recently, naturally left-handed children might be forced to shift to using the right. And many societies—English, French, and south Indian among them—use words like "left-handed" to mean inferior, stupid, or even immoral.

The sources of modern attitudes toward incest are as obscure as attitudes toward handedness, yet Americans have not completely lost their reluctance to approve marriages between cousins. An even stranger flowering of creative ignorance was displayed in England, where, as late as the middle nineteenth century, the law treated marriage with a dead wife's sister as an incestuous union. In many primitive societies, on the other hand, marrying a wife's sister, either after or before the wife's death, was not only permissible, but frequently obligatory, a duty which the wife and her parents expected a man to discharge, and which the man's parents expected the wife's family to arrange.

As the incest tabu emphasized rules for family living, so the struggle between the sexes fostered the development of other social customs. Everywhere, one finds evidence of females trying to win equality, and of males trying to retain the dominance that size, and freedom from menstruation and pregnancy, gave them. Comparative studies of culture bring this subconscious struggle to light in unexpected places. One of the early male strategies was to persuade women that men shared the burden of childbirth and that no child could grow to maturity without male help in overcoming adverse supernatural forces. The most dramatic example of this was the couvade, a widespread custom which required husbands to take to their beds at, or before, the onset of their wives' labor, to receive appropriate condolences or congratulations from friends and relatives, and manfully to try to get back on their feet not too long after their wives had resumed their household chores. Hellenistic writers, such as Apollonius Rhodius, Diodorus, and Strabo, commented on this custom among the Basques, the Corsicans, and other peoples about two thousand years ago. Early explorers and travelers, from Marco Polo on, found comparable customs in China, Chinese Turkestan, India, Borneo, Siam, Africa, and the Americas. In East Anglia and other rural areas of England, from Elizabethan times almost into the present, people thought that the husband was preternaturally susceptible to sickness when his wife became pregnant. It was proper to ask a man with toothache whether his wife, by any chance, was with child. Curiously enough, in World War II, English and American medical officers noted that married men overseas tended to develop symptoms of pregnancy on receiving word that "a blessed event" was in the offing. Statistically, they showed an unexplainably rapid increase in weight, suffered from morning sickness, and after the expected date of birth had passed, exhibited typical post-partum depressions.

In primitive societies generally, aside from those where the couvade occurred in classical form, husbands joined their wives in avoiding certain foods; they might go into isolation for a few days and refrain from touching weapons or going about their normal routine for weeks after the birth. Among the Pomo Indians of California, where the women were recognized as among the most accomplished basket-makers known to modern ethnographers, the men maintained that only they could weave a basket-cradle in which an infant would prosper. Some psychiatrists and psychoanalysts explain the widespread ordeal of circumcision for males as a practice intended to demonstrate that women were not unique even in menstruation, for youths, too, must shed blood before becoming men.[10]

The instinctive struggle between male human nature and female human nature to maintain and entrench male dominance on the one hand, and on the other to equalize female rights and privileges in spite of biological differences, is clearly detectable in other aspects of the evolution of culture. Because of the obvious relationship between females and birth, male claims were usually limited to a mere share in that process. But the dominant male has sought further to justify the advantage given him by size, strength, and freedom from the primary vicissitudes of the reproductive process, by assuming a little of the divine right that kings have sometimes found so helpful. He found the opportunity to do this because of the many inexplicable circumstances of life which can be brought under control only by magic, if at all.

Why was one woman fertile and another not? Why did death come when it did to this person or that? Why was food plentiful one year and not the next? Why were some people always fortunate in what they did and others seldom or never so? Why did it rain or not rain? All these mysteries clearly demonstrated the operation of some arbitrary power. The responsibility of guarding against avoidable calamities engineered by this arbitrary power everywhere fell into the province of the men as protectors and organizers of protection against extraneous danger. But this particular danger called for a different kind of protection from that of repelling hostile forces dispatched by other hominid societies. It presented a challenge not to brawn but to whatever reserve of idle neurons the larger brains of the males could muster to deal with the supernatural.

Understanding the problem required creative explanation of the relation of man to the supernatural: cosmic theories, human origin myths, explanatory myths, personification of supernatural power, and propitiation of personified supernaturals through ceremony, ritual, and codes of individual behavior. With most of this manufactured knowledge, women came to be familiar through ceremonies and rituals at which they were at least spectators. But the men made clear that these exhibitions of magic and miracle were only the public manifestation of a body of secret knowledge which had been given to them for safekeeping, and which men alone could use for the benefit of the whole society. This knowledge could be discussed only in sweathouses, clubhouses, or secret society enclosures, from which women and children were excluded. Women might occasionally acquire paraphernalia or special revelations which gave them power as healers, diviners, or seers, but only men knew the rituals which kept game on the land, fish in the water, birds in the air, the sun and moon in the heavens, and so safeguarded the general welfare of the group. Thus men demonstrated that their dominance rested not only on physical size and strength, but on knowledge, which was divinely inspired and approved.

Without this knowledge, no boy could become a man. Almost everywhere in primitive society, he had to demonstrate his readiness for this learning by going through an initiation, frequently with ordeals, and always with an oath that he would keep what he learned secret from the women and children. To a large extent this was "junk" knowledge, cabalistic words and signs, rituals and their mythological or legendary significance, and finally methods for convincing production of apparent miracles, from conjuring up a spirit voice, to playing the part of a spirit, or dealing with ghosts. One common method of impressing both women and children with the deep seriousness of initiations was staging a mock death and resurrection of initiates. This ceremony not only impressed on the young male that, despite any private misgivings, magic had helped him cross the line from childhood to manhood, but it

73

also showed women that men could re-create life—and in a few days or weeks, rather than the nine months required for its original creation.

To cite the Pomo Indians again, one underlying purpose of the annual "world-renewal" ceremony and initiation was pointed up by gathering all the women and children into a circle, and then valiantly saving them from an attack by hideously painted devils who came rushing down from the hills with fire streaming from the tops of their heads (basket helmets filled with burning pitch). Before the devils came, ceremonial leaders lectured the women on how difficult it was to save those who behaved badly; and the devils lent point to this by waving live rattlesnakes in the faces of those women believed to need a strong admonition. Finally, by superhuman effort, the men present vanquished the devils and drove them back to the hills.

Although the subject has not been studied, one may reasonably assume that the elaboration of such methods of implying divine authority for male dominance is related to the matters which women may control in the society. Notable among these are the right to determine where young people shall live after marriage, who shall inherit tangible and intangible property, and who shall participate in family, sib, and tribal affairs. Female-centered societies, in which descent is traced through the mother, with elderly women exercising matriarchal authority, and inheritance going to a man's sister's children, occur sporadically around the world. It was originally thought that such societies were a vestige of a period when all societies traced descent matrilineally because sexual promiscuity made it difficult if not impossible to identify the father of any particular child. It is now known that probably there never was such a period in human history. Rather, it seems likely that matrilineal descent is just another method of equalizing female with male social status. In many areas where it

The Sexual Dialectic

has been highly elaborated, one finds intensified male efforts to reestablish dominance, as is true among the Pomo, where even chieftainships go to the chief's sister's son rather than to his own, and where sisters occasionally usurp the chieftainship when they lack an eligible son.

Involved in tracing descent, of course, is the universally essential problem of protecting family strength. If two families, sibs, or clans are accustomed to intermarry, then the children resulting from such matches must be so apportioned that both groups gain about the same number of new members. In keeping with the operation of complex brains there must be a rule to follow, and the simplest is that both families either claim all the children of males or all the children of females supplied for intergroup marriages. In the first case, children would belong to the same family and/or clan as their father; descent would be patrilineal. In the second case, children would be affiliated with their mother's family or clan; descent would be matrilineal. Either plan protects the contracting groups, but the matrilineal system leaves the dominant male in a subordinate position, and this is often accentuated by the related custom of establishing residence with, or near, the wife's family. Psychologically, this should create problems for the dominance-designed human nature of the male: his own children belong to a different group; his personal property goes to his sister's children; and he himself lives and works by sufferance on another family's or clan's property. One might expect to find males of limited aggressiveness living under such conditions, and expect, also, to find them seeking spiritual reinforcement of their egos.

The development of a matrilineate is a kind of cultural dead end because it mutes male aggressiveness and female counter efforts. Normal male aggressiveness, mental as well as physical, aimed at enhancement of group status, is damped by a cultural system which rewards dutiful conformance to a

75

subordinate social role. Normal female persistence in seeking equality of rights is diverted into maintaining the *status quo*. In every known society, women may be excused and even admired by their sisters for successfully performing men's work, unless the men have taken the precaution of identifying such brashness as an affront to the supernatural world. On the other hand, men can expect no praise from anyone for doing women's work, even where the women have not identified it as a supernaturally supported specialty. Calling a female an "old man" because of her activities may put her in a mildly ridiculous light among members of her own sex, but calling a male an "old woman" is close to a deadly insult. Matrilineal and matriarchal sociocultural systems confuse the dichotomy based on sex differences in size and strength.

A patrilineal social system is inherently dynamic because females constantly strive to improve themselves by infiltrating activities which appear to carry more prestige and to be intrinsically more desirable, solely because they are almost if not entirely monopolized by dominant males. As this monopoly is broken, the prestige of the activity falls from the male point of view. The male is handicapped because he cannot compete with women in an activity which they perform successfully without losing a little of his self-esteem as a born-to-the-purple, dominant male. His only recourse is to turn the play potential of a larger brain to new and inevitably more complicated activities which men can monopolize for a while at least. Their standing as the principal providers and protectors of the family is under increasing strain today as the proportion of jobs requiring size, strength, and physical aggressiveness steadily declines. At the same time, men inadvertently compound the magnitude of their problem by innovations which further reduce the economic value, the creative challenge, and the attractiveness of female specialties, such as keeping house on a full-time basis.

From an optimistic, ultraprogressive point of view, intersexual competition has done wonders for *Homo sapiens.* It has steadily increased the number of occupations from which a wide range of talents within each succeeding generation could, theoretically, find a method of earning a living best suited to their idiosyncrasies. The process began by expanding the dominance hierarchy for males and their chosen consorts, by making hunting an additional specialty for men, as an alternative to fighting their way to the top, and by making the gathering of plant foods a specialty for women, as an alternative to bargaining on the basis of sex and childbearing power alone. Then mankind proceeded to elaborate on this remarkable idea until the number of specialized occupations exceeded the prospecting potentials of any individual during a single lifetime. Modern American civilization might well be characterized as a culture dedicated not only to the indefinite promotion of change but to the infinite expansion of specialties. It now has ultraspecialties: the doctors' doctor, the lawyers' lawyer, the teachers' teacher, but most of these come to the end of their happy spans without doing much more damage than raising the entrance requirements for the profession, and making many specialties out of one. The ultraspecialists who create real concern are the specialists' specialists at work out on the boundaries of professional knowledge seeking new concepts around which specialties may be built and expressing their delight in this, history's greatest age for the play potential of the human mind, by attempting to turn secondary and even elementary schools into training camps for their own specialties.

This enthusiasm neglects the differences between male and female human nature and between adults of either sex and juveniles of that sex; and it ignores the range of capacities and interests within these categories of human nature. Rapid changes in culture and meteoric departures from old patterns of living may not trouble, indeed may be thought unworthy of notice by, those engaged in the absorbing excitement of discovery. But many others, who must live with the results of such discovery, have an instinctive heritage which appreciates some stability during a lifetime, an opportunity to find a job (itself an *ersatz* way of getting a living) and to keep at it as long as the desire and ability to do so continue. Contemporary talk about protecting freedom gives little evidence of consideration for the basic freedom to live out a life in which the stability and order to which men are habituated, as well as instinctively geared, are not constantly threatened by swashbuckling explorers followed by armies of peddlers.

Currently, it is assumed that whatever creative minds can discover is good for all other minds; their unhappiness and frustration with what is called good for them is no concern of the creative mind, but just a temporary problem which the schools must solve. Some biologists refer to the rapid evolution of the human brain, in size and complexity, as an example of neoplastic pathology which could lead to the extinction of the human race, just as body size apparently brought an end to saurians. The human brain quite frequently becomes so enamored of its own ideas that it will destroy others for failing to admire them, or even destroy its own perfectly healthy body to prove a point, express a mood, or emphasize a pique. Only now is it being recognized that well-intentioned minds, engaged in quite innocent, intrinsically laudable mental play, can collectively create a cultural environment that progressively frustrates an increasing proportion of the human race.

CHAPTER 4

The Guinea-Pig Generation

In assessing the suitability of any cultural environment for human habitation it is not enough to ask whether the adult population of the moment is still alive and functioning. The members of this population are only the survivors of an originally larger generation. Their years of conditioning have acclimatized them and partially immunized them against cultural instability and its psychoneurotic effects. Like individuals long subjected to measured doses of a dangerous drug, adult reactions are muted.

The newly arriving infants and juveniles are the real guinea pigs. They must take whatever psychic dosage civilization is proud to offer and do it with a pattern of instincts selectively chosen for survival during a period of two million years or so, more than 99.5 percent of which was spent as a stone-wielding hunter and plant gatherer. Judging by the size of cranial cavities, contemporary children must face urban living,

79

mass education, and highly artificial economic pursuits with a brain no greater in mass or different in configuration from that of Cro-Magnon children, thirty thousand or more years ago. There has hardly been time for any evolutionary adaptation to urbanized, industrialized civilization, even if some as yet undetected selection process were at work.

Although no one can determine with any accuracy what a child's life was like in a Cro-Magnon caveman's family, something is known about a child's life in primitive societies which were, until recently, still supporting themselves by hunting and gathering, or at best by digging-stick or hoe agriculture and some herding. All these societies may be culturally more complex than those of Cro-Magnon times, but the contrast with modern times, from a child's point of view, is still unbelievably great.

The infant in primitive society seldom survived birth or lived many days unless conditions were favorable and it could be welcomed. For in one way or another, primitive peoples connected births with a supernatural decision. The infant's arrival was evidence of a kindly attitude on the part of some wielder of power in the supernatural world. The infant might be an actual reincarnation of some long-dead ancestor, or merely a ward of some ancestor to provide a resting place on earth for the ancestor's soul. To accept such a blessing from the spirits and then not care for it properly would be the height of folly. If the chosen mother found herself unprepared to accept this responsibility, or faced by some economic or political crisis, the wisest decision was to send the infant back to the spirit world for rebirth later. Abortion or infanticide was not regarded as homicide, but as postponement of a desired birth until the infant could be given the appreciative and grateful attention that the spirits expected.

Consequently the infant that lived long enough to have consciousness of existence had a position of special importance.

It was a representative of the spirit world that could leave if it suffered mistreatment. If it were regarded as a reincarnation, it was automatically endowed with the personality and reputation earned by its predecessor and was regaled with anecdotes —true or somewhat improved—of what the ancestor had accomplished with the personal power that the infant had now inherited. As the child grew, this pleasant but vague sense of importance tended to crystallize into a personal identity and self-confidence in meeting life's challenges. The child felt assured that, through proper behavior and renewal of spiritual strength, it could meet these challenges successfully.

Life in the primitive family group tended to confirm the child's sense of importance. An infant was not only a future asset as a contributor to group strength and economic security, but also an immediate guarantee of respect from other families and of higher social status for the parents. Treatment of very young children reflected both a reverent attitude toward the supernaturals involved and the need for caution in handling an inherently valuable possession. Parents avoided corporal punishment: spanking or slapping was inappropriate for a grandfather or grandmother just returned to earth and struggling to reestablish terrestrial habits. Further, death was a constant threat to young children, and one needed to build their desire to stay, their liking for parents and family. If punishment seemed necessary, every effort was made to make the spirits responsible. There were always spirits whose major function was disciplining children who did not behave as a guest on earth should. Whatever the disapproved activity of the child might be, some spirit did not like it.

Children heard about these omnipresent, omnipotent disciplinarians from the time they were able to listen and understand. Children knew how fierce they looked, and how painful and frightening their anger could be. Their reality was attested because every bump or scratch received in play could best be explained as a warning from the spirit world. In many areas, the hoot of the owl, or perhaps the roar of a lion somewhere in the darkness, was identified as the voice of one of these spirits. Parents or other adults often imitated these voices to demonstrate that supernatural policemen were on duty close by. Drawings or replicas of them might be set up at strategic points. But the crucial proof of these supernatural disciplinarians, in many areas of the primitive world, was provided by their periodic appearance in person. In connection with some kinds of annual ceremonies, adults in disguise would stalk about with crooks to catch naughty children, or knives to cut off their heads, or sacks full of snakes in which to imprison and carry them away. This method of meting out punishment when and where needed left no tangible target for juvenile resentment. The parents could side with their erring offspring and beg the disciplinarians to give them another chance. On occasion, parents shared in the punishment and made it into a calamity which the child's misdemeanor visited upon the entire family. His future behavior was likely to be influenced by the enormity of the penalty as well as by the difficulty of escaping detection and punishment by an invisible watcher who could materialize at will.

But this spiritual backstop for parents was not purely negative. Good as well as bad behavior would be noted, and youngsters could expect a recompense if the spirits were pleased. From the spirits came the power that brought skill, achievement, and security in human enterprise. This was no vague reward; for skills, achievements, and safeguards to security were relatively few and clearly identified in the typical primitive society. The youngster usually grew up in a group composed of parents, siblings, and lineal, collateral, and affinal relatives which presented a microcosm of the culture of the larger society. He observed and sometimes took at least a limited part in all the activities upon which biological survival

82

depended. He had no questions about how one made a living, and he was encouraged to try his hand at various forms of that enterprise as soon as he was physically and mentally ready, without regard to chronological age.

Such training and instruction as a child needed, he could obtain from elders of one sex or the other with all the advantages that come from individual tutoring and active apprenticeship in performing the task at hand or in solving the imminent problem. The "how" that his teachers taught was the result of their own experience. The "why" came out of their accumulated memories of the wisdom of the society. What he learned had a dependability vouched for by community concurrence, and by clear evidence that it had always been thus and thus it would always be. The respect accorded to wise old men and women was undiluted by cultural change for the sake of change, and the resulting rapid obsolescence of knowledge.

The child in primitive society escaped the tension his urban counterpart experiences when instinctive needs conflict with the demands of propriety and morality. The youngster today must remain dependent on his parents far longer than any primitive would have thought decent, yet he is expected to become mentally as well as economically independent of them.[1] Furthermore, he is required to remain relatively static physically while culture and society whirl and careen in change all about him. In primitive societies, on the other hand, culture and society remain satisfyingly stable while he moves as dynamically as his development and maturity permit. A young person does not burst out of minority like a captive animal released from a cage, but advances toward his majority in steps marked by increasing rights and privileges in the adult world around him. Aboriginal societies have many methods of showing young people that they are getting closer to manhood or womanhood. Boys may be encouraged to try their hand at hunting, and girls at gathering food. Their first clear-cut

83

achievements, however humble, are occasions for family, or even wider, celebration. In the typical first-game rite, a boy is the host to adults, who taste of his first small contribution to the family larder and pronounce it the best they have ever eaten, sure proof that the group has a great hunter or gatherer in its midst, a surety against want in the future. This may be followed in the life of a boy by other celebrations as he bags larger and larger game, and he may be buoyed up by the general assurance that when he has completed his inventory of hunting achievements he will be eligible for initiation as a member of adult society, with the right to marry and raise a family.[2] Such ceremonies were apparently universal among Eskimo bands, and general among other hunting tribes of Canada and the non-agricultural northern areas of what is now the United States. Vestiges of first-game or first-fruits rites also occurred among semisedentary agricultural tribes. Among the Eskimo, and other tribes primarily dependent on meat, great effort would be made to help a boy earn his first praise by driving game toward him, letting him take the first shot, or allowing him to deliver the *coup de grâce*. If he set a trap which failed, older hands might surreptitiously reset it, or even supply an appropriate catch from some other trap. They would paraphrase the proverb: one must first experience success to appreciate fully the satisfaction it brings.

In the meantime, he accumulated many outward signs that he was a maturing neophyte in an exclusive company. Perhaps he already had a skull that had been flattened or elongated by pressure in infancy to identifying him as belonging to a tribe of great tradition. He dressed in a common style, wore his hair in an approved way, and gradually accumulated the insignia of his society: circumcision, tattooing; pierced ears, nose, cheeks, or lips; scarification of the body, knocked-out or filed front teeth; depilation of hair in set patterns; painted designs; or ornaments, such as headbands, necklaces, arm or ankle bracelets, or feathers in the hair. All these were conducive to satisfaction in a gregarious species, for they testified to membership in the group, and at the same time gave it importance by setting it off from every other group.

Not all this individual progress, however, was limited to useful accomplishments and superficial decoration. Every group had its own language, differing greatly or only in dialectic detail from every other. It had some kind of philosophy about cosmic plan, human origin, and/or the meaning of life. It had its own kind of music, songs, and dances; its own oral literature which might range from myths, epics, legends, and anecdotes to proverbs and riddles, in prose, and from lyric to epic in poetry. The total array of culture at the primitive level was limited, but it was fully shared by members of the supporting society. If a liberal education be defined as ability to converse with others on a broad, common foundation of knowledge and experience, the primitive man was more liberally educated within his own society than the average civilized man is in his. This, too, provided for the impatient young hominid a ladder of accomplishment which led to a sense of community. The total knowledge available might be limited, but limitation furthered unity, and did not completely restrict the individual, for creative ability could be expressed in perfection of knowledge and its recital, in the artistry with which it was fitted to audience and occasion.

In the absence of writing and printing, the importance of individual memory and talent tended to increase with age and allowed the elderly to approach death with dignity and a sense of usefulness unabated. Quite frequently in primitive society, the goal of age was not longevity, but death while one was physically and mentally equipped for life in the world beyond. This, too, had its effect on the attitude of youth. Where one meets with a belief that infants represent the reappearance of the spirit of an ancestor, or where the giving of a treasured family name carries with it the power of those who held it before, there is an implied responsibility to handle the heirloom carefully and, if possible, to pass it on refurbished rather than worn out and tarnished.

Without question, one striking difference between primitive education and that which the public schools make available to young Americans lies in emphasis on the spiritual in the first instance and on intellectual accomplishment in the second. Part of the primitive effort may be dismissed as based on naïve dependence on superstitious beliefs, but it unquestionably reached an aspect of youthful human nature that modern classroom instruction is obliged to avoid because of the variety of opinions concerning religious conviction held by adults. These range from the orthodox tenets of one or another faith to the denials of the agnostic or atheist, but all proponents insist that if any thought touching on the spiritual is injected into school instruction, it must not disparage their own particular stands. They are not thinking of the magico-spiritual expectancies of the majority of youngsters but of protecting an adult school of thought. The failure of adults to agree, or even seek agreement, on how to meet the needs of a developing mind in this highly controversial area results in the neglect of a powerful stimulus to personality growth. One might say that modern civilization suffers not only from cultural amnesia but also from intellectual myopia and a kind of technologomania.

On the other hand, American Indians, to cite an example close to home, were so convinced that maturity came with an inner awakening that some of them fed their children gunpowder in hope that it would provide a flash of insight as spectacular as that noted at the muzzle of a gun. Out of this sincere search for spiritual enlightenment, properly guided, many other admired traits of character seemed to emerge. This can best be illustrated by the quest for a guardian spirit which so many tribes of northern North America encouraged their young men,

86

and sometimes their young women, to undertake. A classical account of this quest describes the Thompson Indians of British Columbia.[3] There a boy began his questing for a guardian spirit when he was old enough to dream of an arrow, a canoe, or a woman—somewhere between the ages of twelve and sixteen. He might have been preparing for it earlier by hardening himself, by taking cold baths, observing food tabus, and developing himself physically. He might, for example, volunteer to take a whipping at one of the annual midwinter ceremonies and try to remain stoical until the whip wore out.

When his dreams and other omens were propitious, he went out to gain for himself a personal guardian spirit, a supernatural helper who would be attracted by his endurance, bravery, and humility. His purpose was indicated to the tribe and to any spirits which might be present by a coating of red paint on his face, a cedar bark or skin headband, deer-hoof ornaments tied to his knees and ankles, and a skin apron decorated symbolically to indicate the kind of talent he wanted most. This costume not only insured him against casual interruptions from other tribesmen, but set him off from other youngsters as one who was rapidly becoming a man. He was probably envied by some and admired by others, which would help to increase his determination. On four consecutive days, with bow and arrows in hand, he ran until he was bathed in perspiration and could run no more, then plunged into cold water. On the nights that followed these days, he built a fire on a nearby mountain top and in a lonely vigil prayed, sang, and danced until dawn.

All this was a prologue to the real vision questing, which required that he go on pilgrimages alone into the mountains, eating nothing for from four to eight days, the length of the fast depending on his individual fortitude. The more he suffered, the stronger the power he received. It was customary to make these pilgrimages in the winter when the youth would not be tempted by berries, fruits, nuts, and other edibles along the way. He took with him a single sleeping mat, a fire drill, and sometimes a bow and arrows. He intensified the effect of fasting by purgatives and by poking a stick down his throat to cause vomiting. In addition he heated rocks in his fire, threw water on them, and bathed himself in steam. Then he would plunge into a cold mountain stream, pick up the warm rocks, throw them as far as he could, run after them, throw them again, and so on, to insure himself against disease, ill fortune, and laziness. On occasion he would set up small targets and shoot at them with arrows. If he missed, he would pick up the arrows, run about four miles and try his skill again. This might continue all night, and if he did not hit a target, he knew that his greatest talent would not be as a hunter, although he could assure himself of being adequate by shooting some small animal and presenting it as a gift to a very old man.

The vision-quester continued his pilgrimages until, helped by starvation, exhaustion, and loneliness, he had a dream or conviction of having met the spirit of some animal, bird, or plant under extraordinary circumstances. Thus he acquired a spirit which would be his protector through life. His father might help the boy to achieve this by letting him carry some amulet or symbol of his own guardian spirit. When the boy finally achieved the conviction that he had attracted the attention of a guardian spirit, he composed a spirit song; he might, in guarded language, discuss with his father how the experience was to be interpreted, and he might prepare a medicine bag from the skin of the animal he had seen, or other representation of whatever spirit he had encountered. Then he worked on his spirit song until it seemed right and devised a symbolic spirit sign which he painted on rocks in lonely places in the mountains. In this way, a young man gained tangible evidence of a true religious experience, not in order to rise above the mundane affairs of life, but rather to gain supernatural help in meeting those affairs successfully.

88

The guardian spirit superstition offered many advantages. It provided a formula by which an adolescent could bolster his feeling of readiness for the responsibilities of adult citizenship. The procedure which he followed to gain a guardian spirit required a considerable exercise of self-control under circumstances which were psychically awesome and physically painful. Having followed the formula, and thus acquired a secret and personal magic, he could take up the tasks of life with that extra bit of self-confidence that often, alone, determines whether an effort will be successful. But if self-confidence were not enough to overcome ineptitude or chance failure, the guardian spirit superstition offered still another protection to the ego. When the graduate of a vision quest began any task, he was not testing his own ability and skill alone, but the reality and effectiveness of the spirit power he believed he had acquired. If he failed, the failure did not necessarily erode his confidence in himself; it merely indicated that he had not acquired an effective guardian spirit. He could try again and again to get a guardian spirit, and if only mediocre success crowned his best efforts throughout life, there was always hope that at any time these circumstances might suddenly change for the better. The spirit for which he was searching might yet be found, and even when past middle life, he might become a medicine man or a seer, with the proper spirit to back him.

From this account of vision questing, one might get the impression that those who were not psychically sensitive were slated to be failures. Actually, the test of spiritual power was success in meeting the problems of daily living. Only those who had great doubts about future success were likely to persevere in vision questing. If the individual was precociously adept it was clear that he had power, and it needed only to be confirmed by buying the medicine bag of some departed tribesman or by joining a secret society whose leaders could provide an anxiety-dissolving formula. The aborigines of North America

89

were, perhaps, superstitious dreamers, but they were realistic enough to regard performance in life as the final test of any dream. Spirit power, and all the complex formulas for obtaining it or rituals for keeping it, were cultural elaborations in which intuitive answers to the enigmas of birth and death were brought to bear on the journey between and on the wide differences in ability among the travelers. The emphasis on supernatural aid paralleled and supported an equal emphasis on acquiring practical economic skills and social graces through imitation and trial and error.

The earliest toys of the boy were almost invariably a bow and arrows; those of the girl were dolls and miniature household utensils. Much early training was connected with use of these weapons, figurines, or utensils, and with some participation, suited to the child's maturational level, in adult economic pursuits. One might say that primitive child training differed most from child training in civilized societies by establishing for the child the same target at which adults around him were shooting. Adults might be hitting close to the cultural bull's-eye; children might be struggling to make their mark on the periphery, but they felt, nevertheless, that they were in the contest and being judged by the same standards as their elders.

In connection with this primitive effort to let children try a shot at adult targets just as early as possible, another custom sets early societies off from contemporary civilization, that is, the widespread recognition and encouragement of age-grades. Even in a family group which welcomed and encouraged cooperative assistance in economic tasks, youth still chafed at the interminable wait for grown-up independence of action in meeting responsibilities. Particularly among boys, permission to help in an adult-supervised job, although a privilege to be won, especially when hunting was involved, still was less desirable than full responsibility for some meaningful job, and a chance to see what being an adult might feel like. Almost every primi-

90

tive society which had a sufficient number of adolescents encouraged the formation of age-grades, gave them official recognition, granted them certain privileges, and assigned them specific economic responsibilities. These age-grades were primarily aggregations of young males, though less formal groups might also exist for girls. There was never any attempt to have bisexual age-grades because boys and girls of the requisite age tended naturally to divide themselves into separate groups, reflecting physical and psychic differences and divergent interests about immediate activity and the roles they expected to play in adult life.

A good example of age-grading systems—which has been reported by a trained observer who lived among the people described as an adopted fellow tribesman—is that followed by the Ramkokamekra Indians, a tribe living along the Esterão branch of the Mearim River in Brazil.[4] On the technological and material level, the Ramkokamekra were primitive. They subsisted by digging-stick agriculture and hunting with bow and arrows. Their houses were rectangular frameworks of poles, thatched with palm, but only partly enclosed by walls. When whites first arrived, neither sex wore any clothes. They explained to the Portuguese authorities that it was all right for whites to wear clothes—whites probably had something they wanted to hide. For themselves, they preferred to embellish what nature had provided with intricate painted designs, ear lobes pierced and stretched to accommodate ear plugs several inches in diameter, soup-bowl haircuts, and depilation of body hair, including eyebrows and eyelashes. Indeed on the level of making life interesting, the Ramkokamekra were highly creative.

Their villages were wheel-shaped, with a dance plaza as a hub. Dancing and log racing were their principal leisure social pursuits, with dancing at dawn, at sunset, and at bedtime during the summer, and as many as one hundred and fifty organized log races during the year. All the villagers turned out for major log races and even ran alongside the racers as long as age and agility would allow. Logs weighing up to 200 pounds each were carried up to 10 kilometers across country in heat well above 100°F in the shade. Each competing team carried one log, but they exchanged logs midway to eliminate any advantage in weight. Except during this exchange, the logs must not touch the ground, but had to be carried by one man who rolled the log to a teammate's shoulder when he felt his own pace slacken. The girls carried water in gourds; the log-racers carried pom-poms of grass on a stick. Outstanding individual performers were awarded ceremonial spears by the village council and permitted to wear a pair of tiny logs carved from wood dangling from their necks. They also became eligible for election to the Hamren honor society. Women racers, using lighter logs, had comparable opportunities. Ramkokamekran children hardly able to toddle could be observed industriously practicing around the village with twigs on their shoulders.

The first age-grade of the Ramkokamekra was an initiatory step to direct participation in this elaborate social game. Earlier, boys and girls both took part in such female-supervised work as driving birds from the gardens, weeding, or picking off bugs. The girls helped in preparing food and caring for the house. There was, of course, plenty of leisure for purely juvenile amusements such as a wide assortment of pet birds and animals, swimming, wrestling, shuttlecock, stilt-walking, toy bows and arrows, dolls, cat's cradles, tops, buzzers, wood carving, and the like. Not much later than six years of age, however, the boys and girls exhibited the universal tendency to group themselves by sex. Both knew that as men and women they must distinguish themselves in largely separate ways, and their interests turned to such pursuits. The two sexes did join in dancing in the plaza, but the steps they performed were complementary rather than identical.

The Ramkokamekra organized an age-grade at approximately ten-year intervals, with the median age of members about thirteen but including youths up to eighteen who had not been mature enough for the preceding age-grade, and boys down to the age of eight who were physically ahead of their years. These age-grades had an adult adviser selected by the village council, but actual command rested with two older members of the age-grade chosen by vote of the membership. These elected leaders were the only people in Ramkokamekra society who could order others about. Age-grade membership continued through life; each age-grade moved up step by step in social status and privilege as decades passed and new and younger age-grades were formed beneath them. At the end of forty years, those who were still alive automatically advanced into the village council.

An age-grade was actually formed as the number of eligible boys became large enough, and the demands of the older ones grew noisy enough to prod the village council into action. The first decade was largely given over to group instruction and practice in the skills and knowledge expected of an adult. Youths hunted together, built houses together, cleared forest land for cultivation, helped to harvest crops when an emergency existed, and functioned as an athletic team and a dance company. They went through two types of annual initiation ceremonies, each repeated four times during the first decade; one aimed at testing their manhood, through fasting, whipping, humiliation, and strict discipline; the other, at social and spiritual character building. During the initiation periods, age-grade youths were under the direct command of their adult adviser, but during the rest of the year not even the tribal council could order them about as individuals. If the council

93

had work to be done, or complaints to make, it talked the matter over with the elected leaders of the age-grade; when agreement was reached, the latter issued whatever orders seemed appropriate. The village council, however, kept track of the progress of the age-grade by periodic oral examinations of individuals on general knowledge and by observance of their group skill.

From an educational point of view, the age-grade functioned efficiently because every member was stimulated not only by his own ambition, but by a desire to contribute to the group's reputation and earn the respect of his peers. There was undoubtedly a wide range of abilities within each age-grade, but those of high ability did their best to tutor and inspire the others out of group pride. The age-grade had the further virtue of integrating males horizontally across the sociocultural complex, and of providing a formal procedure for communication between age strata.

The male age-grades represented the core of Ramkokamekran social organization, but the houses and gardens belonged to the women; their places of residence determined the village moiety to which their children belonged, and the mother's brother rather than the father took leadership in bestowing names. Girls or women were auxiliaries to the age-grades and other men's organizations. They rose to prominence as dance precentresses, shared in the privilege of being elected to the tribal honor society, and could aspire to elaborate funerals.

It was almost impossible for any Ramkokamekran to feel isolated and neglected. Every individual belonged to a village moiety and to one of two separate rainy season moieties, which divided the population into ceremonial groups. All males belonged to one of six plaza groups for ceremonial purposes and to one or more of six men's societies. Besides membership in societies, every male and female had several friends specifically designated by a socially recognized spiritual linkage between personal names. It was the duty of these name-friends to help each other in any way they could: they swept the ground when any of the others was appearing before the public and served as a claque when the moment arrived for applause. On occasion, if one had an accident, say, a broken arm, a name-friend might deliberately break an arm to share the pain and incapacitation.

The Ramkokamekra also provided checks on arrogance and self-will. Males were expected during their initiatory period to choose a war and hunting partner. This special friend also served as a "Dutch uncle," sure to make a public example of a "buddy" who strayed from socially approved paths. Further, two of the six men's societies kept watch and used public ridicule as an effective weapon to attack and control socially disruptive greed, vindictiveness, or pomposity.

This long description of the Ramkokamekran sociocultural pattern contrasts an integrated society and the industrialized, impersonal, largely unintegrated environment in which young Americans grow up. There are, of course, instances of poorly integrated sociocultural systems at the preliterate level, just as among larger, highly industrialized, technologically oriented civilizations. Matrilineal societies with large accumulations of personal property, including domesticated animals, seem to be particularly subject to conflicts between the sexes and their particular varieties of human nature, with a resultant cultural anomie. But potential conflict between juveniles and the mature, or between their particular varieties of human nature, exist almost universally in societies which have advanced beyond a hunting-gathering economy.

Where a particular people has a history of agriculture, but for one reason or another has largely abandoned this practice, age-grading may still be retained. This was true, for example, of the Arapaho of the Great Plains in North America. They gave up primary dependence on agriculture when the Spanish brought in horses, making it possible to run down and kill buffalo in sufficient numbers to provide a basic food supply. They were undoubtedly influenced in this shift by the fascinating games it afforded: stealing horses from other tribes and warfare comparable to Russian roulette, in that the object was recklessly to expose oneself to death and get away unharmed.

The Arapaho had age-grades in which some details recall the Ramkokamekra. Adult advisers were chosen from an age-group two steps higher, and girls were occasionally used as auxiliaries. But among the Arapaho, age-grades were a series of societies with special names, through which the individual passed in scheduled order. Their responsibilities were largely concerned with policing buffalo hunts and participating in raiding or war parties. When the societies ran out of real duties, they established curious cultural objectives; one, calling itself the "Crazy Lodge," did everything contrary to orders; for example, its members, the Crazy Dogs, advanced when told to retreat from the enemy and retreated when they should move forward.[5]

Throughout the areas of hoe agriculture and herding in Africa, for example, age-grading is a quite generally adopted method of carrying youth through adolescence. Age-grades were common among Bantu-speaking peoples of East Africa. For the most part, turning and draining ground for the women was part of the early preparation for age-grades and so was keeping goats and other animals out of the gardens. The primary responsibility of the basic age-grade was herding cattle. The herding gangs had their own adolescent leaders, subsisted preferably by siphoning milk from cows in rival herds, or stealing food from the gardens of their own and other villages. Among the Chaga, the behavior pattern of herding gangs constituted a separate culture from that in the villages. It included magic formulas, secret languages, and some ancient customs

96

no longer observed by Chaga society, so that it might be said that the children's society had its own culture.[6]

A comparable situation was observed among the Thonga of Mozambique.[7] There a child received relatively little attention from its father who normally had several wives and lived in a separate house which they visited in turn. For several years after weaning, youngsters visited with grandparents, and on return to their home village, lived in special houses for unmarried boys or unmarried girls. Principally, the boys taught themselves and listened attentively to older brothers and other visitors. A herding-gang leader considered it beneath his dignity to accept proffered food, even from his own mother. It had to be brought to him by one of the younger boys. Out on the grazing range, the older boys hazed the younger ones to make men of them. Perhaps for this reason the young males from a herding gang had to undergo a grueling initiation before being accepted as adult citizens eligible for marriage and other privileges. The Thonga initiations lasted several months and involved a semi-starvation diet as well as constant hazing by those who had most recently come through the initiation. Youths who could not take the treatment they received might end in fights to the death.

To balance this rather depressing picture of age-grades allowed to operate without older advisers and of initiations intended to subdue independence of spirit by force, one need only turn to other Bantu tribes, such as the Ngoni and Nyakusa, north of Lake Victoria Nyanza. Both tribes had an adolescent age-grade carrying the economic responsibility of herding cattle, but neither felt that an initiation was necessary to demonstrate readiness for law-abiding citizenship and marriage. The Ngoni so supervised herding activities that they became in themselves a rigorous ordeal, and they topped off this training by requiring five years of military service.[8]

The Nyakusa led their herding gangs to convert themselves into responsible citizens by giving them a philosophy of life and immediately telling them to start developing a society of their own.[9] As among many Bantu tribes, the young herders had to build their own sleeping quarters, but the Nyakusa required them to pick a new village site on which to build. As they grew up, their building skills improved, and they encouraged other young men to join them. They ate at home only occasionally, when they could bring a group of young herders with them. Nyakusa philosophy held that men do not eat with women, nor do youths eat with the aged, for only when a group of like minds sits down together does really free communication occur.

The young men continued to take care of the herds of the old village until they found wives to plaster the walls of their houses and to bring more young herders into the world. In the meantime each young man began to build a herd of his own, which would be worthy to drive before the house when men of his age-grade visited. Pride in the herd extended to pride in a well-plastered house and a clean-swept yard with at least one shade tree. It further extended to pride in themselves, and it was customary to greet visitors at home without clothing.

Eventually, as the old chief aged, and his son, who lived in one of the new villages, reached the age of about thirty-five, there was a *ubusoka* (coming-out party). The symbols of authority—a cow's horn, a cow's tail, and a spear—were handed over to the senior village headman of the young chief by the senior village headman of the old chief. All fires in the tribal area were extinguished and then relighted with a torch from the new chief's hearth. New territorial boundaries were established around each young village, and trees were planted to mark them. The old villages remained as long as the elders survived, but then they were destroyed. Simultaneously, a new generation of young people was being encouraged in its turn

98

to look ahead, to plan a new life for the future, and thus put its feet on the path that leads to *amhala* (wisdom).

The contrast between the Nyakusa and the Ngoni is further interesting as an example of how culture can change under the influence of leadership and chance contacts with other peoples, for both were a part of the Kinga tribe about ten generations ago. Both have continued to maintain herding economies in the same general area; yet they end with strikingly different patterns of culture. The Nyakusa well illustrate the observation that peers, in some communities, may be almost as important as parents in effect on personality formation in childhood. Peers may supplement parents as agents of socialization in rapidly changing, heterogeneous communities, but even relatively stable groups may entrust a large amount of the educative process to age mates.[10]

Generally, every society regards its own culture of the moment as superior to others. Most citizens of a highly civilized country would go further in comparing their own way of life with that of primitive peoples. They are inclined to decide that primitive peoples must have inferior brains or they would not remain happy with so few creature comforts. Yet one of the wisest and most sensitive American anthropologists declares:

"The genuine culture is not of necessity either high or low; it is merely inherently harmonious . . . the expression of a richly varied and yet somehow unified and consistent attitude toward life, an attitude which sees the significance of any one element of civilization in its relation to all others. It is, ideally speaking, a culture in which nothing is spiritually meaningless, in which no important part of the general functioning brings with it a sense of frustration, of misdirected and unsympathetic effort." [11]

That primitive peoples are usually highly superstitious and civilized people less so is sometimes cited as evidence of a difference in thinking capacity.

Superstitions, however, are not the product of inferior brains, but result from logical thinking in the absence of factual information. As a well-trained African school teacher explained, science informs me that typhus results from the bite of an infected louse, but it does not explain why the louse bites one person and not another. The African merely fills in the gaps concerning which science shrugs its shoulders. In fact, certain superstitions regulate human behavior quite effectively. Among the African Azande, a firm belief in sorcery or black magic led the most economically secure individuals to treat their less fortunate neighbors with thoughtful courtesy and promoted friendliness generally. No individual wanted to make himself an obvious target for sorcery, or acquire a reputation which would make him suspect as a fomenter of sorcery in the event of misfortune to fellow citizens.[12]

Any student of Western civilization knows that the decline in superstition among civilized peoples is associated with greater education in experimentally determined cause-and-effect relationships. One might more reasonably remark that the continuation of superstition in Western civilization, despite an increase in knowledge, is just convincing evidence of human delight in magic.

Contemporary Westerners tend to forget that the peoples of northern Europe were still barbarians when the Sumerian, Minoan, Egyptian, Chinese, and even Greek and Roman civilizations were at their peak. Before the earliest primitive settlers set foot upon the soil of Scotland, the first urban community had been flourishing at Jericho for more than a thousand years.[13]

The World Health Organization sent a representative to Africa a few years ago to determine whether there was anything essentially inferior about the Negro brain.[14] He reported that the Negro brain, in gross configuration, was generally

longer, narrower, and smaller than that of European Cauca-
sians, but the difference in size was no greater than that between the average for Caucasian males and females. More
important, he was unable to establish any significant difference
in number of brain cells or neurons. He concluded that so many
factors affected growth, development, and training that nothing definite could be said about African genetic potential.
African diets were generally low in high-value proteins and in
vitamins, notably A and those making up the B complex. The
people were subject to chronic, endemic diseases which are
known to hamper brain development and limit functional efficiency. The typical African culture made few demands that
could not be met at the age of twelve. The absence of written
languages made impossible the development of the kind of
conditioning and learning that Europeans associate with intelligence potential. Finally, African personality ideals and criteria
of maturity seemed to produce a structure of intelligence which
Europeans neither esteemed nor could test.

Studies of the American Negro and the American Indian
have been equally inconclusive. Since individual differences
among members of a given race are always much larger than
so-called race differences, sweeping statements about the intellectual inferiority of people of non-European cultures would
be premature.[15]

Since there is no general agreement on what intelligence is,
researchers are, to a large extent, looking for a black cat in
a dark room when they test for it. One specialist in child psychology remarked that the IQ of children offered a measure
of past achievement in school-allied tasks, but the relation of
these results to inherent potential for general intelligence was
just a hopeful assumption.[16] Critics of the IQ test point out that,
in an effort to make it fair for both boys and girls, all questions
on which the inherent and acquired interests of either sex might

offer an advantage have been cut out; the resulting instrument is an emasculated device which compares the individual with some non-existent asexual ideal. The French Ministry of Education declared that IQ scores handicapped children by putting a basically meaningless label on them; hence it would not approve their use. Those tests are even more meaningless as a measure of relative achievement or potential when applied to children from widely different cultural backgrounds, particularly children from primitive society and high civilization. Getting comparable results even within the limited area of ability which an IQ does test is confounded by totally different languages, past cultural experiences, and lack of motivation for taking the test, or doing as well as possible on it.

It is less important to know what minor differences may exist in the brain potential of the several races, or of the multitudinous individual personalities within a race, than it is to know how close the achievement of a group approaches the last threshold of mental ability and tolerance of its citizenry. This is particularly true when it becomes customary to put the whole range of brain potentials within a population through essentially the same kind of training, aimed at national ideals rather than individual interests and feasible goals. Those at the lowest end of the range, whether for genetic reasons or less than optimal developmental opportunity, may be placed in a situation where they must disconnect themselves from the educational powerhouse or burn the insulation off their psychic wiring.[17]

If those who are already functioning close to their capacity are put under continually greater strain, if those with recalcitrant quirks of character or personality are persistently pushed, society may overstrain the surplus adaptability of a brain first distributed some thirty thousand years ago for routine use around the ancestral cave home. Like the Chinese, not too many generations ago, who insisted that memorizing their classics must be the first step to a successful life, contemporary Americans seem to have lost sight of reality in many of their cultural ventures, particularly those involving young people who are growing up.

CHAPTER 5

The Hurdles of Civilization

To complete the contrast between primitive and civilized cultures from the relatively unprejudiced point of view of an infant or juvenile, it is necessary to examine more closely some key achievements of modern society which bear directly on the instinctive expectancies and aspirations of young people as they advance from neophyte to acolyte in the cathedral of industrialized free enterprise which the people of the United States have under construction.

Infants do have instinctive expectancies and aspirations. If touched on the cheek, they turn their heads to find a breast on which to suckle, but automatically reject substitutes which do not harmonize with a built-in concept of what a breast should be like. When hungry or in pain, infants spontaneously cry, and get red in the face if nothing happens to improve the situation. They appear startled when strange events occur, even explosive noises they have made themselves. They automatically grip rounded objects put in their hands and encourage company with smiles long before they know what a smile looks like or what it means on the faces of others. Without prompting, infants show a curious interest in their surroundings, begin to learn from experience, and generally give evidence of a strong interest in surviving as long as survival seems worthwhile.

One may reasonably assume that these built-in, instinctive reactions are genetically ancient. They occur in babies the world over and give infants a greater obvious similarity than they will later display when conditioned by the cultures into which they happen to be born. One may also assume that the observed likenesses are just the manifest part of a more extensive repertory of instincts that has been accumulating in the primate line and mammalian class for many millions of years. Within limits, these instincts are adaptable to circumstances; they have what one might call pre-adaptability for change. Reworking of instincts involves surplus neuronal capacity, however, and the extent of the available surplus is another possible limitation on the total plasticity of behavior. This is particularly important when one considers the effect on immature juvenile brains of changes brought about by the most capable and mature brains, concentrating on adult interests.

Industrialized, urbanized societies, particularly those with large and steadily increasing populations, have radically increased the infant's and child's problem of satisfying expectancies and aspirations. The family is no longer a readily extensible group supported by a home-based, cooperative economy in which children can play an important role. It must depend for support on working for others in enterprises with no place for children and a declining place for older people. Urban crowding, housing costs, and dependence on widely scattered jobs for a living have tended to make extended-family homes uneconomical.

105

The first problem of the contemporary infant and young child is the nuclear family: father, mother, and offspring; all others are largely strangers. A family, like a fire department, is useful only as it is available when needed. In today's sociocultural system, the captain of the fire department is seldom available except for weekend recreation. Often he does not want even to talk about how he earns a living, let alone try to instruct his son; and he cannot let the boy help on the job. The first lieutenant is frequently in a better position to encourage and stimulate her daughter to learn one basic female occupation at first hand; namely, housekeeping. But she, too, is increasingly away from the firehouse at work or in leisure enterprises in which children would not be considered an asset, even though the event occurs outside school hours.

The nuclear family no longer has the manpower, facilities, knowledge, or time to function as a microcosm of society, demonstrating a full range of cultural behavior and beliefs for the younger generation. Perhaps this has influenced the character of the marriage contract. Proper care of such children as may result is no longer an important part of the compact. The contract, rather, involves two adults—to love, cherish, comfort, and honor each other in sickness and in health. This, of course, is not an unworthy purpose, and, with the population crisis into which the world is drifting, it may be as well not to promote reproduction. Nevertheless, children still are born into nuclear families. Where they are planned for by both parents with full appreciation of the responsibilities entailed, the results are reasonably satisfactory. When death or some other cause dissolves the contract, leaving only the captain or the first lieutenant and damage control officer in charge, the fire department has no auxiliary members to help carry the load. Psychic fires may ignite in children by spontaneous combustion and smolder for years without being noticed.

Worse, children may arrive unwanted, either because contraceptives fail or people are careless about their use. Here one sees another illogical development of culture. Although contraceptives are generally a permissible household remedy, with the possible exception (hopefully momentary) of orthodox Catholic homes, the "sanctity of human life" has been so elaborated as a moral and ethical principle that no error of omission or commission in use of contraceptives may legally be corrected after conception has occurred. The law does not distinguish between a biological process leading to conscious life, and conscious life itself. Rather it has been decided arbitrarily that life takes on sanctity at the moment when two gametes of opposite sexual origins come into conjunction. Yet billions of other gametes with a higher potential for genetically superior lives may be thrown into the discard as a result of this chance conjunction. But the accidental conjunction is protected even if it occurred because of precautionary failure, mental incompetence, or forcible rape. The woman concerned is committed for life, regardless of her wish, unless a miscarriage occurs, or a panel of doctors agrees that her life would be threatened by continuance of the pregnancy and that, therefore, abortion should be induced.

No official, cultural concern is shown for the future of the embryo. Landing on earth in a family circle that does not want an infant, or in the lap of a mother who lacks a family circle, is known to contribute to crippled personalities in a dangerously high percentage of innocent victims of well-intentioned but myopic justice. The numbers involved constitute a threat to the health of society. The United States Bureau of the Census estimates that about a quarter of a million infants each year arrive as uninvited guests and party crashers.

Years ago, it was observed that infants denied the reassurance of simple mothering—being held, rocked, cradled, and stroked—seemed to have a low survival rate.[1] More recently, that report was confirmed by observations made in an understaffed French foundling home.[2] Infants were adequately sheltered there, kept reasonably clean and fed at proper intervals. But there was no time for more attention. The infants cried in a demanding way at first. When this instinctive action failed to elicit a response, they began to lose interest in life and lost weight instead of gaining it; their crying turned into a wailing noise. After four months of this institutionally unavoidable treatment they showed none of the normal infant's interest in sitting up or trying to stand up. Abilities which they had acquired before their arrival began to decline. Some did not reach the 25-pound weight of an average thirteen-month-old baby until the forty-second month. More than a third of the children died before the end of their third year in the home; of those still alive after four years, five still could not walk alone; sixteen others could walk only by holding on to furniture. This experience was contrasted with another, simultaneously going on at a penal institution for women. Inmates with infants were permitted to keep them in an institutional nursery and to tend them personally during certain hours of the day. Hygienic standards were not as rigidly observed as in the foundling home, and the women would never have been selected as paragons of motherhood. Perhaps their mothering was given special warmth by the relief it afforded from the tedium of confinement, but the infants thrived, nevertheless. They were less subject to accidental injuries than the foundlings; they managed to avoid epidemic ailments; and not a single one died in the five years that took such a heavy toll in the foundling home.

Comparable observations on the expectancies of infants, and on the anomie that follows disappointment, have been reported by the contemporary Austrian psychologist, Anna Freud, among others.[3] Evidence that this reaction is not mere cultural conditioning, or a recently developed genetic pattern, comes from many sources. Other primates, specifically baby monkeys, were subject to hysterical panic if mechanical toys

108

were introduced into their cages after prolonged separation from their mothers. But this panic could be averted if a dummy made out of wirecloth, with cradling arms upholstered in terry cloth, was available in the cage. Frightened infants jumped into the mechanical arms, regained their courage, and on occasion became bold enough to attack the toy. The nature of the reassurance they obtained was pinpointed by giving them an alternate choice of dummy wirecloth mothers, without terry-cloth upholstery, but with bottle breasts from which the infants were regularly fed. The baby monkeys were quite willing to accept food without terry cloth, but when they were frightened it was the upholstered dummies for which they jumped. Apparently soft body contact brought reassurance.[4]

An investigator studying goats and sheep at Cornell University read about the expectancies of human infants and tried separating kids from their nannies for two hours or less shortly after birth. This brief but very early interruption of normal licking and body contact seemed to set off a chain of reactions that led nineteen of twenty-one kids in the experiment to die before they were a year old. A control group of kids, born in the same lot in the same period, but allowed to remain with their mothers, sustained a loss of only two out of twenty-two in the first year.[5]

Infant hominids clearly share some critical, instinctive expectancies with the young of widely different orders of mammals, but on the whole they are more resistant to psychic insults than their simpler-brained, distant relatives. They often continue to live even though harboring "an ancient grudge" which makes it difficult for many of them to develop a healthy personality. A follow-up of 166 individuals out of an original total of 248 infants of vintage 1928, after thirty-seven years, showed that one youngster who developed a full-blown schizophrenia as an adolescent pulled out of it and became a perceptive, creative, competent wife, mother, housekeeper, and citizen. On

109

the other hand, particularly if the individual is consecutively baffled by family, school, and the economic system, the results may be socially disastrous. After a few generations of increasing divergence from normal parent-child relationships, society tends to develop potential parents who do not have the least idea of what normal behavior should be and who fight the correctional effects of instinct with neurotic zeal. Even chimpanzees, raised in isolation and so deprived of opportunity to learn by observing others, are frequently so baffled by motherhood, and so inept in what they do, that their infants must be removed for safety.

If the socially isolated nuclear family in modern American society does develop a social heritage of personality aberrancies, it quite frequently joins the ranks of the economically underprivileged and gravitates into poorer neighborhoods. This happens without regard to racial characteristics, but the process is intensified by skin color, or behavioral syndromes, which are traditionally regarded by the larger society as inferior or peculiar. Consequently, environments are created in which youngsters with family-centered personality traumatisms are further confirmed in resentment and suspicion of the "adult establishment." As gregarious young animals, they instinctively seek the company of their own kind: like-sexed, approximately like-sized, juveniles. They will even accept a dog as a boon companion and generous distributor of unquestioning respect, affection, and friendly body contact; but dogs are rare in the environments where they are most needed, and for the most part, discontented youngsters are driven into the company of equally discontented peers.

At this point, adult-centered civilization fails to use a highly important incentive for individual enterprise and motivation toward maturity. Spontaneously created peer groups are ignored if they confine themselves to innocent play, discouraged if they include members with doubtful family connections, and strenuously opposed if they begin to develop cultural philosophies of their own which diverge from those of the family or the society of which the peer groups are a part. In this respect, contemporary adult hominids sometimes act less intelligently than a band of baboons, where peer groups are an accepted part of the social organization and provide the only highly socialized, liberal education that a baboon gets.

The peer group can be, and almost always is, an interim society through which young people pass on their way from the dependent position which they occupy in the family to the independence which they are expected to show as members of adult society. Whether a peer group follows the high road to a culturally satisfactory goal, or meanders off into some low road that leads to antisocial ends, depends, to a large extent, on the recognition that adult society gives it as a progressively more mature, and potentially more responsible, social organization. In primitive societies, peer groups or age-grades have meaningful responsibilities to carry and get meaningful rewards for satisfactory group discharge of these responsibilities. The precocious and highly capable youngster has his chance to learn leadership; the slow-blooming or less capable individual is spared some of the disappointment and frustration of failure by the successes of the group to which he proudly belongs.

Psychologists generally agree on some sequence of stages of physical and mental development through which the hominid, as the world's most complex organism, must pass with some satisfaction on the way to a healthy adult personality. In general, the sequence corresponds with that offered by the anthropologically oriented contemporary American psychologist, Erik H. Erikson:

Basic trust, first in the mother and then in both parents, so that their prohibitions and permissions have meaning. *Autonomy*, where the basic wish for a choice is realized with the conviction that those in whom trust already rests will protect the individual from failures and shame. *Initiative*, which makes room for proposing as well as choosing, with the same basic reliance on parents to protect one from transgressions and guilt. *Industry*, which gives play to the desire to test the workability of the future. During this stage, one needs to be protected from overambition and a sense of inadequacy and inferiority. *Identity*, that puzzled search, at puberty, for some way of connecting what one *is* with what the adult world *expects*, and during which connection of any kind may be seized as a drowning man seizes a straw. *Intimacy*, the search for a mate with whom mutuality of trust may be shared. *Generativity*, an object for which a parental kind of responsibility may be assumed. *Ego integrity*, discovery of some order and meaning for the life that one is living and continues to live.[6]

At the level of family-centered, hunting and gathering economies, boys and girls can move through the first five stages in that sequence by helping in the daily routine. *Basic trust* came from the attitude of the parents and other elders toward children; their permissions—and prohibitions—thus acquired meaning. Gathering plant foods, capturing edible insects and small animals, offered the young of both sexes a chance to exercise *autonomy, initiative,* and *industry.* For the boys, as they approached puberty, a sense of industry merged into an assurance of *identification* in the adult group through joining men's hunting groups. The final transition to adulthood was accomplished, usually, with an initiation and magic ritual, perhaps a death and resurrection ceremony, which eliminated the last vestiges of childhood and gave supernatural assurance that maturity had in fact arrived. The advent of food production by cultivating domesticated plants and breeding and herding domesticated animals did not basically change the process of growing up. It brought together larger groups of juveniles and provided additional opportunities for them to participate in adult activities concerned with economic survival. The peer group or age-grade really came into its own at this point, for many of the tasks involved could safely, and almost completely, be entrusted to the groups of youngsters created by gregariousness. Girls could play at being women by weeding and cultivating. Boys could protect crops from birds or rodents and, simultaneously, try to capture young animals for pets, or bag older ones as game. In certain parts of Africa there was always an opportunity for team rivalry, to turn the soil faster, to drain one flood plain so that it would run onto the land that a rival team had to drain, or carefully to preserve the bugs picked from one village garden for later deposit, with great glee, in gardens tended by juvenile groups from neighboring villages. Similar opportunities for mixing play with work existed in herding, whether goading placid bulls into butting contests, trying to steal milk from other herds without getting caught, or trying to make men out of boys by egging them on to attack hornets' nests with sticks. Yet for all this play there was a serious job to be done, and in doing it boys advanced themselves in maturity. Even in today's circumstances, the young person who goes to work early usually matures faster than juveniles of the same age who remain in school.

From the young person's point of view, probably no aspect of modern civilization is more questionable than the elimination of opportunities for the immature and inexperienced to participate in the adult economic system by holding a job full time or part time. Not only do youngsters who are getting little out of school attendance mature more slowly as a result, but personality distortions acquired in early life are compounded by additional frustration and resentment. Where a number of such young people, who consider themselves misfits, get together, they form peer groups, either within the school or outside, and seek escape through flouting the cultural *status quo*. The attractiveness of these spontaneous peer groups as a juvenile institution, and the excitement offered by opposition to school

113

authorities or the "social establishment," quite frequently recruit additional members from those who otherwise would find
a reasonably satisfactory challenge in orthodox school activities.

Modern American society makes little use of the peer
group as a means of promoting juvenile morale at least in part
because today's large concentrations of adults lack the community spirit which characterized small groups. Instead of
banding together for greater psychic security, contemporary
adults try to establish social space around themselves for privacy and freedom. In whatever neighborhood they settle,
temporarily or permanently, they find it difficult to develop
community spirit. Ethnic origin, family and educational background, religion, politics, occupation, and economic levels
differ in such a kaleidoscopic fashion that unity can be built
only over a long period of time by a *montage* of chance social
encounters. Reliance on time and accumulation of happy accidents is handicapped by American mobility. On the basis of a
20 percent sample, the United States Bureau of the Census
estimated that in 1960 more than half the people of the country
were living in different houses from those occupied just five
years earlier.

Even youngsters who have moved several times find it
hard to learn to put roots down in a portable flower pot. Many
children are quite at home in nomadic tribes which are always
on the move because their friends and relatives, including
peer-group associates, move with them. The difficulty imposed
by moving American-style is not the change in roofs or geo-
graphy, but loss of the social group among which one felt at
home. The need to be related to the world around is as com-
pelling and imperative as any of the physiologically conditioned
needs of the hominid organism.[7] It is not strange physical surroundings which make a crowd lonely, but the absence of
familiar faces. Some parents fail to appreciate exactly what
Boy Scouts, Girl Scouts, Christian Associations, and other or-

114

ganizations for young people have to offer, even though father enjoys belonging to the Masons, Elks, or Odd Fellows, and perhaps a luncheon club, and mother has her book club, or some other social or civic group, which she attends because it is pleasant to know people and talk to them.

The classroom, which has certain superficial resemblances to an age-grade, falls short of attaining this purpose because of historical accident and the cultural devices of adults unfamiliar with the ways in which juvenile human nature differs from adult human nature and forgetful of their own youthful reactions. To simplify enforcement of compulsory education laws, it has been decided that schooling must begin at a definite chronological age. No allowance is made for differential rates of growth and development among individuals; consequently there is no equality of opportunity to achieve a personal sense of readiness, to maximize voluntary insistence on starting school under the pressure of instincts concerned with learning how to survive and with the gregarious satisfaction of doing it as a member of an interim society of "little people." Because, in the early days of public schools, it was not economically feasible to insist on separate schools, classrooms, or curricula for the two sexes, boys and girls are herded together, contravening the instinctive tendency of children at this age to form peer groups of like-sexed individuals attracted by mutuality of interests and goals. The needs of young males are further disregarded by being put into classroom competition with females who are, on the average, as much as two years farther along on the road to maturity. Again, because of earlier concern with economy, schools rely chiefly on women teachers for classes containing young males most interested in finding out how to be adults of their own sex. Later, men teachers are put in charge of classes containing young females most interested in becoming adult women.

The inadequacy of this cultural tradition is intensified by

115

the emphasis which it throws on individual rather than group competition and by the resulting tendency for slow learners and late bloomers to gain notoriety as low achievers. Without question, many of these slip gradually into an ailment which the school nurse can do nothing about—scholastic hypochondria, or chronic retardation. For some, the classification "retarded" may be a kind of emergency exit from an intolerably peripheral position. Stress on individual achievement tends to deplete the sense of belongingness and so to keep the group from becoming an effective unit whose members see themselves, their fellow members, and outsiders in terms of the group's standards.[8]

This observation may seem so obvious that it scarcely merits repetition, but its significance for understanding the problems of youth needs emphasis. The group in which juveniles, hopefully, will finally gain membership and a pattern of living standards is the adult society to which they were born, or some stratum or segment of it. But they cannot postpone the basic satisfaction of belongingness for twenty-one years or more. They try, universally, to give significance to some group of the young by developing special patterns of culture, their own criteria of membership, and their own proofs of exclusive privilege. This occurs everywhere in primitive society where two or more juveniles of the same sex are regularly thrown into contact. It tends to intensify as complexity of adult culture increases the disparity between grown-ups and their offspring and makes the task of qualifying for full participating citizenship more tedious and difficult. Without the practice that juveniles get from organized activities in childhood and from a certain amount of make-believe, they encounter difficulty in reaching the goal.

In his study of the development of moral judgment, Jean Piaget, the twentieth-century Swiss psychologist, concluded that it received its greatest impetus, not from abstract adult precepts, but from the concrete problems of group play and

116

of games with rules. Gradually, small boys come to aspire ". . . to the virtue, supremely characteristic of human dignity, which consists in making a correct use of the customary practices of a game." [9]

The phenomenon of juvenile culture was reported on as early as the 1800s when an American scholar discovered that children in the United States were using rhymed formulas in games and singing songs which they had not learned at home or in school, which did not appear anywhere in print, and which went back to the fourteenth century.[10] Soon afterward, German folklorists called attention to the *secret languages* which children spoke and adults either did not know or had almost entirely forgotten. Further inquiry revealed a hundred and fifty-five examples of such languages of similar construction occurring all the way from Copenhagen to Amoy, in China. One type of such language was used by children in Spain, France, and a wandering tribe of gypsy jugglers in India.[11]

A later study of children's secret languages in America turned up almost five hundred of them. In only one case could the researcher trace a connection between one of these languages and information appearing in books. He decided that for some unknown reason the use of secret languages appeared to be a manifestation of the human nature of children. The practice apparently began as early as the sixth year of life and continued, on occasion, until the eighteenth year, although most cases involved children between eight and fifteen.[12]

Even though the reporters just cited did not appreciate the significance of this material, they discovered that juveniles cannot wait in a vacuum for maturity and a place in adult society. Young people instinctively create interim societies of their own; they build culture patterns to distinguish members from non-members and to make membership appear an exclusive privilege. Adult secret societies and fraternal organizations often follow the same practice, even though nothing more ar-

117

cane is involved than printing ritual instructions backwards so they can be read only by using a mirror. In this, adults are less resourceful than Chaga children in Africa who employed a form of "pig Latin" in which repetitive syllables were inserted between the syllables of orthodox words, so that Chaga became "Chasigasi" in some settlements and "Chatigati" in others.

Undoubtedly the use of Latin as a scholarly and professional language, long after it ceased to be spoken by the general population of Italy, may in part be attributed to its being the equivalent of a secret language which distinguished the learned from ordinary people, and so lent *éclat* to the knowledge that it imparted or concealed. It has been suggested that all secret languages conceal thought from the uninitiated non-privileged; and their widespread use by children reveals a basic need to make what one says sound important, and imply possession of more knowledge than one actually has.[13]

Universal, compulsory education has tended to eliminate this need among juveniles, incidentally, for most of them surpass their parents in years of schooling completed and in orthodox knowledge accumulated, even though their spelling may be unreliable. In many homes, differences in education contribute to a failure in communication at a deeper level than language and create a situation in which instinct and rationality are constantly at odds. The parent's ability to fill the traditional role of guide and adviser is rendered suspect by his deficiency in school learning. He compounds the effect of this by agreeing that school learning is more important than anything else, even though he does not know whether he would have been better off with more, or whether more will benefit the son or daughter in question. Moreover, the parent is popularly expected to take this stand although he may be sacrificing to a dream about a mirage the reality of family influence on a personality that needs it.

Modern civilization, particularly the American version

118

which stresses technology and efficiency, tends to deprive juvenile peer groups of a traditional *raison d'être*—a specific, though limited part in the economic system. The urgency that juveniles feel about trying their hand at survival is undoubtedly exacerbated by their reaching peer-group age with inadequate experience in the exercise of initiative and industry on an adult-mimicking level. They are confused by the problem of gaining an identity in adult society. Almost three out of four juveniles come from urban families subsisting on wages or salaries from jobs that cannot be shared with family members. At best, adults can offer only upkeep and repair jobs on houses and gardens. This work does not directly affect family economy and usually has no relationship to the father's occupation, or probable future occupations of children. The incentive to participate in such activities is weakened because families in lower economic strata are more likely to rent than to own their dwellings and to regard any more than a minimum of upkeep as an unjustifiable gift to the landlord.

Meaningful jobs are equally scarce outside the family *ménage*, even for individual juveniles, let alone groups of them. They are told that in modern America prospective workers must be mature as well as educated. But becoming mature without the experience of working for a living is difficult. On this, psychologists, sociologists, and anthropologists all agree. There are other criteria of maturity, to be sure, but most of them relate to, or depend on, willingness and ability to hold a job successfully: marriage, independently formulated rational action, ability and willingness to make decisions, and to assume responsibility for them.[14] Getting and keeping a job is also prerequisite for showing other attributes of maturity: ability to participate in a wide variety of different activities, experience in meeting frustrations as well as satisfactions, a sense of humor that can be touched by the incongruities of life, self-understanding, and a seaworthy personal philosophy.

Trying to promote maturity without job experience—in other words, without knowledge of how to survive—is one of the most curious and least-acknowledged aspects of the great American experiment. Contemporary Americans seem to assume that this instinctive urge of young hominids can be postponed almost indefinitely if their attention is sufficiently occupied with activities which are good in principle and not obviously deleterious. They are offered toys in profusion: phonographs and records, radios, television sets, games and the equipment with which to play them, books, magazines, motion pictures, amusement parks, playgrounds, lay and religious programs of a character-building type, and heterosexual social events. Most important, school education is provided and made compulsory. For some youngsters, schooling is sufficient. If they have the capacity and interest to do reasonably well, they accept the repeated assurance of their elders that this is the best way to assure survival on a satisfactory level. They do gain a sense of maturing as their accumulation of knowledge mounts, even though the connection between what they are learning and what they may do for a living often seems to be rather tenuous. They are willing to accept a considerable load of such doubtfully pertinent effort as part of the price for diplomas and/or degrees, because of the magic popularly associated with them and the membership which they attest in a relatively exclusive group. Without question, educable young people and the nation both profit from the transaction.

The real educational problem is posed by American juveniles who, for some reason, are not successful in school, who have no hope of getting the kind of employment for which diplomas or degrees are essential, and who remain in school because the law says they must or because they cannot find jobs. For them, the credibility gap between youth and age far exceeds in width and depth that which is said to exist between government leaders and ordinary citizens. They are told that they cannot get a job without more education than they have, when they know they already have completed more years of schooling than average members of the presently employed working force. Statistics are cited, implying that, for every year of additional schooling completed, their expectable income will mount. They are not told that these statistics reflect a period when people with ability to win higher-salaried positions also tended to stay in school longer of their own free will. No one points out that endurance in school will not, alone, overcome personality deficiencies, and that a significant percentage of elementary school dropouts of past decades now enjoy higher average incomes than a significant percentage of college graduates of the same era.

Universal compulsory education, supported by a nation-wide system of free public schools, is one of the world's outstanding educational achievements, but it can be overelaborated. Perhaps it is being overelaborated now, partly out of justifiable pride and partly out of a kind of superstitious faith in the ability of hardworking teachers to perform miracles, not only with their young charges, but on the national economy. Unintentionally, young people are made the victims of a number of cultural delusions: that the United States is entering an atomic age in which all jobs will require more education—although employment forecasts indicate that the overwhelming majority of those now in school will enter employment requiring no more and no different education from that required in the past—that the cultural level of the country can be raised by increasing the average number of years of schooling completed, because of an indirect effect on what people do with their leisure; that a country which requires a high school diploma for digging ditches or service work enhances its superiority; that a shortage of jobs and unemployment problems of rather serious proportions can be overcome by educating all young people for those better jobs in which some shortage is reputed to exist.

121

For the past three-quarters of a century, American industry and business have been increasingly pressed to get along with fewer juveniles in their employ, both to keep jobs from attracting them away from school, and to promote mechanized production efficiency as the highest possible cultural goal. To meet the resulting eliminations of jobs which might be filled by inexperienced minors, more classrooms have been built and national campaigns are waged to keep them overcrowded. Despite this, some 19 percent of the unemployed in March, 1964, came from an age group under twenty which represented less than 8 percent of the population. A still more disproportionate share of this unemployment occurred among non-white young people and it is not possible to account for this on the basis of years of schooling completed. It is extremely unlikely that recent unrest of young people, including rioting, with destruction of property and lives, came out of dissatisfaction with educational opportunities in the areas where this behavior occurred. It is extremely likely, on the other hand, that one important cause was dissatisfaction with employment opportunities. Society may continue to try to meet the problem by spending more money on schools, on busing pupils from one school to another to equalize the color mix, and on vocational training for the unemployed. Yet no attention is paid to the obvious: improvement of the educational program can hardly be the primary need in a nation which already has a higher average of school years completed than any other major social economy in the world. Discrimination against Negroes is countered with more education, even though the limitations of this approach have already been demonstrated by thousands of scholastically able Orientals.

If satisfactory survival were clearly related to the extended education now advocated for all young Americans, it would be less necessary to force them into it. Observations of chimpanzees in the wild make it clear that even the small-brained young of this primate will voluntarily seek to master the intricacies of

122

fishing for termites once they have observed the procedures followed by an adult. Experiments with a cage-raised baboon turned loose in the wild confirm that this holds true even at the lower levels of monkeys. More confidence ought to be put in the ability of hominid young to do likewise if they are given opportunity to observe the need. So much education American-style is based on pretended survival needs which cannot be confirmed by reality that some young people come to feel that they are being denied the right to survive for arbitrary reasons. In the end, they will resort to violence.

When this situation develops in the United States it is labeled "the price of progress." But a dangerously high percentage of young people may feel that they are being denied their natural advance toward a place in adult society. And adults scarcely admit to themselves, let alone explain to young people that, in the course of cultural change, society has forgotten the part that meaningful jobs on a beginning level play in the development of healthy personalities and mature citizenship. Adults may think that a 15–20 percent decline in the number of young people under twenty in the working force, during a twenty-year period when the population in this age bracket increased 30 percent, is not too important so long as they are all eating and going to school. But food is not the only survival requirement to which man has conditioned himself, and one of the earliest of these secondary needs is the satisfaction of winning or earning his food in socially accepted ways.

When cultural change creates a problem for young people trying desperately to grow up and join adult society, common sense dictates seeking a solution elsewhere than in further elaboration of the changes which created the problem. This is particularly true when evidence from other societies and other parts of the world testifies that the same cultural trends are producing the same social problems. The natives of the Palau Islands in the western Pacific are a good example in that they

123

have been under the tutelage, successively, of the Spanish, the Germans, the Japanese, and the Americans. Palau people once depended, as so many primitive groups do, on extended families, peer groups, age-grades, and initiations. The Germans took a dim view of age-grades. The Japanese did also, until they discovered that they could get more work done by preserving age-grades as a reward for completion of basic schooling. Then came the Americans, who knew that the Palauans could not possibly be happy, even if they thought they were, until they were thoroughly educated. A trained observer who spent some years on the spot reported that school children were being cut off from their elders and the traditional wisdom of their culture and so left unprepared to become adults.[15]

The Japanese have undergone an extraordinary metamorphosis from agrarian feudalism to industrialized, constitutional monarchy. The practice of age-grading has almost completely disappeared and been replaced by a remarkable national school system.[16] But Japanese young people have not reached a higher level of satisfaction with life. Recently, Japan has closely rivaled the United States in juvenile delinquency, crime, riots, and revolts of youth. Even the staid British have shown a tendency to react to extensions of compulsory education with more juvenile delinquency. A few years ago the legal school-leaving age was raised one year. The affected age group, which traditionally had gone to work at fourteen, promptly made this fifteenth year a period for experimenting with other approaches to ego satisfaction. In China, there have been two distinct types of juvenile delinquency, one resulting from industrialization and the decline of family-centered enterprise; the other, from the rise of a school system and the equating of family social status with number of years of schooling successfully completed.[17]

American civilization tends to ignore opportunities to acknowledge the achievements of young people in socially admired ways, unless the acknowledgment encourages them to

124

remain outside the adult economy. Young people are rewarded for classroom performance by stars on report cards, special leaves, ceremonial honors, citations and cash awards, or scholarships at higher institutions of learning. But outside the school, social acknowledgment may be limited to the willingness of an industrial or business personnel officer to accept an application from the holder of a high school diploma and to consider him for a job—if he is not pushed out of line by an older applicant with more experience. The value of this preference is often sharply reduced by awareness that the job does not really require the knowledge that the applicant has acquired in high school. The personnel officer is trying to pick a winner, and he assumes that someone who survived high school is a better horse on which to place a bet than one who has not yet finished any race. With a large body of unemployed from which to pick, the employer would be foolish to pass over a high school graduate for an applicant who did not finish, provided that both are clean-shaven and look as if their hair had been cut recently. Without intention, perhaps, the personnel officer thus contributes another statistic in support of the popular belief that modern jobs require what the high school graduate knows.

If a young man will just stay in school, however close he may be to the scholastic borderline, he may be further rewarded by temporary exemption from the draft, and in time of war, or reasonable facsimilies thereof, this may be a valuable reward. Although this clearly indicates a high regard for persistence in schooling, there is no evidence of respect for its results. A native-born youth may finish high school with honors and subsequently render distinguished service in the armed forces, but he does not receive the right to vote or any other adult privilege earlier than the grammar school dropout. (Oddly enough, if a foreign-born resident offers even passably satisfactory service in the armed forces, his wait for full citizenship is shortened.)

As a result, youthful interest in culturally approved effort tends to diminish along with appreciation of citizenship. It is not something that one can earn. It comes automatically if one is born of the right parents or in the right place and lives twenty-one years without committing a felony. The American credo holds that what one gets is worth exactly what one pays for it in cash or effort. Citizenship and the conscientious discharge of its responsibilities are, consequently, not regarded as a privilege granted *summa cum laude, magna cum laude,* or even *cum laude,* but rather *cum grano salis.* This is a departure from all previous human concepts of full membership in a social group. The writers of the American Constitution may not have intended such a departure, but any history of citizenship will show how radical a departure from precedent American practice actually is.[18]

Many people recognize that something is radically wrong with the way in which modern children are reared, but in most cases, lack of knowledge concerning the basic cultural objectives of human society leads only to viewing with alarm, or criticizing the efforts of juvenile human nature to find a more satisfactory solution. Artists, novelists, and poets would hardly stress the plight of children as they do unless some basic fault were involved.[19] Another observer recognizes that schools cut young people off from the rest of society, but regards the formation of peer groups and juvenile societies as one of the potentially evil results, rather than as a neglected answer to the problem.[20] A third scholar comes closer to the heart of the problem, although he describes the schism between age and youth as a withdrawal of adolescents from adult society, maximized by exclusion from adult activities and failure to provide status roles more clearly connected with the serious and significant work of everyday life.[21]

If one were to epitomize American civilization for contrast with older and simpler cultures, one would have to suggest that in size, lack of unity, lack of interest in integration, and technological instability it presents, more than anything else, a test of the adaptive powers of the hominid child. Increases in population, up to a point, tend to promote the significance of the society to which one belongs, but, like increases in the capital stock of a corporation, they also tend to reduce the equity in the whole which one share of stock represents to the individual owner. Americans do not regard lack of unity as deplorable, but welcome it as an evidence of the individual's freedom to believe as he wishes, with the line drawn only at overthrowing the government by force, or breaking rules of behavior which a majority of the people, directly, or through their elected representatives, have decreed shall be the law. Absence of interest in *integration* (anthropologically defined as acceptance of personal responsibility for other individuals in the same society on a reciprocal basis) is somehow related to freedom and to disinclination to be bound by tradition. What one does at any time, beyond his legal duties, has no meaning to Americans unless it is a result of an independent decision, based on logic and/or emotion, to assume responsibility. Humanitarian programs may be adopted by majority vote and still be regarded as a departure from true Americanism, as movements toward a "welfare state" which, in spite of its name, is undesirable. Instability resulting from technological change, far from being greeted with apprehension, is taken for granted, or even praised as the hallmark of progress.

So the child arrives in a family which may, or may not, offer a hearty welcome; which may, or may not, exemplify the norm of the culture; and which, as a social institution, has little practical standing in the community other than what its members have achieved as individuals. If there are any elders about, they are less likely to be objects of reverence and sources of wisdom than to be participants trying just as desperately as the children to hold a place in the front rank of the crowd watching the merry-go-round. The adolescent's most pressing question is "What am I going to be, and how should I prepare to be it?" The only available answer is "Go to school and study hard!" But the value of this advice, even for those who are able to follow it, may be reduced by the widespread criticism that the schools are lagging in filling the needs of a dynamically changing culture. Those trying to stand in the front line of profundity shake their heads knowingly and say that the schools must prepare young people for a future whose needs are unpredictable; and they are sure that the schools are not doing this. One may doubt that they are, that they can—or that they should try.

None of those concerned with modern problems seems to approach them with the requisite sense of humor. None sees anything ironic in greeting as a milestone in progress the solution of a problem that contemporary culture created. In pleading for the application of a sense of humor, which can be described as appreciation of the incongruous, I hope to evoke enough tolerance to make the following pages palatable. Pointing out what, from a child's point of view, contemporary society has lost, has no nostalgic intent to turn backward and recapture some ancient golden age. Rather one questions whether the juggernaut of civilization should be driven at a speed that ordinary prudence would prohibit when traveling over a road as little known as that which lies ahead. No one wants to stop the juggernaut even if it were possible, but one does want to enjoy the scenery and give children a chance to enjoy their theoretically greater life expectancy.

Among the difficulties about speed of culture change is lack of time to become acquainted with one change before another hits. There is no solid experience on which to base a judgment of the new; like astronauts beyond the pull of gravity, one cannot judge which side is up or which direction forward. Without time to evaluate previous changes, one does not even stop to consider whether a new change has worth. The only point now in question seems to be, is change continuing with satisfactory speed?

The free-enterprise philosophy of the American people has so stimulated discovery and invention that literal miracles have occurred in devising and producing both machinery and consumer goods. Although it has occasionally been necessary to protect the free-enterprise system from self-destruction by legal restraint on competitive ingenuity of doubtful public benefit, the over-all result of the system has been to produce a standard of living admired and usually envied, with qualifications, by all the rest of the world. It is difficult for people living in the midst of American civilization and personally unfamiliar with life in other times and places to appreciate what has happened to their culture, and how quickly the change has taken place.

The history of technological achievement of mankind until about twenty-five hundred years ago could be summarized in one volume. Two thousand years of technology compress into a second. Two and a half centuries fill the third volume; a single century fills the fourth; and the fifth encompasses only fifty years. From 1900 on, the problem becomes so complex that historians despair of trying to analyze it.[22] The burgeoning of technology, called the Industrial Revolution, began in England about 1750 but rapidly spread to other countries, notably to the United States. Thereafter, a geometric increase has occurred in the number of manufacturing devices powered by steam and electricity, which imitate or anticipate what man might produce with his hands and replicate these productions at a level of quality, standardization, and cost that handwork cannot hope to match. Agriculture, mining, and the chemical industry have been similarly revolutionized to keep up with the need for raw materials, processing methods, and new combinations of elements which augment and often improve on those supplied by nature.

Economists, engineers, historians, sociologists, psychologists, and philosophers have written scores upon scores of very sound books to tell what happened, how it happened, and why men should be grateful or fearful because it did happen. But none of them, as far as I can discover, has fully appreciated to whom it was, and is, happening—a primate that for almost two million years had been undergoing natural selection for ability to survive as a hunter and gatherer. Whatever opportunity there has been for the processes of evolution to make substantial changes in hominids occurred before they developed urbanized civilization. Civilization did not arise in answer to the needs of Cro-Magnon man; it arose incidentally while modern man was playing with, and elaborating upon, an accumulating inventory of ideas and problems. Elaborating civilization has attracted and intrigued more and more creative minds as it became possible to specialize on objectives not immediately concerned with routine. The harder these specialists work, and the more successful they are, the greater become the difficulties for children.

CHAPTER 6

Toil and Pleasure

‖‖‖

If there is to be equality of opportunity for all young people from middle adolescence on, job experience is required as an alternative to classroom experience. Currently, major reliance is put on universal compulsory school training as a means of preparing young people for successful careers as adult citizens, although it is known that some are not genetically equipped to approach problems as abstractions to be solved through symbolic thinking, and others have been so embittered by earlier experience with adults that they reject all advice connected with the "establishment."

This sizable minority sees school as a frustrating experience which offers no clear evidence of progress toward a worthy goal. Everything that these young people want in life —a reasonably satisfactory means of survival, independence, and some love and respect from others—seems to depend, in the final analysis, on getting and holding a job, or marrying

131

someone who can accomplish these feats. American cultural ideals are in accord with youth's analysis of objectives. The opposition that youth encounters has more to do with means than ends. More specifically, it has to do with popular pride in the educational level, measured in terms of average number of years of schooling completed. It is generally believed that because American culture has more scientists and inventors who have successfully converted the play potential of the brain into remunerative work, every sort of job demands more education. Because American society has more schools, better facilities, and more and better-paid school personnel, it has converted the home of the "Three R's" into a house of magic where, presumably, genetic endowment, personality aberrancies, and motivational limitations can all be reconstituted so as to conform more closely to the nation's ego-ideal.

This general faith in schools as houses of magic is not without foundation. Unquestionably, they have helped to discover and encourage the intellectual talent on which American leadership in many different areas is based. But the educator finds it increasingly difficult to play the role of magician as school populations and the range of talents expecting magic increase. He loses much time trying to pull rabbits out of hats that never held one, or in which the rabbit died of neglect long before the owner entered school. The educator is further handicapped by the antics of those who would like to get out of school and look for another rabbit elsewhere.

School teachers and administrators, who may doubt their magic powers under such conditions—frequently made more tumultuous by picketing, demonstrations, sit-ins, lockouts, and riots—are unlikely to give up the preferred position they occupy as members of one of the most rapidly expanding professional groups in history. Self-interest dictates that they keep trying to accomplish the impossible by demanding more help from the taxpayer and by hard work, enthusiasm, and raising the qualifications for entrance into the teaching field. In the meantime, they can hope that public expectations will be qualified by common sense.

Many non-educational agencies are not at all unhappy with the school system because it gives them a scapegoat to blame for sociocultural ailments. The United States Department of Labor has consistently maintained that unemployment occurs because the most elaborate school system in the world is still not elaborate enough. Organized labor is relieved of responsibility for restrictions on apprenticeships in skilled trades and is free to fight for higher minimum wage laws because of the growing acquiescence in the idea that all young people are better off in school. Industrial and business management, which must compete with the world on the basis of quality, production efficiency, and cost, prefers not to be bothered with inexperienced juveniles for whom minimum wage laws make no reasonable differential, whose ages must be doubly checked for compliance with school attendance laws, whose employment involves added paper work with governmental and union supervisors of apprenticeships, and whose hours and working conditions must be watched to avoid infraction of child labor laws. In addition, there is no special provision for juveniles in unemployment insurance, social security, pension plans, or health and other fringe benefit payments.

This situation results from well-intentioned cultural elaborations promoted by public servants looking for popular causes to serve and private volunteers looking for worthy purposes to push. Unfortunately, neither category of culture-makers can appreciate the problems created in some of the tousled heads they are trying to save.

Work is not a recently acquired hominid habit, nor has it been pressured into existence by the Industrial Revolution. All living animals have brains geared to work, that is, to the use of energy for central-nervous-system decisions and physical activity in order to get food, avoid danger, and survive. Among the higher mammals, and notably the primates, the biological advantage of larger brains with surplus neurons available for handling situational or environmental changes, seems to be clear. The development of such a reserve, over and above routine survival circuits, probably enabled the hominoid line to meet the exigency of structural awkwardness for arboreal life. It promoted the exploitation of hunting and tool use, the family group, and all culture elaboration since.

Much confusion over the sensate behavior of man seems to be somehow related to this duality of function within the brain. On the one hand there is a basic organization trying to perfect adaptation to the circumstances of the moment, guided by genetic mandates, conditioned instincts, acquired habits, and latent knowledge. On the other hand there is always a reserve not involved in the primary mental or physical activities associated with instinctive survival efforts, or the secondary body of dutiful habits associated with group living, and particularly family and kinship group living. This reserve automatically receives the same energy stimulus as the rest of the brain and develops a cathexis which finds catharsis only as main circuits are relieved from pressing survival or dutiful habit activities. The body may be borrowed, if needed, for so-called leisure pursuits uninhibited by visceral needs or societal responsibilities.

This inborn competition between a work potential and a play potential within the individual brain appears to have filled an even more important role in the development of culture than the equally natural competition between differently oriented male and female brains. In the early years of life, before the brain reaches a sufficiently high level of maturity to become concerned over its independent ability to survive, the play potential dominates. Eventually the instinct for survival demands a work program that will assure it and this becomes more important than play. The rule-setting propensity of complex brains leads to the establishing of fixed habits concerning survival and to the defense of rule stability. Whenever the play potential has the opportunity to relieve its own inactivity tensions it wanders widely and sometimes wildly. Out of this activity come discovery and invention, changes in survival and work patterns, an emphasis on specialization, and with the dawn of modern times, the acceptance of high talent in one or another kind of standardized or creative play, as a form of survival-earning work.

The primary function of most individuals with such a talent is not to contribute to the visceral survival needs of society, but in most instances, to help fellow mortals free themselves, vicariously, from the tensions of an insufficiently used play potential. The talented do this by presenting competitive exhibitions of physical strength and skill, or offering relief from humdrum reality through soothing or startling creations in religion, fictional prose, poetry, drama, music, dance, or graphic or plastic art. Of all examples of the play potential functioning as a form of work, however, the most curious and even preposterous, is that provided by the non-teaching scholar, and particularly the experimental scientist. He makes a career out of exercising the explorative aspect of the play potential, sets as his goal the discovery of truth, and often equates the value of what he does with its freedom from practical usefulness to society. As a result, he stumbles on discoveries that vitally affect society, culture, and the natural environment without regard to the pressing social needs of the moment. Many of the educational problems of youth evolve out of these discoveries or out of an effort to anticipate what discoveries may come next.

In the earliest phases of culture development, mental play and the discovery of new specialties of significance to survival and its enjoyment tended to broaden opportunities for the individual and to open new avenues of growth and develop-

135

ment for different categories of minds, body physiques, and personalities. All participated at least part-time in the food quest, and achievement there, by both males and females, contributed to group respect and in turn to a sense of self-importance and security of group membership by those so distinguished. In the later Old Stone Age—with standardization of tool types, designs, and production procedures, with the advent of sacerdotal functions in connection with death, burial, or entombment, with the rise of magico-religious rituals involving a high level of graphic and plastic art, and with the appearance of permanent houses—it seems that opportunities proliferated for self-realization by individuals of diverse personality patterns. In their beginning stages, agriculture and domestication of animals contributed to the same end. They were, perhaps, a little less exciting to the mind than prospecting for natural plant sources, or pursuing and bringing down game, but they were still means of personally obtaining food for personally witnessed group consumption. Under such conditions, dutiful habit was socially rewarded. As has been reported for the primitive Arunta of Australia, when the band came together for its evening meal all shared in what was available, but the successful hunters of the day bustled around the fire with beaming faces; the unsuccessful ones sat quietly at the outer edge of the group.[1]

Agriculture and herding lost some of their charm when the food they produced was distributed to distant places and consumed by unseen people. For a major part of the work product there was no person-to-person homage for dutiful habit well performed. The importance of this loss is indicated by the custom of staging county fairs for exhibiting farm and household products. For that matter, every public exhibit of individual or group products is a reminder that societal approval of work performed is still fundamentally pleasurable and that survival is embellished by an audience to appreciate how well it is being achieved. When a person has a product to show for

136

his labors, he also has an occupation for the reserve potential of his mind, and exhibiting it partakes of a leisure relaxation.

Man's relationship to work and play has been drastically changed by the application of power to machines, and the proliferation of machines to which power could be applied, during the Industrial Revolution. Everyone knows, at least vaguely, what a paradise it has produced for the mechanically oriented creative mind, and more clearly, if not completely, what an awe-inspiring array of goods, services, comforts, and conveniences it has made available for the average individual and family.

Grateful though one must be, nothing is without its price. Truly hard-headed Yankees need to look beyond the down-payment, installments and interest, depreciation and upkeep, to the costs in terms of life essentials. There is a growing suspicion that Americans may be acquiring a vast inventory of physically pleasant accessories which man could live happily without— because he did for some two million years—and giving up, in exchange, certain psychic satisfactions that men in the past never have been able to live without. One of these is reasonable assurance of economic survival. Technological, highly urbanized civilization has removed all but a small fraction of the population from food source areas. Cooperative family production of either food, or goods to exchange for food, has been made impractical. Survival has been made dependent on the willingness of some second party, usually a stranger from another economic stratum, to make a job available. In many cases, the first stranger may have a job to offer, but he is not free to do so until he consults a second stranger who represents a union within whose jurisdiction the job falls. If there are dues-paying union members unemployed, the job seeker, whatever his need and whatever his ability, is out of luck. This loss of control over one's destiny and environment is far more serious than that which gives even a deer mouse the jitters.

137

The American economic system, as presently constituted, has geared itself to serve a group of consumers rather than a community of survival-anxious human beings needing work to keep them happy. It has operated on the philosophy that if some mechanized, automated, or cybernated production system could be devised to produce food, goods, or services of acceptable quality more speedily and cheaply, everyone would, in the end, benefit by adopting it. History has tended to validate this philosophy. Living standards have risen; the gross national product has climbed; new jobs appeared to be created faster than old ones were eliminated. After 1860, for example, research and development so improved agricultural practices that the number of people needed to assure an ample supply of food for the nation dwindled from more than 50 percent to less than 7.5 percent of the population. Almost simultaneously, industry, business, government, and other labor-using agencies expanded fast enough to absorb this vast army of surplus people with no more than temporary dislocations. But when the play potential of human minds concentrates on a field of good ideas, there is no assurance that it will not be overelaborated to the point of absurdity.

From the middle of the nineteenth century on, the invention and incorporation of machinery into production processes became an object of almost mystical faith for industrial engineers. If human workers could not be completely replaced with mechanical devices, the next best improvement was to fragment jobs, arrange them in sequential order, and so organize human labor that it approached the efficiency of a machine, with each worker concentrating on repetitive performance of a single operation, while the work moved past him on a conveyor belt.[2] This idea of utilizing men as if they were just accessory parts on a machine presented so many fascinating possibilities that scientific management and efficiency engineering soon developed into professional specialties. Frederick Winslow Taylor,

138

commonly recognized as the first to hang out his shingle as an efficiency consultant, began his work in 1893 in Philadelphia. What he and his followers did to jobs, as a means of satisfying the human instinct to work for survival, may be guessed from Taylor's best-known statement: "What I demand of the worker is not to produce any longer by his own initiative, but to execute punctiliously the orders given, down to their minutest detail." [3] No wonder that working men organized more and more trade unions to protect themselves from the pioneers whose work Taylor codified.

At the moment, what happened to the content of jobs is less important than what happened to their availability. Common sense makes it seem fantastic that American society could have assumed that machines might be substituted for human beings, indefinitely, without eventually creating a massive unemployment problem. But strangely enough, the substitution went on peaceably for the better part of a century. A growing consumer market for an increasing variety of processed foods, transportation and communication devices, household conveniences, and countless gadgets created new jobs as fast as machines took over old ones, and unemployment never remained dangerously high for long periods of time. Economic depressions did occur, accompanied by widespread unemployment, but this was attributed to temporary economic malaise rather than to an inherent defect in the system. Not until after 1957 did serious concern become general. During the period 1957–1965, the nation was at peace; the economy seemed to be healthy and prosperous; but unemployment rose above 5 percent of the total working force and stubbornly stayed there. It did not drop below 5 percent until the war in Vietnam siphoned off several hundred thousand potential job applicants for service overseas, and abnormally stimulated business and industry by astronomical expenditures of borrowed capital by the Federal Government in logistic support of the armed forces. What, however, will happen during subsequent periods of peace? Some still are not worried, simply because previous periods of serious unemployment have been ridden out without permanent damage. The problem, they maintain, is no more dangerous than those survived in the past; the level of worry is higher because the social conscience is sharper. One also is told of a temporary log-jam created by the demands of American Negroes for job and wage equality; the present problem, as some see it, is created by the sudden calling of a debt that has gone unpaid since the Civil War. Americans have just been lazy, others say. They have not used enough "hard-sell" tactics on consumers; therefore, production demands are below what they should be.

What these defenders of the system forget is that recent unemployment experience occurred in spite of mammoth efforts to reduce the demand for jobs and to maintain consumer buying power. The holding power of our schools has been so increased that in 1960 they held 2,700,000 young people from seventeen to twenty years old who would have been potential job seekers if the enrollment percentages of 1920 prevailed. Voluntary or mandatory pension plans have decreased the number of males over sixty-four in the working force in a period during which the total working force continues to increase, and the total population over sixty-four almost doubled. The effect of unemployment on consumer purchasing power has been eased and some of the desperation has been taken out of searching for new jobs by unemployment insurance which, in 1964, paid out 2.5 billion dollars to 5,735,000 unemployed persons for 75,674,-000 weeks during which they could not find jobs even with the help of 2,000 state-supported employment offices. These figures do not include statistics on certain categories of civilian and military employees to whom the Federal Government made payments in the same year.

Besides these provisions, the working day and working week have been limited, with the incidental effect of rationing

140

the amount of work performed by each individual and spreading the work to be done over a larger number of job seekers. When unemployment continues to be a plague in spite of all these props to the economy, it seems pointless to argue that there is nothing to worry about now, or after the close of the Vietnam imbroglio. Unquestionably, lack of an adequate job supply is one of the most pressing problems facing this nation. Less than six years ago, the Secretary of Labor assured businessmen that plenty of jobs were available, but that the unemployed just were not sufficiently educated to fill them; of the four to five million people then unemployed, 1.5 million had less than an eighth-grade education.[4] He did not explain why the other two-thirds of the unemployed were also out of work even though they had more than eight years of schooling. Nor did he mention that there were twenty million people in the United States over the age of twenty-five with less than an eighth-grade education, of whom at least 93 percent were not among the unemployed, either because they had jobs, or found it unnecessary to enter the labor market.

The Secretary pronounced that "Education is the answer to unemployment," even though the United States Office of Education[5] almost simultaneously was pointing out that unemployment among high school graduates under twenty-five was 17.5 percent, or three times the average for the less well-educated working population as a whole. True, the unemployment average for young people in the same age-bracket who had dropped out of school before obtaining a high school diploma was higher, some 26.5 percent. It seems most reasonable to suggest, however, that this significant differential was owing less to lack of knowledge, per se, than to personality problems which made either finishing school or getting a job more difficult and to the growing tendency of personnel officers to prefer high school graduates to non-graduates when they have a choice at the same price, whatever the job requires. The United States

141

Council on Education, at about the same time, presented independent statistics showing that although unemployment is most prevalent among high school dropouts, it still is three times as high as the national average among recent high school graduates.[6]

Facts like these should evoke more thought before urging young people to stay in school beyond the point where they are interested enough to benefit, or campaigning to shame or pressure dropouts into returning. The real problem is a lack of jobs for young people, particularly for young Negroes. By clinging to illusions which deny reality and continuing to shout the old shibboleths, society widens the credibility gap between youth and age and drives desperate young people to violence. Further, those who do finish high school as their elders advise, cannot help feeling that they are entitled to higher ratings than they get. There still are jobs that can be done just as well by people with less than a complete grammar school education, particularly in agriculture and household service. By overeducating those who would be happy to start a career in agriculture, they are made unsuitable for the job. Then, in order to harvest crops, citizens of neighboring countries were imported until the Federal Government put limits on that practice. As a result, farmers have increased their demands on agricultural engineers to devise mechanical harvesters. California, as the leading agricultural state, provides a number of examples of mechanical harvesters for major crops which only a few years ago were either harvested by hand or left to rot in the fields. Participation in harvesting during school-vacation periods has been one way for young people to get an introduction to agricultural careers, and such careers as general farm hands seem to yield job-satisfaction which exceeds that of industry below the managerial level.[7] Unfortunately, urban school training makes even temporary work at hard hand labor on the farm an undignified pursuit, and mechanization is rapidly removing it

142

from the job market. Increasing emphasis on extended education tends to turn young people away from available jobs of this type, and to build up expectations which the economy is unprepared to meet and the individual is still fundamentally unable to achieve.

Although the effect of mechanization, automation, and management engineering, all aimed at greater production efficiency, is most directly felt in job availability, especially in areas where the immature and inexperienced might expect to get their start, there is a secondary effect which has a bearing on long-term satisfaction with life and on education for it. Mechanization and management engineering tend to bring about changes in the nature of work and its relationship to leisure. Young people must wait for a job. Those who have jobs spend fewer hours at them. For people ill-equipped to develop meaningful uses of non-working hours, leisure presents an additional problem. The high degree of job-fragmentation, specialization, and monotonously repetitive tasks which bring no real sense of personal accomplishment further deepen the difficulty. Too often, work fails to stimulate a positive approach to leisure; the possessor of spare time seeks only relief from pathological boredom.

The human brain tends to function abnormally as a result of persisting monotony in the environment. Protracted driving on long-distance truck routes, or overly long stints of piloting planes during nonstop, high-altitude flights, tends to produce mental lapses and accidents for which the man at the controls, if he survives, is unable to account. Laboratory research on this phenomenon, using human subjects restfully immersed in warm water and nonpatterned light and sound, has demonstrated that the brain ceases to function normally after a relatively few hours of exposure to such a muted environment. Ability to think is impaired, and responses to problems become childish. The explanation appears to be that a continuing bombardment of im-

143

pulses from sensory receptors is not only essential for information purposes but has a continuing arousal effect on the brain. If these messages are repetitively monotonous they are inhibited by feedback and the brain loses effectiveness of function until some time after it is aroused by sensory reports of environmental variations.[8]

Critics of highly mechanized and automated manufacturing or processing systems point out that this kind of repetitive monotony has a similar, though less catastrophic effect on the minds of machine operators and tenders. Moreover, installations increase in number because they maintain or augment production while inhibiting repetitively monotonous demands from employees for higher wages, more fringe benefits, and better working conditions. That is, the number of employees needed for a given operation is decreased. Total production may not increase substantially, because of limitations in the sales market. Nevertheless, the change has a fascination for the owner-producer because he seems to be increasing the man-hour production rate of his employees, has fewer of them to plague him, and is in a position to raise wages. Both employers and organized labor tend to be dazzled by this apparent increase in man-hour production. Neither takes full cognizance of the mounting capital investment that makes this possible. The owner is proud of the progress being made. Organized labor, with occasional exceptions, acquiesces in the diminution of jobs, provided that wages reflect the ostensible progress. Even though the increase in man-hour production rates might more accurately be estimated at 2 to 3 percent annually over the past century, when logical adjustments are made for the growth in capital investment in plants and public investment in education, it often pleases the American ego to estimate an annual betterment of 3 to 4 percent annually, and even to claim an accelerating curve in man-hour production. Organized labor has persuaded the United States Department of Labor to recognize this acceleration curve in production even though sharp-penciled economists claim that it does not exist. The inevitable result has been negotiation on the part of labor for wage rates based on a mirage, greater pressure on industry and business to substitute uncomplaining machinery for never-satisfied human beings, and a continuing build-up of the discrepancy between job supply and job demand.[9]

The entire foundation of America's economic philosophy may need a careful inspection. There is ample evidence from the past to indicate that hominid minds will continue to elaborate on basically good ideas until they become a menace to the welfare of society. Current emphasis on leisure as a substitute for work appears to be a diversionary tactic which ignores the facts that leisure is complementary to work, and that it must be sought rather than imposed. One cannot play involuntarily. Physical survival through meaningful work is the basic problem that must be solved if the personalities making up any society are to remain in good health. For every individual who is able to adjust to an enforced partnership with an inanimate machine or battery of pushbuttons, there is bound to be another who can't. Not many years ago an English coal-mining company decided to modernize by eliminating hand-mining in teams and adopting a remarkable machine which one man could operate. Much to the company's surprise, the mining community promptly developed an epidemic of psychosomatic illnesses: uncontrollable tremors and abdominal pains, stomach ulcers, and the curious involuntary rolling of the eyeballs known as miner's nystagmus.[10]

From studies made of the degree of satisfaction evinced by workers in various occupations it seems clear that satisfaction does not increase commensurately with mechanization and man-hour production efficiency. The man who is sufficiently satisfied with his job to maintain that he would seek it again were he starting life over and given a choice does not usually

145

start his list of reasons with a reference to the amount of money he earns. He is more likely to mention the amount of personal control that he has over rate and conditions of work, including degree of supervision, the fellowship that he finds among others in the trade, and the significance of his group's contribution to society, or to the economic system. As the study by Georges Friedmann already cited emphasizes, this kind of job satisfaction cannot be developed by painting the workshop, improving illumination, opening a canteen, scheduling a coffee break, or hiring a specialist in management-employee relations.[11] These improvements, while all good in themselves, do not reach the fundamental motivations of the mind, as even a deer mouse seems to know.

Leisure is no more of a panacea for decreasing work opportunities or lack of satisfaction on the job than are improvements in work environment and personnel relations. Too often leisure is equated with involuntary idleness or looked on as an antidote for work. The American people have been busily engaged for some time in building a philosophy about leisure which is expected to minimize any inadequacies in the work supply. Work must be recognized merely as a chore to be performed before the purpose of life can be explored. Education should train for work to meet the requirements of the body, but it should also teach young people how to enjoy leisure in order that the highest aspirations of the mind may be achieved.

Unfortunately, many of those who have won more leisure, even, perhaps, as a compromise on demands for higher wages, give little evidence that they are approaching salvation. Depressing jobs, however rationed, tend to promote a depressing use of leisure, a search for forgetfulness through alcohol or other drugs, outbursts of savage self-assertion, brutal amusements, conspicuous consumption, and a predilection for the wild hopes of gambling.[12]

A decade ago, a symposium on leisure as a national goal

and on the progress being made toward its achievement gave little reassurance about either the achievement or the value of that end. Leisure has not proved to be the sphere for self-realization, but rather for passivity, or distractions and vicarious experience.[13] Leisure is described as the great emptiness in which one may seek for means without ends. A surprising number of workers with radically shortened hours have used their leisure to find a second job. The number of these moonlighters in the United States doubled between 1950 and 1957, from 1.8 million, or 3 percent of the working force, to 3.6 million, or 5.3 percent of the working force. The latter figure, by coincidence, produced a national balance between those with two jobs, and those, ostensibly in need of work and looking for it, who were unable to find any job.

In 1958, a well-informed journalist reported on the use of increased leisure in a single industrial city.[14] He chose to study Akron, Ohio, because 15 percent of the workers in the rubber industry had enjoyed a thirty-six-hour week and the extra leisure that it brought, for more than a quarter of a century. Like the participants in the symposium on leisure, he found that one of the commonest uses of more free time was for more work. Not only was moonlighting exceptionally prevalent, but so, also, was the working wife. In fact, a six-hour day, six-day week tended to produce a new family pattern, with husband and wife working different shifts both inside and outside the home, and raising children without the help of hired baby-sitters. Both moonlighting and husbands and wives working different shifts clearly gave work a nuance of variety that brought reasonable satisfaction without true leisure.

Akron workers did demonstrate a catholic taste in their leisure pursuits. The per capita sale of hunting licenses was spectacularly high. Akron demonstrated that the ancient work-purpose of chasing down food was sufficiently attractive to warrant readoption as a pastime. But the workers of Akron also

147

supported a surprisingly high concentration of bowling alleys and spent a higher than average percentage of time on golf courses. If leisure did nothing else, it made Akron the national center for championship bowling and the home of the world series in golf.

Those who defend technology and what it does to job content on the ground that it is a means to a higher end—increased leisure for self-actualization—think of something other than what the average citizen seems to seek in his leisure. More than one sociologist has tried to clarify the concept of the "vast opportunities opened up by leisure" by studying how it was used by people with enough money to set their own time schedules and do what they chose without regard to cost.[15] The activities reported were varied indeed: going to the legitimate theater, concerts, lectures, museums, and art galleries; attending conventions; joining fraternal organizations; playing duplicate bridge; performing community services; reading for pleasure or self-improvement; photography; entertaining at home.[16]

Economic and social status groups differed markedly on worthwhile uses of leisure. Many choices appeared to be dictated by fashion rather than discriminating selection in the light of normative values, since those who have made money enough to achieve high status are not better equipped by their success to make value judgments on the use of leisure than people who are not so rich. If a nation expects its people to find salvation through leisure, it must establish, perhaps, a leisure class trained for, and dedicated to, that purpose, with sufficient prestige to make it the model that the public emulates. The peerage of England, it has been remarked, tended to serve this purpose until new patterns of taxation lowered its wealth and weakened its public image.[17]

More pessimistic observers think that nothing can save a system of cultural values for leisure or any other part of life so long as technology proceeds at its recent pace and is directed solely toward efficient production and distribution at a monetary profit. The low level of benefit from increasing leisure is directly traceable to the entrepreneurial attractiveness of technologically developed mass communication systems as a mean of peddling the piddling.[18]

To the businessman in a free-enterprise environment, most of the foregoing is sheer nonsense. If the public is to be served as a group of consumers, it must be given what it wants, or at least told what it should want in pidgin English and equally hybrid concepts. It is not the responsibility of business to improve people or to question what they do, except when they do not pay their bills or try to avoid debt by shoplifting.

To those who justify continued technological change by the promise of leisure the public's failure to exploit leisure properly is almost unbelievable. Like those who deny the existence of a job shortage and blame unemployment on lack of training for available jobs, the leisure enthusiasts feel sure that the fault lies not in their interpretation of human needs, but in the schools' failure to convey the significance of leisure and its employment. They fail to see that an enthusiastic approach to leisure must be built by satisfactory completion of an episode of work. Trying to interest young people in leisure before they know what their work will be is like frying an egg ten years before breakfast, and then putting it in the deep freeze. The time to educate people in the use of leisure, if education is necessary, is when people begin to anticipate leisure. Whether it develops along normal—that is, socially admired—lines or along socially disapproved lines may depend upon whether jobs are available and well suited to meet both innate and school-fostered expectancies.

The United States is not the only country with youth problems, of course. But these problems show an extraordinary relationship to industrialization, not only in nations well along

149

the same road that America is traveling, but also where westernization has accomplished little but the destruction of traditional systems of sharing adult work and responsibilities with young people who are approaching maturity. It should not be considered unreasonable to suggest that this relationship needs more investigation than it has so far received. One cannot deny that man in partnership with the machine has accomplished extraordinary results in producing and distributing physical necessities, comforts, and conveniences, but the mere thought of this proliferation going on forever is spiritually depressing. At the same time, without reason to check it, the proliferation may well continue until it destroys itself, somewhere on the far outskirts of absurdity. One anthropologist sees seeds of destruction already beginning to sprout; their effect should be checked by studying the health of today's guinea pigs, the youth of the nation, whose social diet is most heavily laden with them.

The social effect of substituting machines for human beings needs to be more closely observed in respect to the availability of jobs and to their changing nature. In particular, it is necessary to check the validity of the assumption that classroom instruction can be substituted for the maturing effect and educational value of work, with no real regard for the talents and capacity of the particular adolescent involved. Businessmen should check the educational qualifications actually needed for beginning workers in specific job classifications. Both management and organized labor should give more thought to the self-interest that could be served by opening the job market for sixteen- and eighteen-year-olds. There is special need of more clear thinking about leisure as a substitute for work and involuntary unemployment as the equivalent of leisure.

More than is apparently realized, accelerated cultural elaboration and change result from the unrestrained enthusiasm

150

of a relatively small percentage of leaders in management, research, and development, who have discovered fields of activity in which they can exercise both their instincts for survival through work and their play potential at a level that affects millions of other people. High though the leaders' technical proficiency may be, socially speaking they often act like children so enthralled with building and loading a cannon that they cannot be bothered with what might happen when it explodes.

As an officer of the United States Bureau of the Budget said a few years ago, in little more than a decade science has been given a role of extraordinary influence in national policy. A generation of scientific and political administrators developed ulcers improving technology; another generation is developing ulcers trying to cope with the problems that improvement has created.[19]

One could well list among those problems the aggrandizing of the scientific mind by those who have it. Increasingly, they are trying to convert secondary and even elementary schools into training schools for future scientists. New textbooks are being written and teaching methods changed to emphasize the abstractions and symbols with which the scientific mind must deal, without regard for the additional hurdles this may throw in the path of the majority of their captives. Science and development seem to work with missionary zeal to eliminate job opportunities for the non-technologically oriented young person, and at the same time to make his enforced stay in school more frustrating. This policy can be described as playing with matches and slow-burning fuses. There is a larger and more dangerous problem: restraining the enthusiasm of free-roving creativity in an age when knowledge and experimental capacity, supported by almost unlimited funds, could easily involve the entire planet in one catastrophic exercise of

151

individual curiosity. Scientists themselves recognize this danger, but they find it intellectually easier to detect it in the work of others than in their own achievements.

The Committee on Science in the Promotion of Human Welfare of the American Association for the Advancement of Science issued a report on this matter quite recently.[20] They point out that the availability of money for large-scale experimentation tends to be more important to the individual scientist than adequate checking of his theories by the scientific community. The possible side-effects of a project on the terrestrial biosphere and the health and welfare of the world's human population are obscured by the gleam of truth which the experimenter thinks he has detected, and he plunges ahead like a phototropic moth caught in the light of a candle. Such was the case in 1958 when a secret, high-altitude nuclear explosion test markedly altered the atmospheric Van Allen belt around the globe before its normal characteristics were fully studied. Other nuclear tests have been made before the fall-out danger from all radioactive elements had been adequately investigated. Similarly, the earth has been sprayed with synthetic insecticides before the dangers from residues were fully known; water has been polluted with synthetic detergents before it could be learned that they were non-degradable. Even now, Americans are engaged in a monomaniacal attempt to get men to the moon and back, without a reasonable estimate of the relation of cost to expectable benefit.

The human brain, released from all social controls, can be as dangerous in the pursuit of truth as it is in the pursuit of power. The intrinsic merit of an idea makes its elaboration appear rational despite the ineffable harm that results therefrom. Man's sense of humor has not kept pace with his ability to conceive and carry through the incredible. As good an evidence as any of this curious distortion in perspective can be found in a recent report on the world-wide progress of industrialization from the Inter-University Study of Labor Problems in Economic Development: Most preindustrial societies will have been swept away by the middle of the twenty-first century and replaced by a world-wide urban society dependent on science and technology and their research organizations. But in the twenty-first century, as today, society will require that its working force be dedicated to hard work and to individual responsibility for performance of the tasks assigned.[21]

At least two consoling thoughts can be dredged from this description of the future. First, it is now scheduled for the middle of the twenty-first century rather than 1984. Second, this Industrial Society may not survive unless its working force accepts a common body of ideas, beliefs, and value judgments. This at least suggests a possibility of changing the Industrial Society into a society which will pay attention to the common body of ideas, beliefs, and value judgments based on the human nature that man has evolved during some two million years of evolution under preindustrial conditions.

All the evidence available from world-wide cross-cultural studies seems to support the conclusion that man will expend great energy at the behest of the instinct to survive, but that he develops anomie unless survival rewards other built-in expectancies. The sense of achievement which comes from working for survival as a member of a group, in ways that the group respects, is just as important as the degree of security, comfort, and convenience that the group shares. The Caribou Eskimo of eastern Canada formerly went through periods of great privation when fishing ice began to melt and snow turned to rain before the spring migration of the caribou from the south. They would sometimes sit for weeks, half-starved, in leaky skin tents, singing and playing games while waiting for the sustenance that the returning caribou brought. Yet when an early explorer tried to persuade a Caribou Eskimo to travel to Montreal with him to complete his record of the language, and described how pleasant it would be to live under a roof, with central heating, piped water, and artificial light, his offer was turned down flatly. All the Eskimos were convinced that there was no finer place or way to live anywhere in the world; the explorer revealed himself as untrustworthy by intimating otherwise.

Modern industrial civilization, heir to the creative riches of a scientific age, is understandably loath to rock the boat which has carried it so far in comparative safety. But it must realize that it cannot continue to throw members of the community overboard to make room for more machinery. To those swimming for their lives it is not enough to promise that if they can make it to the nearest store they can buy water wings, water fins, swimming caps, and weather-resisting lotions better and cheaper than the world has ever known. Neither is it sensible to tell them that a ladder will be lowered to them if they will get more schooling first, nor to try to persuade them that they are on vacation, enjoying leisure, and just as free as the dolphins cavorting about. They need a deck beneath their feet, a reassurance that there is room for them aboard, even if it be before the mast and under the forecastle.

CHAPTER 7

Dropping Out

‖‖‖

Any discussion of the relationship of human beings to the societies and cultures they have created almost inevitably confronts the problem: If group living and culture-accumulation are universal attributes of the hominid family, why do so many individuals find the situations thus created intolerable and either retreat from reality into mental illness or permanently sever connections by suicide?

This is a good question—so good, in fact, that no really adequate reply has yet been found. Occasionally, an ostensible answer can be supplied in the case of individual deserters from the ranks, but nothing has been offered that approaches the simple, universal, elegant explanation that scientists appreciate. Nevertheless, any broad application of anthropology to the problems of modern times must approach such questions.

In this context, mental illness refers to *idiopathic mental illness;* that is, an abnormal or subnormal functioning of the

155

brain for which there is no discernible physical or pathological explanation. Talking about suicides in this context also means those for which there is no discernible physical or pathological cause: not self-destroyers who rationally choose death over a continued life of suffering from disease or a lingering decline of physical and mental powers as age increases, but the vast majority who seek death because society seems to offer no ego-satisfying alternative.

As far as is known, other primates or mammals, in the wild, seldom, if ever, encounter situations which lead to behavior more violent than flight or simple aggression. Anything resembling a neurosis or full psychosis in animals does not apparently occur, except under conditions artificially created by the hominid brain, when flight or aggressive response is no longer practical.

Observations on infant lambs and kids and on infant hominids deprived of normal maternal care suggest that suicide can be brought about through early failure of the survival instinct and a general anomie. But researchers have also demonstrated that reactions comparable to the neuroses and phychoses of mildly or seriously ill hominid minds can be produced in other animals under artificial conditions. A sheep, it was found, could be conditioned to anticipate a mild electric shock on one leg by introducing a countdown with a metronome operating at sixty beats per minute before each shock. Even though the shock was only strong enough to startle the animal, anticipation of the strange sensation was enough to generate a compulsive flexing of the leg in time with the metronome. The intensity of the animal's anxiety was subsequently increased by introducing a metronome countdown operating at one hundred and twenty beats per minute with no electric shock at the end. The mental problems of distinguishing one metronome rate from the other and of inhibiting the compulsive flexing of the leg when no electric shock was signaled produced the following effect: "Within a few days, after thirty or forty repetitions of M-120 without shock, our sheep resists being led to the laboratory. In its restraining harness it is unable to maintain the customary self-imposed restraint. It exhibits a diffuse agitation with frequent startle reactions, bleating, urinating, defecating; irregular, rapid respiration and heart action; and in addition, persistent small tic-like movements of the trained foreleg." [1]

The sheep are reacting against an unnatural environment where electric shocks occur or do not occur solely because of the frequency with which a metronome clicks. One can show further empirical similarities between the reactions of these relatively placid animals and the reactions of human beings to problems of a higher degree of sophistication. Sheep which respond neurotically to metronomic anticipation of a harmless electric shock or no shock may develop a phobia against typewriters because they sound like metronomes. Their flocking instinct is so weakened that they wander off by themselves and as a consequence become the first victims of marauding dogs.

In summing up, the experimenter stated that, when the struggle of a sheep or goat to understand the meaning of what is happening and is about to happen to him becomes too severe or prolonged, the animal inevitably succumbs to neurotic illness. And that illness typically continues through the normal life span. [2]

Confirming evidence is cited from other experimental work, with dogs, in this case. A dog was taught to recognize that two musical notes on an ascending scale signaled that it might obtain a dog biscuit from a dispensing apparatus, and two musical notes on a descending scale meant no dog biscuit. [3] The tonal interval between the notes was then shortened, finally reaching a point where the dog was utterly baffled in attempts to distinguish whether the scale was ascending or descending. In its frustration the dog not only ceased trying

157

to obtain food but refused to eat when supplied. It had to be moved to another environment where it again consented to eat, but still refused to accept the same kind of dog biscuit. If one of these biscuits was put in its mouth, the dog refused to chew and let it drop out. It barked at the biscuits as they lay on the floor, and on one occasion came up and urinated on them, obviously a case of using a patterned reaction out of normal place to meet an otherwise hopeless sense of frustration.

In these experiments on neuroses-like responses from animals, it is important to note that the experimental animals were alone and forcibly restrained from escape. The problem was neither one that they could face as a member of a group, nor one that could be classed as a peril of nature. One could also assume that their frustration was related to that displayed by deer mice and other animals when their expectancies about the environment are arbitrarily changed. The goats were fearful of a mild electric shock, but did not display a full neurotic syndrome until they had learned to anticipate the shock, and then been frustrated in their effort to discriminate between the signal for shock and the signal for no shock. Similarly, the dog was not bothered by biscuits which dropped after one sequence of sounds and did not drop after another sequence of sounds. This was the way that biscuits behaved and he lived with this fact. What bothered him was his loss of ability to predict whether they would drop or not drop. One might suggest that knowledge from which prediction can be made is akin to control of the environment, which another experimenter came to think was a matter of concern for deer mice. Conversely, when animals cannot discriminate between cues, they no longer have this sense of control. Their immediate environment is no longer ordered in the same way; their expectancies are confused, and reality is undeterminable.

Important in this discussion is the problem of whether continuing high rates of mental illness and suicide can be attributed to hominid society and culture, involving complex and conflicting behavior demands complicated by unexpected changes and competitively threatening population density. It is anomalous, to say the least, that civilization, which is popularly believed to be an ever-greater blessing to hominids, has not led to any spectacular decline in these rates. Some statistical studies imply that mental illness is increasing as civilization multiplies its blessings and distributes them more widely.[4] For example, from 1880 to 1934 the number of patients in mental hospitals in the United States increased from 81.6 to 308.6 per 100,000 of population. Such studies may, of course, be unjustifiably pessimistic in that hospital statistics and medical reports reflect the increasing availability of hospital beds and medical services. The rate of illness may have been comparable before the institutions were built, yet not be recorded because the mentally ill were cared for in their own homes and communities with or without the counsel of a family physician.

Statistics on suicide are even more difficult to analyze, because, in any society which frowns on self-destruction as a misuse of the "right to life," there is a tendency to conceal unsuccessful attempts at suicide and to attribute deaths from this cause to accidents, either to save family pride or protect insurance payments.[5] Nevertheless, the number of reported suicides in the United States now exceeds twenty thousand a year (almost twice the number of homicides). It is estimated that six thousand or more actual suicides are recorded as accidental deaths, and as many as two hundred thousand people try to destroy themselves each year, but fail.

Even though it cannot be proved that idiopathic mental illness and related attempts at self-destruction are directly connected with problems created by highly organized societies whose members are too closely cabined by the prescriptions and proscriptions of a complex culture, it should be clear that civilization needs to give thought to this possibility. I cannot

159

share the complacency of those who dismiss this possibility as a new kind of natural selection which removes weak individuals and so strengthens society for its conquest of the future. The kinship between mental illness and both genius on the one hand and delinquency and crime on the other is too close to excuse a fatuous fatalism toward its future incidence. Continued high rates of mental illness and suicide strongly suggest that a laissez-faire civilization is not automatically eliminating either the cultural characteristics that contribute to those deviations or the genetic lines of low threshold that are most likely to produce victims. To maintain, as some theorists do, that the criterion of the success of a civilization is what it does for "society," rather than for the individuals making up that society, seems to imply not only that the whole is greater than the sum of its parts, but that it is utterly independent of the fate of its parts.

Unquestionably, "society" does become more impersonal as it grows larger, and the significance of the individual grows commensurately less; but if the number of individuals whose needs remain unmet continues to increase, the value of a society needs reassessment. Its cambium layer of creative minds may continue to produce growth and luxuriant foliage, but if it is slowly rotting at the core the time will come when unbalanced weight and shifts in the social atmosphere will topple it. Society, like religion, is abstract, and normative, but still emotional. Although it cannot be reduced to any single factor, it is influenced by physical facts, the size of the collectivity, existential values, the complexity of the division of labor, and the characteristics of individual psychology. The social system must offer some reliability and order, and it molds as well as responds to the needs of the individual. Above all, it must supply the individual with the personality goal of some valued role in the collectivity which he finds satisfaction in acting out, partly because it offers identity in a recognized role system.[6]

The relation of these issues to the problem of mental illness can be seen by looking at smaller contemporary societies with a less confusing set of roles. Quite frequently behavior which American society would regard as dangerously psychotic is accepted by other societies as an outlet for frustration within the role parameters of a good citizen, or is perceived as an evidence of his need for a change in role.

When a native of Ifalik, a tiny coral atoll about halfway between Truk and Yap in the Caroline Islands, picks up a club and runs about bashing coconut trees and screaming imprecations at the sky, he is not mentally ill; he is following an established cultural procedure for ridding himself of anger or irritation. The people of Ifalik believe that anger and irritation are caused by malevolent ghosts of the dead who flit about invisibly trying to cause trouble. Therefore, when irritated or made angry by his family or his neighbors, an individual knows that he is under attack by ghosts and must frighten them away. To Ifalik islanders this is the way a sane person meets reality. Only a "crazy" person would take his anger or irritation out on the approximately one hundred and fifty people who make up his society. When an anthropologist visited Ifalik, the local chief explained in pidgin English that fighting could not be tolerated because, if it were, instead of just a few people there would shortly be none.[7] Ghosts are a fantasy, but by accepting them as reality, people of Ifalik find a substitute object for aggression, a means of relieving emotional tensions accepted by the culture and even rewarded by group respect and good will. One might surmise, also, that the "good citizenship" of the injured person would evoke more circumspect behavior from those responsible for his battle with the ghosts. They, too, might suspect that ghosts were at work and try to resist their influence. Even in this small society, with its relatively simple culture, an individual may suffer from mental indispositions, but the society provides a culturally sanctioned safety valve which an outsider perceives as a temporary form of psychosis.

Sanctioned escape seems to be a universal necessity when the individual finds his emotional reactions cabined and confined by cultural rules of the game. He needs a compromise which will relieve his tension and maintain his membership in the group and most cultures provide that compromise in forms ranging from hobbies, the arts, and sports to intoxication, ceremonial torture, and mourning rituals.[8]

The emphasis on leisure activities as a goal of American striving may be in part a rationalization of the increasing need for catharsis as culture grows more complex and tensions mount. This tendency to make a virtue of necessity is useful to human societies everywhere, for it enables human beings to be proud of culture traits which they stumbled upon while trying to deal with the problems created by earlier culture traits. That the mentally ill take over about half of the country's hospital beds as fast as they can be made available suggests that, in American culture, relaxing in a hospital has become one passive equivalent of the Ifalik custom of bashing coconut trees with a club. Presumably, for many people, increasing leisure is not enough to relieve the tensions created by social, economic, or even political problems. Since it is not easy to weigh such possibilities objectively within one's own culture, if mental illness is a refuge from culturally induced tensions, one should be able to cite additional evidence from cultures outside local emotional fences. Consider, then, a recent report on "running *amok*" among the Gururumba, a tribe living in the eastern highlands of New Guinea.[9]

Amok is a well-known form of acute madness among Malay peoples. Like Arctic hysteria, it often occurs without obvious cause and may on occasion spread by the power of suggestion, as did *tarantism* or "dancing mania" in medieval

Italy. A Western observer happened to be in a Gururumba village when a young man, married and starting a family, suddenly ran *amok*. He trampled on gardens, snatched things from children, entered the houses of others without leave, stole whatever small portable goods he could get his hands on, delivered self-laudatory orations, and even shot arrows (without hitting anyone) at those who seemed to cross him. The observer was convinced that the man was truly psychotic. But after a day or two of this behavior, the man disappeared from the village. When he appeared again, a week or two later, he seemed to be quite normal, returned to his small farm and his family, and took up his daily routine as if nothing had happened. The reaction of neighbors seemed as curious as the episode itself. During the attack, the natives gathered, even from distant villages, to watch his antics, often with some amusement. They put valuable articles away, but allowed the "demented" man to carry away trifles, including a number of well-used bars of soap. But when the attack was over, there seemed to be a concerted effort to forget about it and a reluctance even to discuss it.

Patient inquiry finally pieced the background together. The Gururumba are not content with routine lives in which shelter and subsistence are the highest rewards. They take the achievement of these practical goals for granted. What really counts is individual, family, and village status, built on ostentatious courtesies and exchanges of food and goods on every appropriate occasion. In the Gururumba culture pattern, ambition expresses itself through working to acquire a surplus, and then adroitly managing and planning to distribute this surplus so that it will come back and enable one to go through life with a generous hand. But such a system can sometimes put unbearable strains upon the individual.

So it was with the young man who ran *amok*. His family had arranged a marriage which all relatives and the village

163

people considered highly advantageous. This meant that the bride price had to be impressively large. The wherewithal was jointly accumulated by all relatives, but only as a loan to the fortunate groom. He started his married career with a heavy debt and with continuing social responsibilities dictated by the status of his own and his wife's families. He was given land to farm, but did not do well, either because the land was poor or because he lacked a green thumb. Nevertheless, he had to make frequent gifts to his wife's kin to uphold the standing of his own family, and he had so many social duties to perform that he had little time for farming.

Things went from bad to worse. He was afraid that his wife might leave him and precipitate an interfamily quarrel about who was to blame, and what would happen to the bride payment. When a child came, he had to borrow again for the gifts that such good fortune made obligatory. In desperation, he gave up his farm and accepted what looked like a richer piece of land from his wife's family. He did no better with that, and his kin began to press him harder for discharge of debts because he had made them all ashamed by accepting charity land. Another child was on the way. Finally, one morning, he ran *amok*. When the attack was over, he was still a member of the community, but it was recognized that he was no longer an active player in the competition for status. He was no longer pressed to make gifts, or to repay his debts promptly.

Without help from psychiatry, the Gururumba recognize that their culturally idealized struggle for status is not equally advantageous to all members of society, that it leads to psychotic behavior and a retreat from the social reality in some cases, and that individuals so afflicted may be brought back as useful members of society simply by offering them a less demanding role. The dignity of the afflicted person is further protected by blaming his failure to achieve the cultural ideal on a bite inflicted by some malevolent ghost. This misfortune, rather than any personal inadequacy, makes it necessary for a person to change his role. Despite their dependence on superstition, recalling the ghost myths of the Ifalik islanders, the Gururumba are extremely pragmatic in their application of it. An individual who tries to run *amok* without publicly appreciated cause is unceremoniously held over a fire and smoked until he comes to his senses.

An even more elaborate mixture of myth and reality to harmonize individual acts with cultural ideals is found among the Ojibwa (or Chippewa) Indians of the Great Lakes area. These Indians, who were one of the most populous tribes on the continent when European conquest began, lived in a region where winters, under aboriginal conditions, were a challenge to survival. Only by breaking up into small bands and spreading over a vast territory could they obtain enough game to live until spring.

On occasion, one of these family groups might meet with misfortune and either perish entirely, or survive by eating the bodies of its own dead. The Ojibwa, like almost all human beings, loathe the thought of cannibalism. Many peoples have eaten selected parts of the bodies of the dead for ritualistic and magical reasons, but reported cases of relish for human flesh are very few.[10] Even lower orders of mammals and birds seem to use their own kind for food only when the creature is too young to be recognized or has lost its characteristic species identification. Consequently, when an Ojibwa Indian managed to survive a winter through cannibalism he might be expected to lose some self-respect and to be met by society with overt or only partly concealed disgust.

In many parts of the north and northwest, secret societies gain public attention and arouse fear by claiming close relationship with a cannibal spirit. They hold ceremonies in which they attempt to bite people while possessed by this spirit.

165

Among the Ojibwa the cannibal spirit is called *Windigo* or *Witiko*, and he, like ghosts among the Ifalik islanders, serves a useful purpose by being blamed for any cannibalism into which circumstances may force a member of the tribe. The person concerned can save his self-respect because he believes that he would not have done such a horrible thing, even to preserve his own life, had he not been possessed by Windigo.

It is reasonable to believe that this fantasy would also make the cannibal less horrible to his fellow tribesmen. But every culture inevitably elaborates. Playing with the horrifying fascinates the human brain, as the continuing popularity of Bram Stoker's *Dracula* and Mary Shelley's *Frankenstein* bears witness. Consequently, the Ojibwa have made Windigo a general phobia. He is seldom visible and cannot therefore be guarded against. But those who have seen him report horrible details. He is a naked giant whose body resembles stone because he covers himself with pitch and rolls in sand. His heart is a lump of ice, and he has very large feet with only one toe on each. His eyes are swimming in blood, and he has large pointed teeth which are constantly exposed because he has no lips. He brushes trees out of his path as a man would brush grass and swims so fast that his bow wave will upset a canoe. The sound of his voice is so chilling that the legs of those who run to escape him collapse like jelly.

If such a being as this has possessed a man without his knowledge, how can a man's friends know whether the spirit has ever really left, or when he might be back? He may still be there waiting to pounce on others, or in harmony with legends, he can come back at any time. So the Windigo myth both clears the individual morally and ethically for resuming his place in society, and surrounds him with a kind of "typhoid Mary" reputation that, just as effectually, keeps him on the periphery. He lives with the group, but prudence restricts his societal and ceremonial roles. He is not called upon to carry

166

important responsibilities, but he is quite aware that more awe and reverence than disrespect or disdain are involved. After a fashion, his position is comparable to that of a Gururumba who has run *amok*. He lives a life sheltered from heavy cultural demands. One need not be surprised, therefore, to find that some Ojibwa who have never been accused of cannibalism develop a Windigo psychosis and simply adopt cannibalism to prove it.

Not long ago a study of the Ojibwa was made to clarify this point.[11] Out of seventy reasonably well-authenticated cases of Windigo psychosis, only eighteen could certainly be attributed to famine-cannibalism, although seven others might have begun that way. Of those who only began to act like cannibals, nineteen certainly, and seven others possibly, showed that they were possessed by killing and eating a friend or kinsman, or stealing and eating a dead body, not under famine conditions, but solely because Windigo possessed them. Nevertheless, they, too, enjoyed special status in the tribe, received "kid glove" treatment, and under native jurisprudence were exonerated from any incidental homicides, at least as far as "not guilty by reason of possession by Windigo" can be regarded as an exoneration.

When one examines idiopathic mental illness in the United States, with an awareness of what occurs elsewhere, one must ask whether additional culture accretions have mitigated the problems of the individual with a low tolerance for pressure and conflict, either before he exhibits symptoms of mental illness, or after he surrenders to some degree of personality disintegration. It is certainly not possible to affirm that this has happened. The society continues to produce individuals with limited resistance to psychic strains, who may lead reasonably normal lives or become mentally ill, depending on the circumstances they encounter. The law requires that every embryo physically capable of birth be pushed into life without regard

167

to the welcome parents are prepared to offer, or to its chance of developing a healthy hominid personality. Regardless of individual talents, interests, and early-developed alienations, children are placed on a compulsory school assembly line and kept there for an arbitrarily established term of years, in heterogeneously sexed groups of pupils and teachers. They are subjected to a shotgun type of education aimed at fitting them for no particular job and no particular social stratum. Then they are turned out into a world which has ignored their needs for simple job experience in a monomaniacal quest for production efficiency. They may survive juvenile years without satisfying their built-in needs for personal maternal care and membership in an integrated family, go through adolescence with limited constructive peer-group experience, and then face an indifferent adult society which provides no culturally accepted program for neophytes. The only legally sanctioned group to which all feel eligible is David Riesman's "lonely crowd."

The American credo attributes virtue to this system, perhaps because those who survive can call themselves self-made men. But for the majority it is a system designed for the accumulation of doubts and anxieties. Without membership in a group of some kind, the hominid, young or old, is abnormal. Hence juvenile gangs and criminal society are successful in their recruiting efforts; fraternal organizations are popular; and the United States has acquired its reputation as a society of "joiners." Only in the company of others does the average hominid find reason and strength to meet the vicissitudes of life. Even catastrophe can be borne when a person shares it with a group to which he belongs.[12] What disturbs him are the problems and conflicts which he cannot share with others. Exiled remnants of the pre-Communist society of China on Taiwan have one of the lowest rates of psychosis on record.[13] They not only share a catastrophe, but they are held together by the dream of someday reconquering their homeland. Other

factors, of course, are involved, including freedom from debili-
tating diseases and malnutrition. Where such diseases prevail,
as in the newly independent nations of Africa, non-industrial-
ized people are said to rival New Yorkers in incidence of neurosis.[14] Inadequate diets intensify feelings of incompetence,
anxiety, and shame and lead to a high incidence of neuroses
and psychoses, whether in primitive societies and cultures, or
among slum dwellers and minority groups in civilized nations.[15]

The effect upon mental health and the general welfare of
the members of a society which is exerted by unified beliefs,
and a clearly defined economic system with a place for all, is
perhaps nowhere better illustrated than among the Hutterites
of the United States and Canada.[16] The Hutterites are a Protestant group organized by Jacob Huter in German-speaking
Switzerland in 1528. Early religious persecution and subsequent
governmental opposition to them, as stubbornly non-conform-
ist, brought four hundred or more Hutterites to the United
States in 1874–77, after a number of shifts from country to
country in Europe, ending in the Russian Ukraine. They are of
particular interest to anthropologists because of their remarkable cultural stability and rather strictly maintained endogamy
over a period of more than four hundred years.

Briefly, the Hutterites are highly religious, communal
farmers, having separate family living quarters, but a common
dining room, treasury, and store. Economically, they have been
highly successful, buying new farms as old ones become over-
staffed and dividing each flock by "swarming." Except for
adopting better farming equipment as it becomes available,
they have maintained their culture with little change, even
though living within the rapidly changing cultures of the
United States and Canada. They have maintained rather successfully many of the societal and cultural characteristics which
high civilization tends to abandon. Groups are small; they have
unity of belief and behavior; and membership is an exclusive

169

privilege. They dress alike, and differently from non-Hutterite society, because non-Hutterite society has changed and they have not. Only in the last generation or two have they given up making their own clothes and shoes and permitted buttons rather than hooks and eyes on clothing. They operate their own schools, yielding to teacher certification requirements as this becomes necessary, but closing formal education at the age of fifteen.

Since 1762, when a group of forty-nine Carinthian Lutherans joined forces with their decimated ranks, the only outsiders accepted by the Hutterites were a widow and daughter and one orphan boy in the early 1800's, and about thirty adults and children in the 1930's. By 1950, the original four hundred or so immigrants to the United States had increased to more than eight thousand people living on communal farms scattered widely through North and South Dakota and Montana in the United States, and Alberta and Manitoba in Canada. There are only sixteen different family names among the Hutterites, but the group has continued to produce large numbers of healthy children (averaging ten per family), contrary to the popular belief that close inbreeding is genetically dangerous.

Because the Hutterites are stubbornly different from their American and Canadian neighbors, and keep to themselves, they are all considered to be slightly queer, but when they were studied, with the cooperation of their leaders, it was found that the incidence of mental illness among them was substantially less than in the surrounding, more highly civilized communities.

Life for these hardworking people is relatively uncomplicated even though rigidly prescribed. Hutterite children are not immune to nail-biting, enuresis, thumb-sucking, temper tantrums, quarrelsomeness, disobedience, untruthfulness, or cruelty to animals, but it is quietly expected that they will grow out of these childhood problems, and apparently they do. The adults drink wine with their meals and are not averse to a glass of beer when they go to town, but they have no record of alcoholism. Neither do they have any recognizable juvenile delinquency or crime. No evidence of breaking community rules could be discovered except an occasional surreptitious sale of spare-time handiwork, some trapping of fur animals, and work for neighbors in order to get money for goods not obtainable from the common store. Hutterites of lesser ability are expected to do only what they can; those of more than ordinary ability seem to find adequate goals in community leadership. This is not an environment in which genius proliferates, but neither does it raise many intolerable conflicts for those who exceed or fall short of average ability to adjust to group demands. Occasional cases of neuroses or psychoses appear, and it is in the Hutterite attitude toward the afflicted that one finds echoed a cultural concept of reality which the mentally ill can accept, and a cultural niche which offers them protection without loss of dignity or respect.

An outsider sees an inconsistency in Hutterite attitude toward the mentally ill. Community leaders will, in some instances, discourage marriage between families which have shown a susceptibility to mental illness, thereby indicating an underlying concern over the probability that susceptibility, at least, may be hereditary. Yet this does not affect the general belief that neurotics and psychotics are privileged people chosen by God for a special kind of testing, and that, somehow, the entire community shares in the testing by the understanding and sympathetic cooperation it extends to the afflicted. There is never a drawing away from the mentally ill, or any encouragement for them to withdraw from Hutterite reality. The community, rather, rallies around to help. The individual is relieved of responsibilities to whatever extent seems necessary and is treated with a deference which exalts rather than demeans. This attitude is said to be responsible for the remarkably favorable prognosis for those who succumb to mental ailments; they may not fully recover, but they are enabled to carry on in some limited capacity.

In reviewing current knowledge on mental problems in relation to culture, some psychologists are more impressed by the Hutterite success in treating mental illness, than by its low incidence.[17] Undoubtedly, the Hutterite treatment does not work for everyone. One cannot reduce either the causes or the cures for mental illness to this level of simplicity. The point here—and one made by other observers—is that an uncomplicated culture in a closed group may be conducive to mental health for those with low resistance to tension and conflict, and that a culture which provides limited participation for those of limited strength has therapeutic advantages.[18]

As the American psychologist Harry S. Sullivan declared, a pronouncedly schizophrenic personality, brought to that state by failure or disappointment in interpersonal relations under culturally established rules, still continually strives for self-respect and status in the eyes of other people it judges to be significant.[19] If such persons are held for some time in a mental hospital, they are exposed to the danger of finding their fellow patients more significant than the doctors or the staff. They accept an institutional culture as more rewarding than the culture they left. On the other hand, even among patients who escape from hospitals or leave without the doctor's blessing, as high a proportion as 50 or 60 percent may find on their own a new niche in the outside world, which enables them to carry on without return to the hospital.[20] Their ability to do this seems to depend in significant measure on success in finding a job which enables them to participate in society without meeting the strains that initiated the original breakdown.

The kind of work that society offers the individual may be one important factor both in preventing and treating mental illness. Japan, a rapidly industrializing culture, handles its mental illness problem with about one-seventh as many hospital beds per hundred thousand people as have been needed in the United States, another psychologist concludes, because there are still many small-job niches in Japan's industrial economy, because hospital care may be contributed by family members themselves or by a special practical nurse hired to tend the patient, and because group therapy by Buddhist temple groups adds religious impact to the treatment.[21]

There seems to be a growing realization that the gregarious instinct is still strongly operative in many cases of mental illness and that shutting a patient off from society while trying to discover what social situation may have contributed to his illness is like cutting off an arm in order to facilitate removing a splinter from one finger. At Cowell Memorial Hospital on the Berkeley campus of the University of California it was customary, before 1960, to separate mentally disturbed young people from the campus community while probing in depth for some underlying cause of the disturbance. Then the entire procedure was changed. The disturbed individual was allowed to continue in college on some limited study schedule while counseling and treatment proceeded. The results were spectacularly encouraging. With some protection against the problem as the student saw it, 65 percent of the schizophrenics and 83 percent of the severe psychoneurotics managed to carry on successfully. The prognosis for recovery was improved and hospitalization was reduced to about one-eighteenth of the average for the State as a whole. The psychiatric staff reported that these data tend to verify the belief that prompt intensive treatment in a community setting helps to prevent the permanent psychological crippling that prolonged custodial care in large mental hospitals tends to produce. The institutionalized patient often begins as a person with a recognizable identity, whatever his problems may be, and ends as a mere "mental case."

Perhaps a highly mechanized culture, such as that operated by the United States, commendably concentrating on efficiency, but less commendably ignoring the needs of individuals for a share in the production process, may contribute to the general tax burden by inflating the demand for institutions in which to incarcerate unused or slightly defective people, starting with public schools and ending with public prisons and public hospitals. American behavior is not caused by apathy toward human problems. It results, rather, from exuberant enthusiasm for doing what is seen as good. Then, rather than cautiously retreat a little, the same exuberant enthusiasm is diverted into developing an antidote. There should be some more logical middle ground. As has been found in studies of the people of Nova Scotia and of Africa, a maximum of sanity seems to be promoted by a reasonable amount of social organization, a reasonable amount of cultural complexity, and a reasonable amount of stability.[22] Each person has his own optimal level of complexity in situations he can deal with comfortably and effectively.[23]

Job competition tends to sort people out on the basis of ability to handle the work assigned, but the American credo, exemplified by its school system, seems to be based on the theory that all abilities can be brought nearer to equality by steadily raising the minimum average of school years completed. This is part of America's mythology, for the evidence shows that extending the period of schooling for all increases the difference in achievement between the able and the less able, as far as academic knowledge is concerned. Since schooling does not decrease the range of abilities, those on the lower end of the range find it hard to find and hold jobs that they think school has prepared them to fill. At the same time, young people with craftsmanship abilities, or even good judgment in life situations, who could earn an equality of respect under other circumstances, are subjected to more frustration, and

174

even begin to lose their youthful enthusiasm for achievement. All this tends to increase the chance of later trouble, rather than help diminish it.

Suicide may be related to mental illness, just as what is called *mental illness* may be a symptom of psychic inadequacy. Some eminently sane commentators maintain that at least a few psychoses and suicides are a normal flight from an insane situation which culture has helped to create. Explaining suicide is even more difficult than explaining mental illness because suicide involves the sane as well as the neurotic or psychotic. One *can*, however, make a few general statements about suicide. As far as is known it occurs only in human societies. Although some primitive societies assert that their members would not think of it, they are more likely to recognize that under certain circumstances suicide is the wise man's choice and a culturally accepted course of action. One can say that complete proscription of suicide is peculiar to civilized, Christian nations, reflecting the Biblical implication that life alone has value and that death is its enemy, both in the physical and in the spiritual sense because sin brings spiritual death. The Bible, however, does not specifically categorize suicide. When the counselor Ahithophel hangs himself because his counsel was ignored, this action is mentioned without comment. Matthew records just as matter of factly that Judas hanged himself after confessing his betrayal of Jesus and casting down the pieces of silver.

Among primitive hunting and gathering societies, death was preferable to life with infirmities; if the aged could not persuade others to dispatch them, they might kill themselves, violently, or by just sitting down and waiting for death. Often it was thought to be better to begin afterlife while still active and in full possession of one's faculties. Where war captives were enslaved, suicide might be preferred to slavery. Quite frequently, suicide was the only honorable antidote for any public shame or unrevenged insult. Suicide, or self-injury lead-ing to death, was often an evidence of deep grief over the death of a loved one, though there is an implication that widows grieving for dead husbands in the customary manner expected onlookers to restrain them—as was also customary.

Suicide in modern civilization is anomalous because the suicide gets no cultural praise, and the kinship group no respect or social prestige. Custom and the instinct for survival join to condemn suicide, yet it persists; in some places, a special watch must be kept to prevent people from killing themselves, in and out of mental hospitals. More than three hundred and fifty in-dividuals, for example, have jumped from Golden Gate Bridge which spans the entrance to San Francisco Bay.

The nineteenth-century French sociologist Emile Durk-heim, in his classical study of suicide, concluded that the sui-cide rate is determined by the degree of meaning given to life by a society and the culture it supports. The rate tends to fall when large numbers of people are united in a common enthu-siasm.[24] The same general conclusion is supported in the find-ing that whether associated with psychotic symptoms or not, most suicides tend to occur in environments where family and group affiliations are minimal, and to be promoted by loneli-ness and a sense of failure, of hopeless anger and despair.[25]

Louis I. Dublin, the well-known American statistician, suggests that loss of family and group affiliations intensifies loneliness and sense of failure. Divorced persons have a very high suicide rate. The widowed rank next, and those who have never married rank third. The lowest rate is found among married people who have continued in that status without interruption by separations, divorce, or death. More men than women succeed in suicide attempts, but more women make the attempt and fail: their plans are impractical; or they take steps to assure that they will be saved before death occurs.[26] One cannot be sure why people commit suicide even when they leave notes to explain. More than three-fourths of these give one of three reasons: ill health, domestic troubles, or disappointment in love. But the unmentioned reasons must include a little hate, a little fear, a little despair, and the end of patience in coping with them.[27] It is generally agreed that behind the ostensible cause, the situation that triggers action, must lie a state of mind that has developed during a fairly long time. Among holders of industrial insurance policies, most of them skilled or unskilled workers, the rather spectacular improvement in labor conditions from 1911 to 1920 seemed to lead to a better state of mind, for their suicide rate dropped from 16.5 to 7.3 per 100,000. In the middle of the Great Depression, the rate moved up to 12.9; with the advent of World War II, it fell again to 6.4 per 100,000, considerably below the rate for the population as a whole, and particularly the rate for people whose economic and educational position made the comforts and conveniences of civilization widely available.

Continuing high rates of mental illness and suicide indicate that civilization is not gradually making life more satisfactory for all people; nor is it selectively eliminating those genetic lines which have a low resistance to the stresses which change, population crowding, competition, and restless mobility tend to impose. It is not even certain that suicides and those who succumb to mental illness ought to be eliminated. The social and cultural conditions which they find intolerable are not necessarily desirable for those who manage to stay out of mental hospitals and refrain from self-destruction. Every culture seems peculiar to those not brought up in it, but those who find it insufferably peculiar even though they were brought up in it may reflect rather basic conflicts between the subconscious equilibrium of the average hominid mind and the ambitions of the creative mind. One cannot be sure whether the most tolerant or the least tolerant are the most sane. One anthropologist comments that the discernible difference be-

177

tween a culture and a psychosis is the number of their respective communicants.[28] The larger the population of mental hospitals, the less certain one is that the people outside are sane. The mental hospital may be the only dependable escape from the insanities which are encountered elsewhere.

Experimenters' judgment about sanity and neurosis or psychosis may be questioned when it is based on the reaction of experimental animals subjected to electric shock. The shocks are mild and harmless; hence the abnormal behavior of the animal is called *neurotic*. But do the animals know that this incomprehensible experience is harmless? It might be an introduction to death, and the animal's reaction might well be interpreted as an instinctively normal one without which the species would have died out long ago.[29] One can apply a similar line of thought to the kind of environment that civilization provides: If most people lack freedom, spontaneity, and genuine experience of self, the individual is not aware of that lack as a defect; hence he does not feel threatened, isolated, or inadequate. Social scientists, however, cannot identify the behavior of the majority with sanity, nor can they accept any given culture pattern as normal merely because it is generally practiced.[30]

CHAPTER 8

Routes to Rebellion

Juvenile delinquency and adult crime, like mental illness and suicide, are interesting here as aberrant forms of behavior suggesting either that evolution cannot produce a line of hominids fully adapted to the demands of civilized living; or that contemporary civilization—despite its claim to greater security and health, and more varied interests, comforts, and conveniences than the world has ever known—is falling short in distribution of its blessings, or failing to recognize that some of its demands are out of harmony with biological imperatives.

If the number and magnitude of problems created are reasonable criteria of significance, then juvenile delinquency and adult crime are more important social aberrations than mental illness and suicide. The neurotic, the psychotic, and the suicide seek escape from social or cultural dead ends; they harm others only incidentally. The delinquent and the criminal are in open revolt against the society in which they live and attack both property and persons. Moreover, there is better statistical support for concluding that this category of aberration is spreading. If it has cultural causes which can be corrected, it is urgent that they be defined and mitigated.

A recent report of the Federal Bureau of Investigation indicated that major crimes, such as robbery, aggravated assault, burglary, and grand larceny, have been increasing at the alarming rate of 10 percent a year. Crimes of all sorts lead to annual arrests aggregating one for every twenty-seven people in the population. Federal and state prisons are overcrowded by a continuing load of more than 200,000 inmates and the situation is unlikely to improve so long as more than 25 percent of all arrests involve juveniles under twenty-one years of age. The manpower loss—hundreds of thousands of law violators and additional hundreds of thousands engaged in apprehending, trying, and imprisoning them—is staggering; the dollar loss is astronomically greater; and the effect on public morale cannot even be estimated.

Juvenile delinquency and crime are not, of course, peculiar to high civilization. They occur on all cultural levels in every human society for which adequate records exist. The great disparity between what a primitive society would identify as its crime record, and statistics like those cited for the United States, is partly attributable to expanding definitions of crime, to greater sensitivity about the infringement of personal rights by individuals, heightened irritability in large concentrations of people who are strangers to each other, and to the efficiency of professional police departments and courts, operating under written laws.

In primitive society, a given act of aggression may be a crime only if it is directed at a member of the same community, clan, or tribe. Successfully carrying it out against traditional rivals, or potential enemies, may be regarded as commendable bravery. If aggressive action does exist within

180

the same community, the circumstances preceding and following the event may determine whether the public classifies it
as a crime, a justifiable reprisal for past injury, or merely an
offense which may be expunged from the record by payment of
damages (wergild). Adolescent cattle herders in Africa stole
garden produce from neighboring villages and took milk from
cows in rival herds. They were expected to forage for themselves, and it was up to the owners of property to protect it
from pilfering or to catch and whip the pilferers. The adolescents often had elaborate magical formulas to protect them
while pilfering or guard them against subsequent capture.
Quite recently in the United States, particularly in small rural
communities, petty theft and damage might also be treated as
a matter to be settled between the victim and the offender, or
the offender and his family. Today, in large cities, the victim of
any kind of molestation by juveniles is more likely to call on
the law for help, and he is more likely to need that help. For
he is dealing with adolescents whom he does not know and
who have no stake in the economy to restrain their resort to
violence.

Many activities of adolescents, since time immemorial,
could be classified as misdemeanors or worse. The current tendency for simple, individual misdemeanors to grow into vandalism and crime is not a result of any change in the genetic
character of juveniles. What has changed—and this warrants
stress—is the cultural pattern of customs relating to children.
They are no longer so fully protected as primitive children
were against entering the world as economic and social burdens on resentful parents. Their anticipation of welcome membership in larger social groups is not promoted by early membership in a joint family economy. They have no system of peer
groups carrying a meaningful responsibility for some fraction
of the economy of their communities. In fact, American society
takes pains to prevent the formation of peer groups by making

181

school coeducational and permitting teaching to be miscella-
neously bisexual. There is no awareness that the formation of
peer groups is not prevented by that policy; that it merely
makes sure that those groups will be secretive and that their
activities will be led by their most alienated members.

Opportunity for recreation does not help here, for even
play without clearly discernible relation to adult activities loses
its attractiveness to the adolescent. In this respect a comment
by Erik Erikson, the contemporary American psychoanalyst, is
most pertinent:

"Theories of play which are advanced in our culture and
which take as their foundation the assumption that in children,
too, play is defined by the fact that it is not work, are really
only one way in which we exclude our children from an early
increase in their sense of identity. . . . No wonder, then, that
some of our troubled children constantly break out of their
play into some damaging activity in which they seem to us to
"interfere" with our world; while analysis reveals that they only
wish to demonstrate their right to find an identity in it. They
refuse to become a specialty called "child" who must play at
being big because he is not given an opportunity to be a small
partner in a big world." [1]

One problem, as pointed out earlier, is the shortage of
meaningful work in which American adolescents may participate. The inherent needs of children for at least a limited role
in the world of work has been lost sight of in enthusiasm for
other cultural goals: production efficiency, protection of children from inappropriate labor for overly long hours, protection
of the rights of the adult worker through unionization, and
equalization of economic status by minimum wage laws without adequate consideration for the salability of the services
offered by the immature and inexperienced.

The paradoxical attitude toward work, evidenced by indifference or opposition to work-experience for the young in a

culture which expects everyone to paddle his own economic canoe, is further exemplified by the rejection of employment opportunity as one basic prophylactic against delinquency. Yet at the same time leading penologists urge the expansion of meaningful work opportunities in prisons as a means of rehabilitating criminals and combating recidivism. If work has even a minor value as an alternative to crime, it would seem to be common sense to make it available to delinquents before rather than after their trouble becomes chronic. When delinquency starts, those who turn to it are not demonstrably worse than non-delinquents. It is estimated that very few active young people reach the age of seventeen without taking a chance at some unlawful activity. Those whom the police apprehend each year are not much more than 2 percent of those who could legally have been apprehended if they had been identified. The overwhelming majority of youngsters manage to straighten themselves out, more by chance than inherent virtue, depending on whether reasonable alternatives are open, and provided that they are not given intensive training in delinquency while locked up in a reform school or its equivalent.[2]

American society seems to be just as pigheaded about the kind of life children should lead as the automobile industry was a few years ago about the kind of automobiles their customers might buy. Not until a flood of foreign cars deluged the market did designers and producers realize that there might be more available garage space and more sales opportunity for cars slightly less massive than a battleship. Similarly, society seems unable to let young people experiment with small ambitions. There appears to be something reprehensible about admitting limited ability or being attracted to a job of no higher status than that held by a working parent. If this is not a reasonable interpretation of the contemporary American attitude, then insistence on schooling beyond the point where the return justifies the cost must be attributed to adult monopoly of the

183

job market. This makes it impractical to hire inexperienced, immature minors even if jobs might be found for them. Many of the discontented may be kept in school solely in hope that they will get into less trouble there than they might if they walked the streets.

This hope might be reasonable if going to school were more widely recognized as an adult avocation, and if, somewhere along the line, a youngster were convinced that he had completed his term as a child and really begun a new regime as an apprentice adult. To the extent that school tags its clients as non-adults, it becomes progressively less attractive for those who are desperately in need of assurance as to how and where they fit into the adult world, when they well know they are headed for some level lower than that of the professions. Hope for the discontented in school would have more chance of realization if youngsters could find, within the approved educational structure, some of the assurances of progress toward adult goals that preliterate societies convey through membership in age-grades, with a few adult-related responsibilities and privileges.

In many instances, the only activity that makes sense to the juvenile may be membership in an organization like the junior traffic patrol. Here, at least, he has a meaningful job to do, a sense of responsibility to be discharged, a bit of privilege to enjoy, and some authority to wield. For the first time in his life, perhaps, he is distinguished from the "lonely crowd" by a uniform or some insignia to be worn, by a code of disciplined behavior, and by participation in a learning group which has an immediate, practical application for the instruction it receives. Junior traffic patrol groups are about as close to highly successful, primitive age-grades as anything that civilization has to offer. But for older adolescents, as their personal need for identity becomes more urgent, there may be nothing but athletic teams or student activities, which are sometimes described

184

as playing in the "economy size sandbox." These have their place, and are highly challenging to some adolescents. But to others, they are "kid stuff," and for want of something better to do, the discontented organize social clubs, exclusive cliques, and undercover "in groups," which do their best to create purposes sanctioned neither by school authorities nor parents. If supervision cannot be avoided in these organizations, the most adventuresome may turn to out-of-school gangs. It is not delinquency and crime, *per se*, which *attract* young people, as much as it is the orthodox pattern laid down for adolescents that *repels* them. Unruly or delinquent behavior in young people may represent legitimate revolt against the external environment.[3]

Evidence that membership in gangs directly contributes to delinquency and crime is overwhelming. Unfortunately, the gatherers of such evidence seldom consider the possibility that the prevailing cultural attitude toward gangs helps to strengthen this undesirable relationship. Almost every healthy male juvenile welcomes toleration by, and membership in, a peer group. He is pleased by every fact which makes membership a privilege: only boys are eligible; entry is restricted to a vaguely defined category of "real guys"; the group has at least the rudiments of a special culture, including knowledge, beliefs, styles of dress and ornament, private vocabulary, signs and signals.

In modern civilization, however, particularly in poor urban areas, it is hard to get certain essentials for a viable subsociety, notably a headquarters and earned economic resources. It is difficult to turn a street corner into a headquarters without complaint from some "square." There is no public domain to be foraged for food, and few if any economic enterprises by which members can contribute to the common larder or treasury. Everything desirable belongs to somebody else; even the means of acquiring things, jobs that earn pay in cash or kind, seem to

185

be under selfish or surly guard. In such a situation pilfering can become a subsociety duty, a contribution to the welfare of a neglected small public. But if an individual gets caught by law enforcers, he is not praised for bravery; he is labeled a delinquent, and he begins to recognize society as the enemy rather than a despised assortment of untouchables. The process that dramatically singles out the young offender from his group puts him into a different world. He has been tagged, and this experience plays a major role in making a criminal.[4]

When a few members of a gang have been marked "potential enemies of society," it is quite normal for the group to accept this designation as one of its enviable marks of honor. For those already proud to look like a "punk" or "tough guy," even though never involved in illegal acts, arrest can be a "palm with oak-leaf cluster." Gang demeanor plus a police-blotter decoration increases the probability of later arrests, and finally a scholarship to a reform school or its equivalent.[5] And such custodial institutions have built a remarkable record for turning amateur delinquents into semiprofessional criminals. The Cambridge-Somerville study of delinquency and crime found that 78 percent of the young people who had been isolated from society with other delinquents went on to more serious crime later. Another 7 percent continued to pile up a record of minor offenses. Only 15 percent managed to stay clear of subsequent conflicts with the law. Where the great majority end is suggested by an analysis of the population of New Jersey's maximum security prison at Trenton.[6] Eighty-four percent of the inmates had served time before; and their repetition of offenses was not the outcome of mental defects, for 55 percent of them rated average or better on standard IQ tests.

Civilized society operates under one basic handicap when trying to convince the delinquent that "crime does not pay." It cannot make effective use of supernatural controls at the juvenile level. The nature of young children has not changed. Whether born in highly civilized or still primitive societies, they generally seem eager to accept imaginative, magico-miraculous explanations of causality. The change has occurred at the adult level; modern adult society no longer unanimously accepts the creditability of intuitively transcendental thought. Young children may accept the idea of supernatural beings who reward good behavior and punish bad, but they lose faith as they grow old enough to discover that these supernaturals are "just for kids." Loss of society-wide conviction about super-natural sanctions for moral and ethical codes is an inevitable outcome of growing sophistication based on scientifically derived knowledge. What may more logically be regretted is the failure, so far, to develop an effective substitute guidance system.

Many studies of delinquency and crime in the United States have tried to determine the difference between the delinquent and the non-delinquent, or the criminal and the non-criminal, to suggest changes in cultural practice which might eliminate such differences. Early studies tended to concentrate on proving that those cultural practices which the sponsor of the study believed to be undesirable on other grounds were also responsible for delinquency and crime. The campaign to protect young people from obvious abuses of child labor led to the theory that work of any kind at an early age, and subsequent neglect of education, were important causes of crime. One representative example was an inquiry, financed with the help of the United States Children's Bureau, some thirty years ago, at the Preston School of Industry in California. The researcher tried to determine more exactly what part early entry into the labor market played in promoting delinquent behavior. The histories of 213 Preston inmates were compared with the histories of 213 non-delinquents of about the same age and background who were still in high school. No startling conclusions emerged. Although 95.3 percent of the delinquents had entered the labor market early, so had 80.3 percent of the non-delinquents. To further equalize the record, it was revealed that "street trades," reputed to be the most dangerous in their influence on the young, had been followed by twice as high a percentage of the working non-delinquents as of the working delinquents. The study determined the most important characteristics of the delinquent group, relative to school and jobs, were inability to keep up with their age groups in school, early dropout, and difficulty in obtaining work.[7]

Far more exhaustive studies have been made later. One of the most painstaking was published in 1950. The subjects of this study were five hundred delinquents remanded to the Lyman School for Boys in Westboro, and the Industrial School for Boys in Shirley, Massachusetts. They were compared with an equal number of non-delinquents, matched as to age, IQ, age of entering school, home neighborhoods, and national and ethnico-racial parentage. They were equally underprivileged individuals from equally underprivileged homes. The delinquents had a higher incidence of families of low education with records of desertion, separation, divorce, death, physical ailments, and alcoholism, but the non-delinquents were, in many instances, successfully surviving the same types of family situation. The delinquent boys more frequently sought substitute gregarious satisfaction in gangs—more than 50 percent as compared with about 1 percent of the non-delinquents. It appeared that one basic family problem of the delinquents was related to parental ideals, attitudes, temperaments, and general behavior.[8] The study, however, failed to uncover any statistically significant relation between delinquency and such factors as health, intelligence, size and economic status of family, immigration conflicts, age of school entry, membership in clubs, introverted personalities, or emotional stress related specifically to school failure. The investigators decided that the most significant factor was a personality which found it easier to react aggressively to an unsatisfactory situation than to submit passively. Contrary to popular notions about the delinquent, they tended to be extrovert athletic types, aggressive, impulsive, and adventurous, ready to resist authority openly with hostility, defiance, suspicion, destructiveness, and sadism. Delinquency was their response to feeling inferior in intellectual or other matters, and their method of escaping from further failures, defeats, and isolation in the same situation.

One could dismiss such findings, perhaps, if they stood alone, but they seem to be confirmed in principle by all the major studies that have been made. In the 1930's, other researchers failed to demonstrate the validity of any of the major, popular explanations of delinquency, after studying the backgrounds of 7,278 delinquents for the National Commission on Law Observance and Enforcement.[9] More recently, the data accumulated during the Cambridge-Somerville Youth Study have been reviewed, and generally comparable conclusions emerged.[10]

The Cambridge-Somerville Youth Study is of special interest because it dealt with young people of pre-delinquent age in neighborhoods where delinquency was common. The original object was to find out whether delinquency could be prevented by assigning personal counselors to a representative sample of boys from such a neighborhood. The counselor's job was to become as intimately acquainted as possible with family situations and personal problems and, as friend and adviser, to ameliorate or at least counterbalance the delinquency-promoting forces. Proper controls were established by choosing two matched groups of boys, with 325 individuals in each group, and assigning counselors to one group only. It is doubtful that any more intensive—and expensive—scientifically planned program to combat delinquency has ever been tried. It was finally abandoned because the results achieved during the first decade

189

offered no encouragement whatsoever. The boys who had personal counselors ran afoul of the law just as frequently as those in the uncounseled group, but they did benefit incidentally; they received fewer and lighter sentences for what they did.

Various attempts have been made to explain the failure of the Cambridge-Somerville experiment. One inquiry concluded that counseling would have worked better if it had begun earlier, at ten or even younger. For when the records of the counseled and non-counseled groups are compared by age of entry into the program, it seems clear that the younger boys were benefited. But for this discussion certain other analyses of the study are of special pertinence. True, only 30 percent of the unbroken, cohesive families included in the study produced delinquents, as compared with 50 percent of the broken homes. If, however, one singles out families characterized by the counselors as quarrelsome and neglectful of their children, without regard to the integrity of their structure, then one establishes a classification of families where 70 percent do produce delinquents. If family break-up alone were a crucial factor, then the age of the child at the time of break-up should affect the delinquency statistics. But the data showed no significant difference associated with the child's age.

In summarizing the family situations which did seem to influence the incidence of delinquency, firm and consistent discipline was its most effective preventive, particularly when supported by stable maternal affection. Overt expressions of affection from the father were shown to be less important. It is noteworthy that an earlier study also found "firm and consistent discipline" important as a preventive of delinquency. The fathers of delinquents were characterized as maintaining this kind of discipline in only 5.7 percent of the cases studied, whereas the fathers of the non-delinquents were classified as firm and consistent disciplinarians in 55.5 percent of the cases.

Parents' religious beliefs did not seem to affect the incidence of delinquency, except when the mother was strongly Catholic. Such families were somewhat less likely to produce a delinquent. Finally, rejection of a delinquent child by both parents occurred too frequently to be accounted for by mating preference of like personalities. The key to this double rejection, it was suggested, was the infant's coming when neither parent wanted it.

The more thorough a study of juvenile delinquency is, the greater the emphasis laid on the family as a social unit. The family needs to meet the group-membership expectancies of the infant, from an original feeling of basic trust up through firm and consistent guidance in experiments with autonomy, initiative, and industry. The compatibility of the individual's personality with the regimen imposed by school may often be set firmly before the fateful first day of schooling. The youngster may be looking forward to expanding his relatively successful group relations at home, or he may be looking for support from peers to protect him from a second experience like that he is trying to avoid at home. The boy's being required to sit with girls may, in such cases, be a disturbing fact that starts him off on the wrong foot. The introvert with problems may be able to sublimate them by achieving success in school. But the extrovert who arrives with problems may find in school work only an object for suspicion and belligerence, and his chances of fitting into an academically oriented group are thereby limited. He is likely to look for companionship among others reacting as he does.

A pioneer study of gangs in Chicago, almost forty years ago, estimated that gang sanctions dominated the moral and ethical codes of some 10 percent of the city's 350,000 young males between the ages of ten and twenty.[11] The satisfactions offered by membership in a status-conferring gang were more attractive to the restless and discontented than anything that either home or school could provide. The gang gave peer-

191

group fellowship, a chance to be regarded as something other than a child, excitement to relieve the monotony of waiting to grow up, and a sense of security in a world of rather aloof adults. Gang members headed toward crime not only because success in minor depredations gave them a sense of importance, but because organized crime offered them friendly and profitable recognition while law-abiding citizens always played the part of inevitable enemy. Too often the bad guys wear the whitest hats.

With increasing enforcement of compulsory school attendance and with the growth of secondary school enrollment, the restless and the discontented found it harder to join gangs as truants or dropouts. They also found themselves constituting a greater percentage of the school population, and able to operate in the school on a basis comparable to that developed by street-corner gangs. Innocuous cliques and clubs took on a gang atmosphere as a result. School officials found it necessary to ban the so-called social clubs unless parents accepted responsibility for directing and controlling their activities. In many instances, parents did accept this responsibility, since they thought that social affairs, well chaperoned, would be better than what otherwise might occur. But these social activities often proved to be only window dressing. The juvenile culture pattern supported by the social clubs, like the hidden part of an iceberg, drifted in accord with deep currents that would have turned some parents grayhaired if they had investigated scuba-style.

The majority of young people accept the tasks set for them by the schools because they have no preestablished prejudice against them, and either win satisfaction through achievement quite easily, or believe that they ultimately will win such satisfaction. A disturbingly large minority either cannot achieve or has no interest in achieving satisfaction in orthodox ways and, making a virtue out of its aberrant interests, organizes subsocieties with special cultural rules and ideals. Like the old-fashioned gang, cliques are another example of youthful gregariousness growing wild. One does not require a delinquent type of mind to account for this; it arises from a positive need to fill the vacuum which modern civilization sets aside for juveniles. That need may be accentuated by unhappy family situations. A sense of inferiority, arising from lack of ability to achieve in the school situation or stubborn opposition to achieving in adult-commanded but child-oriented tasks, provides a common ground on which the restless and discontented can meet. From this point on, the development of a clique is motivated by the same purposes of the central nervous system that account for all cultural developments. A sense of difference from others can be a mark of inferiority or superiority, depending on conviction; and a conviction of superiority can be buttressed by arbitrarily developing more differences and restricting membership to the group that displays them. The often bizarre character of the behavior of a high school clique is dictated in part by the conventional and undistinguished traits of high school culture as a whole. The particular direction in which the clique elaborates on behavior may be determined by the social status of the families from which the majority of the members come, but in detail these behavioral traits are ascribable only to a play-urge unchastened by experience and the responsibilities carried by adults. Dress, coiffure, language, gestures, social activities, codes of ethics and morals are all obvious avenues of departure from the orthodox. Approach to the orthodox is unthinkable in a group which achieves superiority by being exclusively different. Departures from the orthodox are limited only by amateur judgment on the chance of escaping reprisal. For, even without formal organization, cliques within schools can dominate the lives of youngsters who are ready to sacrifice anything for acceptance by an exclusive peer group.

The magnitude of the problem which this presents is indi-

193

cated by a pilot study made in the Los Angeles secondary schools. This showed that, far more than generally realized, the high school clique is an important opponent of school purposes and public aspirations for the younger generation. Among 3,288 high school students, in the opinion of the students themselves, about 732 could be classed as non-conformists and rule-breakers. Of these 732, about 652 were recognized as "insiders" who belonged to the self-claimed superior "in" group. These 652 deviants from the expected behavioral norm represented about 40 percent of the "insiders." The other eighty individuals represented 6 percent of the non-"insider" student body. Of the students recognized as delinquents by the school and other public officials, 90 percent came from the "insiders" sub-culture. Groups of "insiders," made proud by their self-developed group distinctiveness, may drift into delinquency much as out-of-school gangs do, by acting on the belief that all non-members of the sub-culture are fair game for exploitation. Outsiders are the "suckers," dwellers in what Milton called a fools' paradise. Weaker non-member students may be bullied and victimized by "conning" or extortion. Success in this kind of enterprise may lead to pilfering from stores, vandalism, and joy-riding in borrowed cars. The need to market stolen goods creates a point of contact with professional criminals; the search for new activities encourages dealing with purveyors of marijuana and other narcotics.

Only a few centuries ago the restless, aggressive youngster had a reasonable chance of living through the long wait for maturity as a recognized and participating member of an extended family group. Industrialization, urbanization, and other economic and social changes have reduced the power of the family as a social force and helped to make the security of the youngest citizen within that group a gamble. Consequently, during the first 30 percent of his average life expectancy, the youngster sits, figuratively, in one of the last rows of the social

194

gallery, unable to express an opinion on the drama of life except by stamping his feet, making an airplane out of his program, shooting spitballs, or throwing pop bottles. When he is grown up is no longer a decision made by his family and those who know him, but by a law fitting an average which scarcely exists and by personnel management which saves itself trouble by accepting these arbitrary classifications.

In many respects, republican government *has* restored to popular will some control over culture change, most markedly *vis à vis* the religious leader who ruled for a number of centuries. In this and other areas, however, the popular will attempts to express itself through elected representatives who, at all levels of government, listen carefully to only the loudest voices. They are particularly vulnerable to organized efforts by those who make a career out of adding decibels to some segment of the popular voice, not just for the profit that it may bring, but for the sake of a hobby and a conviction. Often, the partisans of education, for example, are building their own sense of importance by setting new and higher requirements for those who aspire to take their places. Youth cannot often speak effectively for itself and may confirm the exasperation of those who speak for more youth controls, by breaking out of its cage, much as a wild animal would, when opportunity permits.

The president of the Carnegie Corporation declared, in his 1962 report, "In our society we could do much more than we now do to encourage self-development. We could, for example, drop the increasingly silly fiction that education is for youngsters." Certainly nothing about education damns it more tellingly in the eyes of those who want to get on with life than the fact that attending school is almost exclusively a childhood chore. Not far behind this observation is the second, if education were really important it would not have been possible for so many to rise to power without it.

A study of the moral crisis facing free society, which in-

195

cludes the problem of reorienting deviant groups and resolving the present vacillation between punishment and rehabilitation for those who deviate, observes that juvenile delinquency may be the price Americans pay for progress, with its rapid social change, for a free labor market, with its population mobility, for aspiration to a higher level of living, with its inevitable burden of envy. Americans want their mass production economy, with its great cities and often unrewarding jobs. They want their children to enjoy life, and they want to enjoy themselves; hence children are given less responsibility and parents often reject the burden of supervision.[12]

In defense of the American people one should add that they usually act without malice. They create problems because they go about with their hearts on their sleeves and their minds unbuttoned. Criminality cannot be dealt with merely by efforts to rehabilitate those who have become criminals, important as this is. Neither can their number be reduced merely by smashing juvenile gangs, even though 75 percent of certain groups of young criminals may have a gang background. These efforts can succeed only if society finds something more challenging for seriously discontented youth than prolonged incarceration in schools. As gangs are brought under control, their place is taken by cliques of "insiders" within the school, or by "flower children" in "hippy" settlements. Society must realize that there is an irrepressible need for membership in a group with which the youngster can cope during the purgatory which family circumstances may make of his adolescence.

This cannot be dismissed as a problem for less fortunate families alone, because desire to be a member of an organized group of fellow adolescents can affect the lives of those who have never known what life in a slum, or poverty and deprivation are like. Even the prosperous want their children to be popular among suitable people of their own age. Yet the group parents approve may be rejected by their adolescent children

who, albeit in rare instances, have so great a need for relationships with significant age-mates, even though they can be found
only in a gang, that the most probable alternative to such associations may be a severe mental disturbance.[13]

Part of the problem arises from the increasing emphasis
on the legal fences which border every path of righteousness.
As their number grows, staying outside the fences becomes
increasingly difficult, especially for adolescents with adventurous minds. Parents may count themselves lucky if an adolescent reaches his majority without having been declared
guilty of stepping over a fence in a moment of exuberance, or
deliberately knocking it down in a gesture of defiance. Society
is understandably concerned over the residual effects on the
individual of experiencing arrest, booking, and being found
guilty, because that process may affect social status and economic opportunity. Some writers maintain that Americans have
a "guilt complex" deriving from the Protestant ethic. But most
writers fail to appreciate that the growing obsession with situations involving *guilt* is related to the increasing incidence of
shame which complex cultural situations can bring about.

Erik Erikson puts shame chronologically before guilt in
the emotional development of the child: "He who is ashamed
would like to force the world not to look at him, not to notice
his exposure. He would like to destroy the eyes of the world." [14]
Erikson is credited with being one of the few students of child
psychology to recognize that shame is equally important with
guilt in the emotional reactions of the developing personality.
Guilt involves self-condemnation by the superego or conscience.
To some extent it may be expiated by undergoing punishment,
either self-imposed, in the form of penance, or prescribed by
society, in the form of fines or imprisonment. *Shame,* on the
other hand, is a more subtle emotion, for which neither the individual nor society provides a ready antidote. It is connected
less with breaking some rule of behavior than with failure to

197

achieve some accepted standard, or to recognize that a given situation involves a standard reaction. Habitual and indiscriminate use of derogatory, shame-arousing judgments on juvenile shortcomings can be a parental mistake only slightly less destructive than walking away in obvious disgust. Subconsciously the juvenile is faced by the contempt of the social unit to which he belongs, and behind it the fear of abandonment by his parents and death by emotional starvation.[15]

Still another view of shame emphasizes the discrepancy between the intent of an action and the social situation. The young person assumes he is one sort of individual living in a particular situation, and suddenly learns that his assumptions were false.[16] When actions are thus revealed as shameful, the ego is not castigated by "conscience" but rather is mortified by failure to live up to its own self-image, or ego-ideal. Escapes from mortification are not easy. In primitive society they often lead to mental illness or suicide. In civilized society, where guilt and the expiation of it are more clear cut, the individual may come to regard crime and punishment for it as an escape from the hopelessness of shame. It is suggested, for example, that indecent exposure in public places is often subconsciously motivated by a search for escape from the unbearable shame of sexual impotence.[17]

Stress on shame and its relation to guilt implies neither that all criminal careers start as shame-escaping enterprises nor that schools have a monopoly on mortifying situations which encourage delinquency. Explaining delinquency and crime is not that simple. Shame reactions may antedate first enrollment in school, and the classroom situation need merely fail to offer an effective cure for a pre-existing ailment. But shame is often overlooked in the search for explanation of delinquency or academic failures, and as a result, time, energy, and money are wasted on procedures which exacerbate a difficulty having its source in family situations, home conditions, or just severe acne. No souls are saved by criticizing teachers and administrators as if schools were institutions established for psychiatric care of youth. Attention must also be given to the customs and traditions of society at large.

However, the retarded and frustrated youngster compelled by law to continue school beyond the point where he has even the slightest sense of achievement, or of progress toward adult identity, may have only truancy and delinquency as an alternative to neurosis, psychosis, or suicide. If he has any force left in his personality, truancy may seem to be the best solution of an otherwise hopeless situation. As a chronic truant, he can pay a set penalty and have done with it. In addition, he may discover that, for the first time, he has earned prestige and gained status, at least among a few equally frustrated peers, and this may lead to further misdemeanors in order to maintain gang status. "Flower children" and the users and purveyors of marijuana, LSD, and the like, appear to be following a similar emotional pattern.

Membership in a minority group which believes itself unjustly assigned to an inferior position in society, and which has become painfully sensitive about its distinguishing characteristics, undoubtedly plays its part in the shame syndrome; it may promote crime in order to win economic status and political power which members feel unable to achieve quickly enough in any other way. In the recent history of the United States, public concentration on one or another minority group as a butt for ridicule has led to increased prominence of that group in crime.[18] The period when the Irish were called "micks" and "hod-carriers" was followed by a period of Irish dominance in public corruption. They were succeeded as butts by Jews, the "kikes"; and then Italians, the "wops"; and both groups, for a time, produced more than their share of leaders in organized

199

crime. Latin Americans have shown the same tendency; currently Negroes are disproportionately represented in police and court records.

One can better appreciate the relevance of the facts just cited to the problem of juvenile delinquency and crime by considering in how many respects America's adolescents constitute a minority which has spent perhaps sixteen to eighteen years overcoming a biologically imposed inferiority of size, strength, and maturity. It is then confronted with arbitrarily established requirements for release from minority status, requirements based on non-existent averages and taking no account of individual talents, achievements, and interests. An intensive study of five thousand high school juniors and seniors showed that, regardless of family background, the situation of being no longer a child but still not an adult evoked a large percentage of low self-esteem, particularly among boys.[19] This sense of not getting anywhere adversely affects their standing in the eyes of fellow students and produces a significantly greater incidence of psychosomatic ailments or neuroses. Such reactions may be accentuated by precocious physical development which removes even the consolation of being a typical member of a group of people in limbo.

Whether expressed or only subconsciously sought, the normal goal of every young person is to grow up and join the ranks of adults. Many illegal acts by youngsters are motivated rather by desire to do what adults are doing than by any attraction to the act itself.[20] Among these marks of adulthood are drinking, gambling, and automobile driving. They are explicitly enjoyable because adults enjoy them.

I am not suggesting that there is any panacea for juvenile delinquency and crime, but to avoid a continuing increase in such aberrant behavior, society should pay more attention to the basic needs of young people as slow-developing, long-dependent primates instinctively and experientially attracted to peer groups which are emotionally and practically fostered by adult society and help to prepare members for survival in the mode directed by their own society and culture. This requires that jobs be available for young people when schooling offers neither challenge nor benefit enough to warrant the cost of buildings and teachers. The final test of life is satisfactory adjustment to society, its culture, and its aspirations. Schooling is one of the essentials, but available jobs are equally important. If the individual is to be prepared for these experiences, he needs the kind of healthy personality that a real welcome to family life and continuing concern on the part of one or more family members produces. In other words, Americans need to begin making radical changes in the culture pattern. To those who shake their heads and say "Culture can't be changed," I recommend closer study of the changes that have already occurred and of the reasons for their occurrence.

CHAPTER 9

Education as a
Cultural Compulsion

||||||||||||||||||||||||||||||||||||||||||||||||||||||||||||||||||||||||||||||||||||||||||||||||||||||||||||||||||||||||||||||||||||||||

If we think education is defined as any process by which a brain learns to modify its reactions to specific combinations of sensory stimuli, then in a limited sense education is as old as central nervous systems capable of storing up memories; it is at least as old as the flatworm which learns to cringe when a light flashes because it remembers that an electric shock follows. Self-education in the light of experience is within the capacity of the simplest organized central nervous systems, and it occurs spontaneously. Learning is usually classified as ontogenetic and instinct as phylogenetic; if that is so, then readiness to learn appears to be one attribute of phylogenetic instinct. At every level of psychic complexity, living depends on learning from experience.

If the definition of education be restricted to learning

202

which is stimulated in young organisms by older organisms of the same species, education is still very old, at least as old as young which require feeding and care after hatching or birth. The young of both birds and mammals learn from their parents to modify instincts, and this teaching also occurs spontaneously. This leads to the conclusion that both learning and teaching are to some extent instinctive. Even an infant hominid begins to learn spontaneously, and most mothers begin to teach automatically, as a necessary step in establishing mutually satisfactory, cooperative relations with their infants and discharging equally strong instincts to care for their young.

The culturally elaborated educational process encountered in twentieth-century America is not generally recognized as a continuation of a process of adjustment and naturalization which began instinctively long before the age of school entry and which continues profitably only to the extent that primary instincts are fostered, and the basic motivation that they provide is expanded and redirected by conditioning. The problems engendered by this oversight are compounded because the methods and content of education themselves constitute a complex of customs which constantly expands, reorganizes, and elaborates. It is an important focus of societal attention. (One might add that the educational complex has elaborated because about two million Americans are teachers or school administrators and personally concerned as well as publicly charged with maintaining, building, and demonstrating the importance of education.) When expectation is disappointed the public blames those who operate the system rather than weaknesses in the system itself. The educators perforce must defend themselves, although they are aware that American civilization could not continue without the existing system or one very much like it.

This seems to be an age of educational pyramid-building; the size of the pyramid is somehow believed to symbolize faith in democracy, equality of opportunity, and the freedom of the individual to use to the full whatever talents he may possess. Americans seem to believe, quite sincerely, that all the ideals to which they ascribe high value will be more nearly achieved if every young person is required to climb the educational pyramid. To justify this effort these young people are told, without intent to deceive, that the higher they climb the more successful and happier their lives will be. An anthropologist must conclude that this faith is in part a cultural delusion. For it rests on the observation that those with the ability and motivation to climb the educational pyramid are also, generally speaking, those who succeed. From this observation, Americans jump to the conclusion that climbing the pyramid has some magical effect which will help everyone, even though he must be coaxed, coerced, or carried above, say, the eighth tier.

No one knows when teaching became a specialized profession, but it was probably about the fourth millennium B.C., in Mesopotamia, with Egypt not far behind. Before that time, the knowledge and skills required for any occupation were largely exclusive to it and could best be learned by working with, or listening to, the most successful available practitioner of the art concerned, whether it were hunting, fishing, farming, building, pot-throwing, fighting, healing, governing, or maintaining religious ceremonies and rituals. During the fourth millennium B.C. the first true written language developed, as distinguished from earlier sporadic use of personal identification marks and pictographs. By 3500 B.C., the city states and temple estates of Mesopotamia were keeping records and communicating by impressing some two thousand different characters in clay tablets and then firing the clay to preserve the record.[1] Producing or even reading such records required long periods of memorizing symbols and practicing with the impressing tool, or stylus. A working scribe could not do a job and, at the same time, instruct an apprentice. Professional teaching, and schools where the necessary supplies for teaching could be kept, became essential with the invention of writing.

The late Sir Leonard Woolley, the English archaeologist, describes such a school, dating to about 1780 B.C., which was excavated in the ruins of the ancient city of Ur, where Abraham was born, on a now dry channel of the Euphrates River in southern Iraq.[2] School records and classroom work preserved on two thousand almost indestructible clay tablets give a surprisingly clear picture of a typical school in those days. It was private, subsisting on tuition payments and catering almost exclusively to the sons of important people, from government and temple officials to military officials, sea captains, managers, archivists, accountants, and the like. Occasionally a philanthropist sent a boy from a lower social stratum to school; one boy in this Sumerian school was identified as a waif saved from an attack by a vicious dog and subsequently befriended by his rescuer.

The curriculum of the school was by that time graded to carry a student from childhood to maturity and included arithmetic and geometry as well as reading, writing, and literature. The older students were titled *junior scribes* and helped the teachers instruct beginners. Then as now, apparently, there were reluctant pupils, but then the rod was used with vigor. Pupils came to school in the morning, carrying their lunches, and they were punished if they dawdled on the way, or if they arrived improperly dressed. Whispering or standing up without permission was prohibited.

Although this school was clearly dedicated to the instruction of boys, there must have been schools which accepted girls, for women served as professional scribes in the city, and in later centuries schools were operated by women. At another site in the city of Ur, a woman named Bel-shalti-Nannar conducted a school from 555 B.C. to 539 B.C., and in her records she mentions that her earliest predecessor in the same building had begun teaching about eight hundred years before.

Pictures on vases show schools in operation in Greece, homeland of the modern Western alphabet, as early as the sixth century B.C. Professional teachers in ancient Greece were divided into three classes: grammarians who taught reading, writing, and some arithmetic; musicians who taught the seven-stringed lyre and lyric poetry; and athletes who took care of physical education.[3] As early as 2000 B.C., school was the way to preferment in Egyptian society, as described in the classic advice of a father to his son, *The Teaching of Khety, Son of Duauf,* probably written during the Eleventh Dynasty. This document emphasizes that the man who could read and write was equipped for the profession of scribe; he sat with the great and near-great and might himself aspire to greatness. It follows, then, that the first professional teachers carried some of the prestige of their more primitive predecessors who were asked to teach because they were successful practitioners of some valued art and had status in the community. To them, the supercilious aphorism, "Those who can, *do* and those who can't, *teach,*" did not apply. Even those teachers who later were described as slaves, were captured instead of killed because they were talented and were relatively scarce and valuable.

From pre-Christian Greece almost to the end of the Middle Ages in Europe, school education continued to be primarily a privilege of the already privileged and a kind of professional training. The scribe continued to hold independent professional standing, but the art he professed gradually came to be recognized as only part of the necessary equipment for other professions. The teacher became primarily a professional who was expected to know the art of the scribe though he might not be one, as was also generally true of those who knew the art, but served in the medical profession or in the priesthood.

The Church, the principal social institution requiring professional people trained in the art of the scribe, also became the principal organizer and administrator of schools. As early as 1179, the Third Lateran Council recognized that not all the best priests would be recruited from the upper classes and granted permission to offer free education to selected children of the poor. Within a century, the demand for scribes who were not dedicated to the priesthood or another profession but who might serve commercial enterprises grew so heavy that towns began to operate schools competing with those under the local cathedrals.

An entirely new attitude toward basic education in the three R's was introduced by the decline of feudalism, the breakup of baronial estates, and the rise of towns. Twelfth-century England was plagued by hordes of people whose ties with the land had been broken and who were concentrating in cities or ceaselessly migrating on the public highways hoping to stay alive by begging, borrowing, or stealing.[4] The old manorial system, however unjustifiable serfdom may seem to modern philosophy, at least kept discontent below the breaking point. When it fell apart, the peasants moved from security to freedom, and many starved in the process.

Some of the social changes which were forced by the breakup of manorialism affected education.[5] In the fourteenth century, England tried to halt the movement toward the cities by making idleness unlawful and restricting aimless wandering and begging. At the same time, localities were required to take care of their indigent poor and not just drive them to the next town. Under Richard II, it was further required that individuals continue at the trade and in the place where the first twelve years of their lives were spent.

Landowners, appalled by the hegira from farm to city, requested that schooling for children of the villein class be prohibited, because people who should be working the land were using school attendance as an excuse for idleness, which periled the safety, honor, and freedom of the realm. That attempt to hold people on the land failed, but fourteen years later conditions had so deteriorated that rural families were forbidden to apprentice their children in the cities unless they were independent farmers, owners or renters of land to the value of 20 shillings or more. But the law had the revealing clause: "Provided always, That every Man or Woman, of what Estate or Condition that he be, shall be free to set their Son or Daughter to take learning in any manner of School that pleaseth them within the Realm."

Here was the earliest implication that the individual had an inherent right to gain an education, although only if he could get it for himself, in one way or another. Within a generation, under Henry VIII, came a further discovery: if people could not support themselves, the state had a right to see that they were taught to do so. New laws empowered the government to pick up any child between the ages of five and thirteen who was caught begging and to put him out as an apprentice. The Elizabethan Poor Law of 1601 codified and amplified earlier laws.

When the Puritans left England in protest against religious intolerance and set up their own system of intolerance in the New World, they brought with them the lessons that England had haltingly learned. They agreed with the views of Martin Luther:

"I hold it to be incumbent on those in authority to command their subjects to keep their children at school; for it is, beyond doubt, their duty to ensure the permanence of the above-named offices and positions, so that preachers, jurists, curates, scribes, physicians, schoolmasters, and the like, may not fail from among us. . . . [If authority may command service in war] with so much the more reason ought they to compel the people to keep their children at school, inasmuch as here upon earth the most terrible of contests, wherein there is never a truce, is ever going on, and that with the Devil himself." [6]

New Englanders were keenly aware of the needs that Luther stressed, but they had problems which Luther did not envision, namely, local self-government and the rights of parents. Literacy and some familiarity with numbers were essential to participating citizenship, but there was also a need for families to utilize the labor of all hands if living were to be possible in the new land. The need for workers often conflicted with the need to set aside time for school. In 1640 and 1641 the General Court of Massachusetts Bay Colony first gave serious consideration to the need for labor, exhorting all citizens to see that their children and servants put early morning and evening hours, then being wasted, to better use. The following year, in spite of possible concern for the rights of parents, the legislature took a first step toward compulsory education. The selectmen of towns were made responsible for seeing that parents and masters of apprentices trained their charges properly in both learning and labor.

This was rather like ordering all citizens to learn to swim in the absence of sufficient water to swim in, for few schools were available. So in 1647, the General Court took the fateful step and passed a law requiring every town of fifty households to support a schoolmaster to teach reading and writing, by either fees paid by parents, or a general tax on all citizens. Perhaps recalling that Harvard College had been established eleven years before, it was also required that towns of one hundred households or more maintain a schoolmaster competent to prepare students for college. Towns failing to abide by these laws were to be fined five pounds.

The right of the individual to buy an education had long been taken for granted, but the statute of 1647 implied that the education of children involved the welfare of the colony. This generated opposition both because it infringed on the traditional right of a parent to the fruits of the labor of his children, and because it suggested a tax on those without children to provide education for the children of others. The needs of an increasingly complex culture came into conflict with the independence of its constituent families. The needs of culture won, not because of any clear conviction on the part of the electorate, but because of action taken by the General Court of Massachusetts. This decision, with which almost unanimous agreement would be expressed today, established a precedent for the American concept of universal compulsory education. It presaged a profound change in the relations of the family and the individual to society and illustrated how culture might change, for the better—or for the worse, on occasion—through elaboration of a basically sound idea without adequate consideration of its optimum limits.

The actions of the Massachusetts General Court did not immediately revolutionize education within the colony. Nor did it have much influence on other colonies, but we cannot say that national progress suffered because education continued to be a limited commodity to which many citizens had no access. The fluctuating rate of development in the American system of education cannot be fully explained without attention to the cultural changes which radically altered the environment for children. By the first quarter of the nineteenth century, with the continued development of steam-powered machines in industry, demand for cheap and relatively unskilled labor created a demand for working children. Consequently, numerous objective observers thought that many factory owners had closed ranks with the Devil in finding work for idle hands and were providing it for so many hours of the day and week, under such unhealthful conditions that both education and longevity were in peril. A few employers tried to ease this situation, created by competition, by opening the first Sunday schools in factories and even in homes in order to provide training at least in the three R's. But those efforts were hardly sufficient to restore a balance between labor and learning. Some factory owners were said to have threatened that if children were withdrawn from jobs, the whole family would be discharged.

By the early 1820's, an investigating committee of the Massachusetts legislature reported that hundreds of youngsters were working about thirteen hours a day, six days a week, and that they were receiving no education in a state which prided itself on leadership in this regard.[7] One of the first American labor organizations, the New England Association of Farmers, Mechanics and Other Working Men, charged, in 1832, that two-fifths of all factory workers were under seventeen years of age and working from daylight to 8 P.M. The Working Men of Philadelphia had addressed questions on public education to candidates for political office as early as 1829; in its 1830 platform, the Boston Working Men's Party declared one of its chief objectives to be "the establishment of a liberal system of education attainable by all."[8]

Laws were passed to deal with this situation. By modern standards, the legislation was mild enough, requiring only that children under twelve—later, under fifteen—could not be employed unless they had attended school for at least three months during the immediately preceding year. But factory owners connived with parents, in what they felt to be a defense of freedom and justice, to defeat enforcement of these laws. Hence, people fighting to stop exploitation of child labor, and those concerned with the education of future citizens, joined in an effort to make school attendance compulsory. If all children of a given age were required to be in school, it would be easier to make sure that they were not employed in undesirable ways. But this complete exclusion of work from the experience of future citizens was not generally accepted.

Not until 1847 did Horace Mann, for example, begin to advocate compulsory school attendance. He admitted that this

211

policy might invade family rights, and he probably foresaw the difficulty of teaching pupils against their will and the will of their parents, but he could see no other way of curbing the cupidity of employers who supported parental freedom for the sake of their own profit. Finally, in 1852, Massachusetts passed the first state compulsory school attendance law, requiring all children between the ages of eight and fourteen to spend a minimum of twelve weeks in school each year. But many decades passed before compulsory attendance, even at the elementary level, was more than a pious hope. The program lagged because of cultural inertia against the change affecting the authority of the family, the cost of providing schools and trained teachers, and the reluctance of juveniles to delay their participation in the work of the community. Real life offered no convincing proof that education was the *sine qua non* of either survival or social preferment. Exceptions were too numerous to prove any rule, particularly in family circles of modest talents and ambitions.

Indeed, just four generations ago only nine states in the Union tried to make education compulsory; three generations ago there were still only twenty-seven states with compulsory school attendance laws. Moreover, the goal of these laws was generally surprisingly modest, chiefly insuring that young people could read, write, and count. What has happened in the last seventy-five years in education would scarcely seem possible without the aid of a magician and a silk hat. United States Office of Education statistics for 1961–62 show that 44,553,000 young people were in full-time attendance in public and private elementary schools that year.

With some pride, the American people could report not only that 99.1 percent of all children six to thirteen years of age were enrolled in school but also that 97.6 percent of the fourteen- and fifteen-year-olds and 79.6 percent of the sixteen- and seventeen-year-olds were in school. Although, if a young person found a job and he and his parents insisted on a working permit, he could usually be released from school at about sixteen.

Many factors contributed to this phenomenal development: the Protestant need for a personal approach to religion through reading the Bible; the common-sense conviction that literacy was a *sine qua non* for a self-governing people; and the obvious need to protect children from exploitation in business and industry. These three motives were sufficient to start the American system of education on its way. Most citizens agreed that everyone should know how to read, write, and manipulate numbers. The problem was providing elementary education for those who could not afford to pay for it and who would only reluctantly give time to it. Many were equally reluctant to share the cost of raising other people's children. This reluctance perhaps gave coeducation its impetus. Maintaining one school and one teacher for boys and girls was financial problem enough, without worrying about separate facilities and personnel for each.

The move toward education at all economic levels was accelerated by increased mobility of the population as transportation and communication developed; the extension of suffrage; and the growth of organizations which could bring pressure on local and federal governmental bodies. The Sunday School Union, state lyceums, the National Lyceum, the Independent Order of Odd Fellows, and Masonic lodges added their voices to an increasingly strong chorus in favor of public education. But none of these organizations showed more concern than the early labor unions. Organized labor had good reason to support public schools and, later, compulsory attendance at them, aside from basic democratic concern with equalizing educational opportunity. The struggle for a reasonable working day and a living wage was made more difficult in areas where the labor market was glutted by cheap child labor. Children could not be organized without the support of their parents, many of whom had not yet been reached directly by unions. By joining philanthropic movements on behalf of education, organized labor could gain a strategic advantage while fighting for all underprivileged children and, incidentally, meeting the criticism that unions were wholly self-serving organizations.

Horace Mann and other pioneers in the movement for free public schools would undoubtedly be gratified to see how conscientiously the American people have accepted the irrefutable logic of free schools, but they might find it hard to understand or discover logic in all that cultural elaboration has added to the basic idea. The two sound principles that every child needs a basic education and that every child must be protected from avaricious exploitation through long hours of employment at inappropriate labor have gradually been amended to imply that the longer an adolescent can be kept in school, and kept from working, the better off he will be.

The early struggle to promote literacy and the subsequent fight against child labor clearly started a cultural movement that has continued with increasing vigor even though its original objectives have been achieved and new ones have had to be manufactured. Now that compulsory school attendance has embraced all but a fraction of 1 percent of American children, and sweatshops have been eliminated, the emphasis has shifted to continuing education, if possible, until chronological maturity and to discouraging remunerative work because it often tends to divert interest from the culture's educational ideal.

Interesting evidence of this shift is given by the 1923 report of the director of the Helen S. Trounstine Foundation for Social Research. The struggle against child labor should not be confined to enterprises in which labor presumably might be unhealthful or inappropriate. Nor, the report declares, should society proceed as if working for pay were undesirable. Rather, school attendance should be promoted as a positive good, and as the only dependable preparation for life. Even work on the family farm, apparently, does not always have the values and virtues once attributed to it. Since, however, work is sufficiently attractive to lead youngsters to leave school even when that is not economically necessary, schools and their holding power must be improved.[9]

A somewhat similar shift in approach is indicated by the first publication in a new Department of Labor series on child labor.[10] Protecting the child from labor unsuitable for his age or undesirable for other reasons remains a purpose of child labor laws, but first place is given to preventing leaving school early for any reason and to assuring that development will be well rounded. The danger of relaxing compulsions and restrictions was illustrated by experience during World War II, when the availability of jobs led some two million youngsters under eighteen to leave school and go to work. The steps taken by the Federal government to ameliorate this situation are listed as laws fixing the minimum working age, maximum hours, minimum wages, and penalties for contractors who break these laws, including withholding benefits from sugar growers who allow youngsters under fourteen to participate in cultivating or harvesting or permit anyone under sixteen to work more than eight hours in any one day. A concluding statement on what the law should be, ideally, declares that no one under eighteen should be allowed to take a job except under a working permit from school authorities.

The curious fact about this movement toward *more* education for *all* is the inadequacy of the evidence to support its universal need. Although insufficient education has been blamed for the disturbingly high rate of unemployment in the United States on the basis of some unidentified report that one-third of the unemployed had less than an eighth-grade education, nothing was said about why more than 90 percent of all the people in the United States with less than an eighth-grade education seemed to be getting along all right. More important, no evidence was offered to prove that the *only* handicap preventing one-third of the unemployed from finding work was an education which stopped short of the eighth grade. Both low school achievement and limited success in holding a job may be results of personality handicaps, intellectual and/ or emotional. The army of the unemployed began to shrink in 1965, not because the unemployed had meanwhile raised their educational level, but because the draft was stepped up and governmental spending for support of the armed forces in Vietnam began to spiral.

The more one studies the enthusiastic campaign for more education at all levels of intellectual capacity, in the light of man's past history and contemporary cultural problems, the less easy it is to accept some of the current slogans and shibboleths. The average college graduate, it is remarked, makes more money than the average high school graduate, and the high school graduate earns more than the elementary school graduate. One can readily see the fallacy of imputing differences in earning capacity solely to the number of years of schooling completed, without regard to differences in the average ability of the groups compared. Some people, undoubtedly, could have gone on with school and made more money had they been motivated to do so. Others, just as certainly, could not have increased their job capacity significantly by any given number of additional years of school attendance. People who have intelligence, intellectual curiosity, and drive usually want to complete high school and college. But they do not succeed because they went to college; they succeed because they have intelligence, curiosity, and drive.[11]

Even among those who do well in school and who persist

216

to the bachelor's degree, the master's degree, or a doctorate, character attributes other than those required to win a degree are a potent factor in determining earnings. The National Science Foundation recently found that engineers and scientists without a Ph.D., who achieved supervisory positions, received substantially higher salaries than those with the Ph.D. who had not achieved supervisory status.[12] Even within occupations where the Ph.D. is a basic determinant of salary, ability to lead others commands the highest remuneration. This, of course, is a truism, but it may be underemphasized in the advice and training forced upon many people in the public school system.

Nobody wants to face the possibility that, for many young people, the real difficulty is not their disinclination to continue in school, but their lack of a choice. They are told that they cannot expect to find employment unless they have more education. This is asserted in order to get them to attend high school. It is repeated in order to encourage them to finish high school and to go on to junior college. School counselors try their best to sort those who could benefit from staying in school from those whose continued presence is not only of no help to them but perhaps a less than desirable influence on others. But counselors' efforts are partially thwarted by the lack of jobs for young people. Assertions of altruism might be suspect, were it admitted that most young people have no alternative; many must stay in school or walk the streets. The national faith in education spares public concern. Schooling cannot possibly do any harm; even those who seem most immune to it are probably benefited more than they realize. They cannot expect to appreciate this until they get older. So with a clear conscience, Americans embark on national campaigns to keep "dropouts" in school.

Whether one accepts them fully or not, studies by social psychologists ought to encourage reexamination of the national

217

faith in education.[13] One study dealt with one hundred and five non-delinquent school dropouts, all average in achievement on intelligence tests, and all from middle-class white families. The investigators concluded that 75 percent of this group suffered from character problems more serious than simple conflict neuroses, and that in the case of the boys in the group, these problems had begun to develop long before they finally decided to leave school. The study implies that leaving school is not a decision lightly reached in this age of faith in education; the situation cannot be dealt with by simply pressuring these young people back into school. Many of the boys were potential dropouts before completing elementary school. They were already bodies equipped with central nervous systems incipiently in revolt before they met any really serious school problems. For them, school and its typical demands did not provide the right answers; one may question whether anything short of a complete change in environment over a considerable period of time would have led to permanent improvement.

Even if one doubts that high school dropouts in general would show such a high percentage of serious personality disturbances as was found in the selected group of one hundred and five, there are other reasons for questioning the benefit to be derived from a wholesale campaign to prevent dropping out without regard to the reason for leaving school. There is particular reason to question the intellectual honesty of assuring potential dropouts that they will have a significantly greater chance of finding employment at a higher wage if they remain in school. In spite of an improvement in education considerably greater than that of the labor force as a whole, people under twenty carried a greater share of unemployment in 1963 than they did in 1948. This process is continuing, and anyone who promises a potential dropout from high school a greater chance of finding work if he suffers through two or three more years of high school is ignoring the facts.[14] The most recent additions to the labor force may be better prepared educationally, but they are confronted by employers who prefer greater maturity and experience. Another factor must be considered before promises are made to potential dropouts; namely, skin color. Recent statistics on unemployment show that in 1964 the unemployment rate among white males who quit school at the eighth grade was lower than the unemployment rate among non-whites with four or more additional years of education.[15]

But the basic question is whether there *is* a real need for intensive effort to increase the level of education in the United States in order to keep up with a technological, computerized age which has put men on the moon and is aiming at flights to Mars and outer space. Listening to the trumpets calls for a "Yes!" but looking at the score seems to show that the trumpets are improvising. Without question, the demand for professional, technical, and kindred workers is increasing very rapidly. Between 1940 and 1960 the percentage of the working population engaged in occupations requiring high-level technical training rose from 7.5 percent to 11.4 percent. The money spent on research and development by the Federal Government, industry, philanthropic foundations, and universities increased from 5.15 billion dollars in 1953–54 to 14.04 billion dollars in 1960–61.[16] But a 3.9-percent rise in occupations demanding extended higher education did not represent a great new demand unmet by educational growth. For the output of professionally trained technicians increased faster during those twenty years. Further, the percentage of clerical and kindred jobs requiring no technical education rose 5.4 points in the same period. The only significant decline in job availability was in agriculture, domestic service, and day labor, occupations which, in about 60 percent of the cases, had few or no educational requirements.

219

Looking at the whole job picture, one does see a general rise in educational requirements, but not so preponderantly at the higher levels as it pleases Americans to believe.

It scarcely seems vital to divert people already approaching the dropout stage back into school unless enough motivation remains or can be aroused to make the diversion meaningful. But the American culture trend glorifies education. Somehow the increasing demand in the area of advanced technology becomes an urgent reason for keeping everyone in school longer, even though this field currently provides jobs for only about 7 to 8 percent of the working force.

One-third of the students in the fifth grade do not complete high school; there are a million young people a year who leave high school without a diploma.[17] Nevertheless, 91 percent of the male students and 88 percent of the female students remain in the classroom until they are sixteen. The United States has reached a cultural stage where jobs as well as goods are manufactured, and it would make sense to manufacture jobs to fit the people who need them, rather than to go on turning out jobs blindly and screaming at the unemployed, and especially at the unemployed young, that they must grow to fit some job that is available, or is believed to be available. This might work —if, at the same time, they are assured that they may apply for social security when their unemployment insurance runs out if they cannot find an appropriate job.

The situation facing the scholastically handicapped may be summed up as a closing off of opportunity because failure at school fosters poor work habits and thus makes jobs hard to hold even when they are obtained. English young people have an easier time because the less-mechanized English economy offers more unskilled jobs suitable for fifteen-year-olds who are then easily initiated into the adult world.[18] Freedom of choice in what a hominid does at any moment is a necessary corollary to the enthusiasm which he brings to the doing and the satisfaction

he derives from doing it. When school becomes a "must" because there are too few jobs available, or because they are
fenced off with laws, the "land of promise" reneges at just the
point in life when fulfilling this promise is vitally important.

What happens when jobs are not available at the psychologically right moment in the lives of the young can be illustrated by the experience of the City of New York. Some
twenty years ago, when it became apparent that orthodox
schools were driving a few pupils to desperate rebellion or complete anomie, attitudes which had a damaging effect on the
entire student body, it was decided to herd these difficult pupils
into a separate, special "600" school. Since then, it has been
necessary constantly to increase the number of 600 schools until
there are forty-four, with five thousand enrollees, all transferred
at the request of teachers in the regular schools. Nevertheless,
trouble has continued. In 1958 the superintendent of schools
decided simply to expel several hundred pupils as incorrigible.
When this resulted in one school being destructively vandal-
ized by a gang of expellees, the mayor of the city promptly
instructed the superintendent to take the incorrigibles back,
because it would be disastrous to have them wandering around
the streets. His punch line, as usual, was "If present schools
don't meet the need, build others." [19] All over the country,
Americans go on building "others." The cost of construction
and the $500 a year per student spent on operating schools
might better be spent to create jobs. It would be worth trying.

A staff report to the Congressional Committee on Labor
and Public Welfare lists among the nation's educational problems some 1,117,800 mentally retarded children, 972,000 mentally disturbed, and 486,000 with major learning disabilities.
These children need something more imaginative than a "stamp
out dropouts" program, although many of them are dropouts
or "never-enters." The school system itself, as the great highway
of youth, may, unwittingly, contribute to the problems such

221

children meet. The New York State Department of Mental Hygiene observed that mental retardation was largely an occupational handicap among school children. For the number of a given age group reported as mentally retarded rises as the group progresses through school, and then drops when the age group leaves school to make its own way in the world. Two out of three children who are not quite able to do school work cease to be identified as retarded after they leave school. Presumably they make a more satisfactory adjustment to life than to school. Yet one cannot ignore the emotional impact which segregation because of asserted mental subnormality can have on children.

Other studies support the conclusion that morons, subnormals, defectives, and the like, identified by IQ tests, when out of school make surprisingly adequate adjustments. The great majority of them not only become self-supporting, but show a rise in IQ to the dull-normal level or higher. During World War II, one hundred and seventy-seven boys transferred from regular schools to the Wayne County Training School as mentally retarded were released because of the labor shortage to find jobs if they could. In school they tested at a mean IQ of 71.8, but when released, 80 percent of them found jobs, some in skilled categories, and their IQ seemed to have no bearing on the jobs they were able to perform satisfactorily. Those who rate highly on an IQ test may be gifted only in school-like activities; those who rate poorly on an IQ test may have abilities the test does not sample.[20]

One might question whether contemporary enthusiasts for education pay sufficient attention to the hit-or-miss relationship between formal education and achievement that seems to prevail. Many geniuses had very little orthodox schooling, or lived before such institutions existed, including the producers of some of the Magdalenian Age cave murals of France. Michelangelo was an apprenticed assistant to a Florentine artist at the age of thirteen. Fourteen Presidents of the United States managed to discharge the responsibilities of their office with less formal education than is now considered necessary for a common laborer. About 10 percent of the men and women in *Who's Who in America* in the mid-twentieth century were elementary or high school dropouts. Undoubtedly all would have profited by more education, but their example shows the need to be cautious about what is said to young people who think they have been in school long enough.

Any society takes pride in its most remarkable culture elaborations, builds a folklore which explains and justifies them, and dismisses criticisms as inconsequential. Americans have good reason to follow this tradition in respect to their educational system. There has never been anything quite like it. One favorite item of folklore is that the public school system is the means America has devised to equalize opportunities. The equality guaranteed in theory is, in practice, delivered by the public school system. That is, a boy of high talent born into a family of little means and low status, without much hope or ambition, gets a legally enforced training which shows him a way out. School opens a road to advancement, literally a route to a new world, which develops the future promise of the younger generation rather than conditions it to the despair and defeat of the old.

Unquestionably, the schools do perform this function. Many young people who have managed to hope, no matter how hopeless their surroundings, may be helped to find a way out by schools. Perhaps they would have found it without free public schools, but their chances would have been less, and perhaps their usefulness to society would have been far more limited.

Nevertheless, since public education functions in a society which has basic inequalities built into its structure, American schools not only help some people to rise, they and their personnel also operate to keep many aspirants from rising.[21]

Prisoners of Culture

The self-made man is a national ideal in the United States, and Americans proudly assert that, for those who are willing to work, this is truly the land of opportunity. The assertion is less relevant to the present than to the past; even with free public schools, today's youth finds it more difficult to advance from the lowest rungs of the ladder to the highest than youth did a generation or two ago. The school, again, presents itself as a tougher assignment than the practical problems of the world, particularly for those who have given up or have become belligerent even before they start. Americans are said to believe in themselves because they notice successful people most—particularly those whose material success is obvious. More pointedly, the self-made man in America is proud of what he has done and makes no secret of his lowly start. There is an equal amount of social mobility in Europe, according to some American sociologists, but the European who has climbed high prefers to say nothing about his climb; he is happier if people think that the position he occupies in society is one to which his family has long been accustomed.[22]

America as a nation is committed to the belief that ten years of education is an absolute minimum for all citizens, whether they are headed for a white collar or a blue. It seems convinced, too, that high school graduation is equally desirable for all citizens, regardless of their life plans, and that junior college should be recommended. All arguments which support these beliefs are accepted without question, no matter how questionable the logic on which they are based. Those who look at the evidence more critically are almost disregarded, or if criticism is admitted to be valid, then it is concluded that society needs not less education of the kind now offered, but more education of a different kind. A 1964 report on man, education, and work made for the American Council on Education states that contemporary urbanized society increasingly denies youth opportunities for work. Yet, since adults measure status in terms of jobs, having a job symbolizes acceptance into the adult world.

The report then proceeds to make fifteen recommendations, all concerned with the need for greater emphasis on vocational and technological education in line with predictions that professional and technical workers, who represented only 4.3 percent of the working force in 1900, will constitute 14.3 percent by 1975. No one appears much impressed by learning that clerical workers, who represented 3 percent of the working force in 1900, will constitute 16.2 percent of it by 1975, and that, in fact, all groups of workers except those in agriculture and ordinary labor are on the increase. Perhaps it would be impossible to justify emphasis on more education if it were admitted that almost 60 percent of the young people now in school must earn their livings as clerks, salespeople, or blue collar workers.

It is further suggested that much of the apparent demand for more and more highly trained scientists and engineers may be artificially created through wasteful assignment of those available.[23] The armed forces have recruited small armies of scientists, engineers, and technicians to develop weaponry, much of which is functionally duplicative and subject to eventual cancellation. Private enterprises recruit their own separate corps of engineers and scientists, not to meet current needs, but to make themselves eligible for future government research and development contracts. These highly trained people may spend years at nothing more useful than preparing elaborate proposals for such contracts. Highly trained scientists and engineers are often held in jobs that could be just as well done by technicians, because their employers hope to have more appropriate work for them later. Hoarding slightly used engineers and scientists is regarded as prudent foresight in the highly competitive American industrial system. Overstaffing is regarded as a safety factor and is encouraged by the attitude of government contract negotiators who prefer to pay high costs to a favorably known organization rather than risk failure elsewhere. Even universities and colleges, constantly worried by their poor success in holding top teachers against the higher salaries offered by industry, do not use the men they do hold to best advantage. Of 176,000 scientists and engineers in the employ of colleges and universities in 1961, fewer than half were teaching. The rest were pursuing their own programs of research, or devoting their talents to administration and other miscellaneous jobs.

This shortage of scientists and engineers, artificially created though it is, feeds the national vanity. It is a proof of progress and a confirmation of American leadership in modern technology. It assures adults that stress on the need of more education for the younger generation is prudent preparation for the future. Anthropologically and culturally speaking, this is "par for the course" in any successful and self-respecting human society.

The way to impress people with the importance of a group is to increase the requirements for membership. This occurs, almost as a matter of course, in every successful professional group with high regard for its own importance, whether it be in medicine, dentistry, pharmacy, nursing, law, theology, or the academic scholarship that earns the Ph.D.; among city managers, librarians, police officers, teachers, or any other specialists. It might be said that the attitude of the United States toward education derives from the same motivation. It is not especially important what the educational requirements are, provided that they are time-consuming enough to lend dignity to the already established members, many of whom probably could not meet the newly recommended requirements if they had to start over. Americans enjoy feeling that one really cannot get along in their civilization without at least ten, and preferably twelve or sixteen years, of classroom instruction.

226

What other country has so high and exacting a culture? That twenty million adults already functioning successfully somewhere in the culture stopped school at the eighth grade or earlier is inconsequential.

As I was writing these pages I received a letter from a local high school, one of the best college-preparatory schools in the area, which said:

"Whether your needs are inside or out—an hour or a week —we have capable young people who are ready to assist you: babysitting, typing, housework, general cleaning, waxing and ironing, general office work, delivery, sales, janitorial, yard work, lawnmowing, service station help, stockroom, auto waxing, carpentry, painting, etc."

Strange, that young people must beg for work as if they were asking alms while Congress is passing more legislation to support them in comparative luxury if they will just go to school and stop trying to work for pay. Every significant study confirms that people drop out of school, not because of economic necessity, primarily, but because of boredom generated by an interminable course of training which the people concerned are convinced will not benefit them, and which they know millions of people are getting along without—although some of the latter do join in insisting that it *is* essential for youngsters.

One cannot understand the intense faith of the American people in education without admitting that it may be tinged with belief in magic. If the teacher has the right touch, the dullest subject can be illuminated, the dullest mind be made brighter. The great eighteenth- and nineteenth-century educators—Rousseau, Pestalozzi, Herbart, Froebel, Spencer, Montessori, Parker, and John Dewey—have sounded their siren notes and Americans are demanding that their own hardworking teachers produce the miracles which all these worthies assure us good teaching can produce. In this connection we might well recall a conversation between a juvenile and an elder in the fantasy world of Lewis Carroll:

"'In our country,' said Alice, still panting a little, 'you'd generally get somewhere else—if you ran very fast for a long time as we've been doing.'"

To which the Red Queen replied, "'A slow sort of country! Now, here, you see, it takes all the running *you* can do, to keep in the same place. If you want to get somewhere else, you must run at least twice as fast as that!'" [24]

CHAPTER 10

The Future of Youth

Assuming that the information presented so far is convincing, there still remains the question: "What is to be done about it?" This question cannot be answered in detail. There is no ready-made formula of fixed steps to be taken in ritualistic succession. One can only indicate the basic changes in cultural habits which must be made. Beyond that, the answers depend on the intricacies of ingenious elaboration that the human mind is certain to create.

The existing variations in culture from society to society and place to place throughout the world have all arisen from the creative activity and common modes of operation of the brains of individuals belonging to a single species of primate, *Homo sapiens*. Which variation of the many equally practical ways of skinning a cat is best in a given situation depends on the established habit patterns of the society involved, the size of the population, its existing environment, and its aspirations

229

for the future. To build a new play for a thespian family with an established tradition of good acting and bad, for performance on a stage loaded with inherited scenery and furnishings, requires patience, tact, and a readiness to amend the script in both stage business and lines.

It is equally important to remember that, as the company of actors increases in size, the *dramatis personae* with bit parts require a larger stage and a directorial flair for the spectacular, if crowding and chaos in the wings are to be avoided. If the cast is to be satisfied there must be space on the boards and a line in the program for each member. If the actors are to gain the satisfaction that audience approval generates, they need an opportunity to rehearse their parts and to try on costumes, before what is for them, opening night.

All this is made difficult by the number of juveniles in the cast, and by the number of "plays within the play" that have developed. Further, no one knows where the central plot of the play should lead, or whether the play will turn out to be a comedy or a tragedy. Only the title of the play is known but most men feel that "Civilization" has wonderful possibilities as a bit of cosmic drama. "Civilization" has been playing to ever-larger audiences for thousands of years, although the cast changes from generation to generation. Some scholars conclude, therefore, that the play perpetuates itself, automatically presenting parts to each "poor player that struts and frets his hour upon the stage and then is heard no more." Every star, with his supporting cast, not to mention scene painters and shifters, impresses his unique personality on what he does, and that which excites applause is what his successor tries to emulate. The play is continuously changing, owing solely to the efforts of the human beings involved in it and to the mood of the audience, which is made up of players not at the moment on stage.

Some people, admitting the truth of what has just been outlined, despair of giving the plot of the play more logical direction, because this would involve a better understanding of the human brain; and the brain, they believe, like Tennyson's "flower in the crannied wall," is as full of mystery as the whole scheme and purpose of the universe. Part of this awesomeness results from the difficulty of dealing with brains *en masse*. The customs of a society develop their peculiarities not as a contribution of any single brain but through gradual accretion from many individual ideas. The difficulty encountered in bringing about voluntary cultural change cannot be credited solely to individual resistance to changing established habits. There is involved, also, the *interdependence of habits*, that is, the number of habits affected by a change in one; the *centrality of habits*, that is, their relationship to the core pattern of the culture; and the *number who share the habit*, that is, the number of individuals required to change their attitude toward the habit. One could say that the formula for estimating the difficulty of change is IC^n.

Culture may be more difficult to change in a small, primitive society, because the pattern is more closely integrated, and the number of individuals involved, although small on an absolute scale, is very large relative to the total population of the society. The converse tends to be true of large societies with highly complex but not closely integrated cultures. Nevertheless, even in primitive society, culture does change, slowly, as a result of internally originating ideas which elaborate on and make more significant this custom or that; rapidly, as a result of outside ideas or pressures which are compatible with some phase of the culture pattern.

The Plains Indians of North America, for example, rapidly turned to using horses after they were introduced by Spanish explorers and settlers, notably in the vicinity of Santa Fe, New Mexico. The Spanish did not force the horse on the aboriginal tribes; in fact, they were constantly struggling to prevent horses from being stolen. The natives, themselves, aggressively initiated this culture change. One may guess that the movement was started by nomadic hunting tribes. They had a transportation system of sorts—in some cases using the domestic dog—which could be elaborated and made more ambitious by acquiring horses. These tribes were accustomed to driving others from their hunting territories, or to being pursued when they encroached on territory claimed by stronger tribes. Many of them depended on meat from buffalo herds which was difficult to secure on foot. The horse, like the rifle, was an aid in their established way of life. But by the time that the French and English got to the Great Plains, even some sedentary, agricultural tribes had turned to hunting buffalo on horseback; patterns of culture all the way to the Canadian border reflected the increased range of mobility, the speed, and the sense of power and exhilaration, that the horse brought. It was difficult for the first travelers in the northern Great Plains to believe that the Indians had not always had horses.

Then came the steady invasion of whites, restriction of territory, and the decimation of the buffalo herds. The tribes were left with a pattern of culture which no longer functioned, and again one finds evidence of the way in which individuals influence culture. Seven samples of post-conquest tribal histories illustrate the variety of reactions which occurred.[1] An account of the Southern Ute of Colorado is particularly pertinent because it identifies the individuals who directed the course of Ute culture on the basis of personal charisma.[2] The Utes were both tribally miserable and individually desperate. One band chief argued that it was better to retreat into the hills with their old culture; another, that the time had come to move toward the culture of the whites. The tribe split up in consequence, with half sticking to its old language and customs, and half making an attempt at agriculture and the English language, in separate settlements. The first leader guided his followers into poor country which offered no temptation to white

232

aggression. The second encouraged his followers to turn to farming and accept education and they adapted to the new conditions quite effectively.

History offers many examples of the influence of leaders on the course of cultural movement, and leaders frequently strengthen themselves by claiming special revelation from supernatural authorities. Among American Indians, the most notable leaders were Handsome Lake among the Iroquois; Smohalla among the Nez Perce; John Slocum among the Squaxin and other Northwest Coast tribes; and Wovoka, the Paiute, whose Ghost Dance cult spread halfway across the United States and provoked some of the final uprisings against white domination. Western civilization is replete with such leaders, right down to the group of patriots who engineered the revolt of the American colonists against George III of England and subsequently proposed a Constitution of the United States as successor to the Articles of Confederation, thereby establishing a framework for political, economic, and social change of worldwide influence.

Taking account of history, this chapter suggests culture can be changed by the forethought and agreement of leaders, provided that the proposed changes are compatible with the instinctive and acquired behavior patterns of the people concerned. Culture traits are not Chinese paper dragons to which individual human beings can impart nothing more than mobility and a semblance of life. Human beings must assist in the regeneration of paper dragons. New dragons will be accepted as legitimate if they continue to show a family resemblance and may even excite special praise if they exhibit idiosyncrasies which embellish the complex of traits to which dragons belong. True, the viability of a culture is not measured by the degree of satisfaction of the least privileged individuals in the supporting society, but rather by the over-all advantage of the society relative to others. Nevertheless, a society's ability to gain or hold

233

such an advantage, through change or resistance to change, is strengthened by a sense that all economic and social levels participate in cultural advantages. Where opportunity for gaining advantage on an individual or familial scale is reasonably well distributed, the society gains internal strength, and culture remains relatively stable. If opportunities are unequally distributed, the society is subject to disintegration even though its total advantage relative to other societies is so great that it dispatches missionaries everywhere to spread the faith of its leaders and promise salvation to mankind.

Arnold Toynbee, in his study of history, poses a question: "What is the weakness which exposes a growing civilization to the risk of stumbling and falling in mid-career . . . ?" He replies by stressing the role of creative persons and minorities. But these can be effective only if they can make the uncreative rank and file follow and imitate them.[3]

With a rather similar thought, I am trying to summarize the kind of changes in American culture which should be sought in the light of available evidence of biological and cultural evolutionary changes in the past. The need for guidance in this regard has recently been further stressed by the observation that men can alter their external environment to fit physical and psychological needs, but they still have the innate responses developed for adaptation to conditions which no longer exist. The persistence of those needs and responses can be a source of physiological and psychological conflicts under the usual conditions of modern life.[4]

The United States is obviously among the most highly advantaged societies on earth, offering a higher level of satisfaction to the average individual member in more diverse ways than any society in history. But it also falls into that category of societies where the degree of satisfaction is unequally distributed: sizable minorities are either markedly above or markedly below the average by culturally established quantitative and/or

234

qualitative criteria. That a high average of satisfaction gives the society an advantage over others is a reason for national pride which the minority can appreciate only vicariously. Their sense of personal participation in the achievement is diluted by discontent. They find no comfort in knowing that their under-privileged condition leaves them better off than the average person in less-advanced societies. They are concerned with their share in the privileges which their own society offers.

Currently, newspapers, magazines, and television and radio programs, are filled with evidences of discontent: passive or active protests against the war in Vietnam; peaceful or violent reaction of black Americans against their exclusion from full and equal participation in the advantages that American society has achieved; acts of civil disobedience by both advantaged and disadvantaged groups in order to bring about change by some method faster than that provided in the normal democratic process; an increase in vandalism, violence, and illegal activities by adolescents and young adults, against societal practices, institutions, or authorities which represent what is called *the establishment;* and a continuing increase in delinquency and in crime directly aimed at the property and the lives of ordinary private citizens or public leaders. These are multi-faceted problems, and each incident has its own kaleidoscopic array of contributing and inciting causes. The following summary tries to point out certain general trends of American civilization which, in the light of man's past, tend to set the stage for discontent, whatever the form and occasion of its manifestations.

Americans are all aware of and some, secretly at least, are amazed by the increase in goods and services which high culture has stimulated researchers, developers, independent inventors, and production and distribution engineers to provide for the public in the last two or three generations. No one in his right mind would want to turn the hands of the clock back to a time when they did not exist, even though, on occasion, he is happy to escape to some sheltered haven where telephones, radio, TV, the stench of automobiles, and the roar or scream of high-powered engines can no longer be heard, smelled, or seen. Even though it cannot be accurately measured, the effect on the individual nervous system of being surrounded by all these "conveniences" is probably itself significant, but one's chief interest here is the change in important facets of social organization and culture pattern which *production* of these "conveniences" has brought about.

From the point of view stressed here, three major shifts in ways of living have occurred since the foundations of civilization were laid: the development of agriculture and animal husbandry, beginning some ten thousand years ago; the rise of city states and the development of a written language, beginning, perhaps, six thousand years ago; and the proliferation of metropolitan centers of manufacturing and commerce, beginning with the Industrial Revolution about two hundred years ago. The last has had the most drastic effect on the life of the average individual. The ways in which life has been changed are too numerous to list, but one can concentrate on some major changes which have affected the family, and the relationship between young people and their society, particularly the character of the work offered them when they try to become adults.

The family probably arose as a means of assuring protection and support for infants and dependent juveniles by group recognition of a male who would be responsible for each reproductively active female. Throughout the history of hominids, this pairing of males and females formed the nucleus of an extended group of lineal, collateral, and affinal relatives, all contributing to the immediate social environment of the child and to the development of a more or less autonomous, economic unit. It tended to be a microcosmic replica of the larger society of which it was a part and provided a fairly extensive culture-

236

conditioning environment for future adult members of the larger society. Its positive effect was heightened because authority balanced responsibility; that is, the family, in many cultures, was free to choose the time when it could most satisfactorily discharge the responsibility of bringing children into the world. Society influenced this choice by offering public respect and social status to potential parents who saw their way clear to bearing and properly rearing an effective addition to the adult community. The need for such limitation on family size varied from time to time, place to place, and circumstance to circumstance. Agriculture and domestication of animals decreased concern over food supplies and offered an expansible area of usefulness for growing children. Societies with available means of transportation and the power to establish colonies were more favorable to rapid population growth; and so were societies seeking to build up their defenses against aggression. In fact, as civilization began to spread in a still sparsely populated world, the birth rate became one measure of internal strength and external influence. Then, as population increased, and areas available for expansion became difficult to find or acquire, society after society found itself faced with a problem of natural increase and cultural sanctions against primitive ways of meeting it.

The biological seeds of human life, with sowers increasing in number on a fixed planetary surface, threaten to become the seeds of civilization's destruction. Families, as social units, have already lost much of their functional efficiency where urbanization, industrialization, and standards of housing and living have advanced most rapidly. Within the past century they have typically shrunk to a nuclear unit of a male and female adult, lacking collateral, unpaid adult assistance, either for routine child care or adequately broad sampling of the society to which the child must be enculturated. The family, as a citizen-producing unit, has been isolated from the total culture while,

237

at the same time, the variety and complexity of the demands made by culture on its citizens of the future steadily increase. Moreover, civilization, in the past few millennia, has developed abstract theories concerning the sanctity of life which deprive the family of full freedom to decide when it is materially and spiritually prepared to assume responsibility for a future citizen.

The modern ethic, based on Judaic and Christian philosophies and frozen into juridic principle, denies the desirability of this choice. Unborn life is vouchsafed a sanctity beyond human interference. This policy ignores the clear indication, in both the Old Testament and the New, that life must be free from corruption and evil to deserve the name. If an unborn child is offered less than a reasonable expectancy for developing a healthy personality, it is denied a real right to life even while society virtuously insists that it must continue to exist.

If Americans are sincerely looking for a means of correcting the discontent that seems to plague so many young people, this is the area for initial action. It makes no sense to permit children to be brought into the world under circumstances which give birth the appearance of being a penalty or a horrible stroke of bad luck. If bearing children cannot be recognized, morally and legally, as a privilege to be enjoyed only by those willing and prepared to assume the concomitant responsibilities, society faces a long and disappointing wait for an effective solution to its youth problems.

The longer society puts off admitting the relevance of parental convictions on the decision to allow conceptions to proceed to birth, the worse off it will be. Each succeeding generation of parents who have themselves just managed to survive birth and childhood as unwelcome immigrants further decreases the chance of subsequent normal parent-child relations. Furthermore, if the world is to meet the threatened catastrophe of overpopulation, there is no more appropriate place to begin than in homes which are forced by convention to have children which the parents do not want. The number of such homes may be too small to have an immediately dramatic effect on the birth rate, but recognition of them will emphasize for others the priority which should be given to the rights and expectancies of infants and children, and help to create a public attitude without which family planning programs and birth control campaigns are a waste of time and energy. The magnitude of the problem and the need to use every psychically helpful support to solutions are indicated by the geometric pace at which population is now increasing. It has been estimated that world population could not have increased at a greater average annual rate than three hundred persons for a million years before the Christian era. But with higher food productivity, this rate has steadily increased to an annual average of twenty-seven million for 1925–62. Projections into the future indicate that it will probably be necessary to find room for an additional billion people on earth by 1975, and another billion by 1982.

Despite dire predictions made a century and a half ago, food shortage and starvation have not proved to be controlling factors in population growth. World population has more than tripled since the early nineteenth century, without marked effect on the per capita available food supply or on the accelerating rate of reproduction. It is now predicted that food to support population growth can be provided for an indefinite period—if the smell, taste, and appearance of the food is ignored. But what of the effect of a regimented existence in a teeming, polluted world from which wilderness and the fantasies of nature have disappeared, and where the individual has lost the "elbow room" which assures quiet, privacy, independence, and initiative. It is now known that the famous lemming migrations occur because of the intolerable effects of crowding on even a simple mammalian brain. When population density exceeds the threshold of lemming tolerance, these animals start a pell mell trek, attacking those who get in their way and strik-

239

ing even against those who are also trying to escape on nearby, parallel courses. Lemmings make no claim to superior intelligence in the class *mammalia. Homo sapiens* cannot claim this alibi for letting population density reach an intolerable level.

The second major constellation of problems which changes in social organization and culture pattern have created is closely related to, and frequently intensified by, the family situation just mentioned, but it affects all juveniles whatever the status and internal adequacy of their families. In the broadest terms, that constellation is concerned with the sociocultural conditions and practices which substitute for, or supplement, such efforts as the family traditionally made or still attempts to make to help to prepare juveniles for adjustment to, and membership in, adult society. These conditions and practices include the effect of other families in a neighborhood, educational and recreational facilities and services of local communities, and state and national laws and policies relating to juveniles.

Efforts to build character and stability into American neighborhoods are handicapped by lack of agreement on what is a desirable basis for either character or stability. Families seldom show any common patterns of belief or interest, religious, ethical, civil, or political. Most families are part-time residents; they work, shop, and seek entertainment outside the neighborhood. Many are just transients. The 1960 census found that 38.3 percent of the people enumerated had been living where the census-taker found them less than six years. Of those born more than five years before the census was taken, some sixteen million had moved from another state. Such migrations may have a profound effect on the personalities of children because of the disruption of social ties. Nomadic peoples are or were constantly on the move, but they moved in groups, and wherever they stopped was home, because each individual was still surrounded by the same relatives and friends. The lonely crowd is made up not of people who are strangers to their physical surroundings, but of those who have no personal ties with the people around them, and this kind of loneliness strikes juveniles harder because they have had less time to develop defenses against it.

Even under primitive conditions, with relatively small societies and simple cultures, children are somewhat isolated from society outside their own families. They are so markedly different from adults in size, strength, knowledge, and skill that they constitute an underprivileged group. Automatically, they turn to each other for compatible companionship. They form social groups in which they will not be underprivileged and from which they can derive that ineffable feeling of participating membership so important to gregarious primates. Age-grades can, in effect, establish a continuing parallel society in which slowly maturing hominids can learn what it means to be a fully privileged personality while waiting to outgrow their second-rate standing in adult society. Infants the world over are more like each other than they are like adults in their own society. Juvenile peer groups the world over frequently share more attributes than do the adult societies and cultures from which they are derived. The presence of organized and recognized juvenile peer groups would give neighborhoods and communities a stability of likeness at the level where it is needed most.

Unfortunately, American society gives more attention to peer groups for its senior citizens than for juniors. As a nuclear-familied, technologically sophisticated society finds it increasingly difficult to give its older members useful and challenging work, it has produced plush ghettos and tenement hotels, where oldsters with nothing much to do may have at least the gregarious pleasure of doing it together. Even that kind of peer grouping is probably less successful than it could be. Land developers and community planners do not take into account the resulting separation between settlements of understaffed,

241

underequipped, and often overworked and semi-neurotic nuclear families, and settlements of remnants of families where neurosis develops for lack of mental challenge by things that need to be done. Functional differentiation of housing for these two types of settlements is undoubtedly important, but their effectiveness might be enhanced by keeping the settlements close together.

Despite transportation achievements, many small jobs remain undone or half done, and willing part-time workers remain idle, because bringing them together costs time and money. This is equally true of people isolated in slums by circumstances beyond their immediate control, and of older people who hopefully follow a pied piper from some suburban real estate office. Many subsequently discover that it would be pleasant to have an occasional respite from doing nothing together, and they could have this respite by planning to put their dwellings nearer settlements of young families whose members often feel the need for a respite from doing too much, not well enough, alone.

The greatest problems are more directly concerned with failure to employ peer groups as an aid in the development and maturation of future citizens. Even the effect of America's frenetic mobility would be eased for youngsters by the presence of established and comparable peer groups with their own specific responsibilities for matters of adult concern. In this, as in many other areas, however, culture has been elaborated in ways which not only do not promote peer-group development, but interdict it. Interest in peer groups appears as personalities begin to seek for opportunities to take initiative action. But just at this crucial stage, boys and girls are herded into coeducational schools, which are incompatible with peer-group operation except on an extracurricular basis. This runs counter to the invariable tendency of young hominids, when the choice remains open, to group themselves by sex, and to turn to older persons of the same sex for mimetic guidance and specific information on how to reach manhood and womanhood most quickly and successfully.

Coeducation affects boys more adversely than girls. Most teachers in the elementary grades are women. In the typical family situation, where male economic activities are carried on outside the home, the boy enters school with more unanswered questions about how to win identity in the male moiety of adult society, than girls have about identity in the female moiety. Girls usually have some opportunity to observe and to work with a woman in one of the basic occupations for females—housekeeping. For the girls, supervision by women teachers maintains continuity in the process of learning how to behave like a woman. For boys, it seems to be another sidetrack off the main road to manhood, no matter how effective the teacher is pedagogically. Finally, boys and girls are grouped by chronological age without regard to girls' being a year or two ahead of boys in physiological development. Male pride may stimulate some individuals to meet this unequal competition, but it generally slows down the girls and discourages a significant percentage of boys sufficiently to make them seek out peer groups which rank their members by other criteria than success in school.

If one considers the influence exerted by this situation on personality aberrancies which a boy (or girl) may bring to school as a result of earlier familial and neighborhood experience, it is not difficult to see a combined effect that lays the foundation for authority-resisting cliques, truancy, gangs, delinquency, and crime. The argument that better male-female relations in later life are fostered by encouraging early close acquaintance is not supported by the rise in the American divorce rate in the years since coeducation became general. What common sense leads one to expect, and what seems to be the result, even when a young ape and a young human are raised to-

243

gether, is a sharing of superficial mannerisms. Perhaps this accounts for the current difficulty in differentiating the boys and the girls on the basis of hair style, clothes, footgear, and ornamentation, such as earrings, necklaces, bracelets, and anklets. Among "flower children" the resemblance in dress and hair styles between the two sexes is phenomenal. Even language patterns and philosophies seem, at times, to become nearly identical.

The schools, on the whole, succeed well in sifting out and training an increasing number of young people with the wit and will to go on to college. But they have also been turning out a disconcertingly large minority of aberrant individuals who need psychiatric treatment, or who join cults, become chronic delinquents, professional criminals, or patients in mental hospitals. Very serious consideration of the reasons for this situation is needed, as is bolder experimentation in an effort to correct it. One is concerned not only for those who enter school with some distortion of personality resulting from earlier life experiences, but also for those who may be influenced by both the presence of potential aberrants, and by the problems that schools, as presently constituted, seem to raise in central nervous systems which, though normal, are least tolerant. Removing some of the barriers to the organization of peer groups in the elementary schools is suggested as a first experiment. But something more must be done as the members of these peer groups become teenagers, if today's children are to profit by the experience of primitive societies.

One important key to the success of age-grading appears to be progressive sharing of meaningful adult responsibilities. A few experiments along this line might be initiated in the schools. To use a homely example, the curricula of schools are, in general, progressively more difficult; there is a ladder, or various different ladders, to be climbed. But the only ladders leading to a tangible goal are those hooked to the registrar's window at a college or university. Young people with special talents also get along fairly well. Just as the academically oriented student sees the completion of preparatory school as a job which pays off in admission to college, scholarships, and prizes, so members of athletic teams, musical organizations, dramatic groups may find a real challenge for their talents and something equivalent to a job which pays off in public praise, peer prestige, and tangibles, such as trips and financial assistance. Unpalatable as a continuing diet of abstractions and symbols may be, persistence gives these young people a reasonably satisfactory reward. But climbers who do not have special talents, whose abilities do not require college, and who have no intention of going there see the secondary school ladder ending in midair. Many youngsters who need a job for a goal cannot see that the rung above them is any closer to that goal than the rung on which they happen to be standing. Increased responsibility for those on the upper rungs of the ladder— some kind of job experience as part of the curriculum—might change this.

It would pay society to add to the rewards that advancement on the academic ladder offers. Even teachers in the ancient city of Ur recognized this thirty-seven centuries ago. The Ur school for scribes, the first which has left detailed records, gave titles and assistantships to its older students. They had jobs and were no longer ordinary juveniles. Some similar system might be introduced into secondary schools, even if it required establishing assistantships for every member of the regular operating staff and paying nominal wages for a few hours of work a week. Anything that will contribute to a sense of progress toward adulthood is important. If there are not enough part-time jobs within the school, then civic agencies, industries, businesses, and private citizens should be asked for further

245

help, not with any expectation of getting efficient workers at low cost, but rather with giving job experience and adding an essential missing ingredient to education.

Some readers, at this point, are undoubtedly wagging their heads to and fro and thinking, with a quiet, condescending smile, that this is just another "egghead" idea. Perhaps, but it is also an idea that is built into the instinctive concern for survival in the minds of young people. The "egghead" knows it cannot be put into effect tomorrow. He is suggesting that if something is not done, and promptly, about jobs for youngsters who are approaching or have already reached complete frustration in the school system, Americans may expect more headaches than all the patent medicines in the country can relieve.

Restructuring school curricula to include some equivalent of a part-time job may be sufficient for some young people. It will enable them to feel that they are making more progress toward being adults than is now possible in the traditional, semi-custodial institution for juveniles. Others probably need a more radical change from school to job, and hopefully to continued education at night, along lines applicable to the work they are doing.

The National Alliance of Businessmen, under the leadership of Henry Ford II, recently began a campaign in fifty major American cities to find jobs for the so-called hard-core unemployed: people whose police records, educational and skill levels, health handicaps, or general attitudes have barred them from consideration for even the lowest level of jobs. The goal of the campaign is to persuade employers to hire one or more such persons, to give them on-the-job training, to help them get remedial education if needed, and so to show them that America still is a land of opportunity for everybody. Employers may undertake such a program singly or in consortiums. Whatever expense is incurred beyond the value of the work

246

performed can, under conditions set by contract, be reimbursed from a federal appropriation of 244 million dollars.

Although it is too early to predict the outcome of this campaign, it has every practical argument in its favor. Certainly it is a simpler and more realistic approach to problems of unemployment and poverty than that taken under the Economic Opportunity Act of 1964, with a funding commitment of 160 million dollars. The major emphasis of this program was on training people how not to be impoverished. Unemployment is recognized as one of four major factors producing poverty, along with inadequate education, poor health, and dilapidated housing. But in accord with the high rank of education in the American credo, the program of attack on poverty dispersed its efforts over remedial reading, literary courses, homemaker services, consumer education, job training, and vocational rehabilitation. The last two facets of this war on poverty are particularly curious in view of the fact that the Federal Government and the states have operated a joint program in these areas for more than sixty years, and expenditures have steadily risen to more than 400 million dollars a year.[5]

American faith in the magic of education seems to be limitless. Adequate food and shelter are recognized as essential to the elimination of poverty, and there is general agreement that the traditional American way of obtaining food and shelter is through working at a job, but instead of making sure that there are jobs available for all the impoverished who are capable of working, the government offers the unemployed an opportunity to go back to school with all expenses paid, even though the course deals with how to spend money wisely after one gets it. Well intentioned though this may be, it does not get at the primary problem of providing useful work for those who are impoverished. Hopelessness is one of the psychic problems which the government stresses in its definition of

247

chronic poverty. There would be no better antidote for this than a meaningful way to win survival through one's own efforts.

Business and industry, as the primary beneficiaries of democracy with free enterprise, must assume their share of responsibility for this insistence on education whether needed or not and the belief that jobs will thereby be created. The reputation of free enterprise for miracles of invention and production has been built in part on discrimination and economy in employment. But evidence seems to be accumulating that more jobs must also be created for the people who need them for psychological as well as economic reasons. The first to be aware of this need are those with physical, social, or mental handicaps—often transitory handicaps that a job, plus all that it connotes in security and self-respect, would soon correct. There is an urgent need for business and industry to join with the schools in matching men and women to jobs. The schools cannot perform the miracle of fitting all people for the kind of jobs that the nation likes to think are available. A reciprocal effort must be made to fit jobs to people, using all the ingenuity of which free enterprise is capable.

The need for philosophical soul-searching is indicated by the fact that jobs for prison inmates have been vigorously opposed for several decades in spite of a general consensus among penologists that American society as well as the prisoners would benefit. The battle cry of "No Prison Labor" is obviously aimed at limiting competition from the products thereof, but it also implies that jobs are a privilege rather than a basic necessity for good citizenship. Blind and crippled persons who are still capable of doing excellent work in jobs created with their handicaps in mind are poignantly aware that management seeks to avoid the planning that would be required. Racial minority groups are equally aware that their job opportunities are not equal to those of the white majority

248

even when educational qualifications are more than fully met. And, finally, young people under twenty-one have learned by experience that they cannot find jobs in the number needed.

Resentful action on the part of the young is already quite apparent, particularly from those who have a double handicap of color and youth. During the last quarter century, large-scale migrations out of the Deep South have made blacks realize, for the first time, how really underprivileged they are. Racial prejudice and past denial of equal opportunities have left many of them unprepared to demonstrate the fallacy of prejudice by successful competition in the job market. The message blacks get is that they cannot move from the position in which history has left them. The result has been organized protest, riots, and violence in major cities throughout the country. The need for cooperative action to correct this situation is obvious. The Economic Opportunity Act, well-intentioned though it was, stressed emergency training programs to prepare the unemployed for some assumedly available job. The National Alliance of Businessmen's program takes the more direct approach of putting the unemployed to work first and then training them.

Perhaps the plight of the Afro-Americans will arouse the nation to the deeper problem, affecting whites as well as blacks, of an increasing shortage of jobs resulting from mechanization and almost fanatical concentration on production efficiency. Unemployment is not confined to racial minorities or to the least well educated. It reaches serious proportions among people of all skin colors who are less than twenty-one or are beyond middle age. On the average, unemployed applicants for jobs who are below twenty-one have completed more years of schooling than the employed population above that age. This is also true of young Afro-Americans. Their problem is not primarily a deficiency in formal education, but lack of the experience and maturity that earlier entry into the job market has been observed to provide. Clearly, when the chips are down, education is less important than experience and maturity as a guarantee of efficiency in the majority of the thirty thousand-odd job classifications making up the American labor market. Clearly, too, there are more job applicants than jobs; employers are taking their choice—and tens of thousands of young people, ready and eager to step into the adult economy after an exasperatingly long wait, are pushed away. At the moment, the draft takes some of the heat out of this situation but the heat has been sufficient to burn a considerable amount of private property. If nothing can be done to lower the temperature before the much-desired end of the Vietnam war, trouble may be expected to increase.

Two vital questions must be raised if the situation is to be improved. Can the internal strength and prosperity of the United States be maintained by concentrating on producing efficiently, without regard for the citizens who need jobs even though they have not yet acquired efficiency? Secondly, is the welfare of society best served by continuing advocacy of longer schooling for all categories of jobs, without regard to actual job requirements and individual talents?

In answering the first question one must remember that, in the American culture, the instinct to survive, involving subsistence for a family as well as oneself, can be satisfied with dignity and public respect only by winning a job. Without a job, the person must either give up his dignity by accepting alms or give up public respect by engaging in criminal activities. In answering the second question, one must remember that job experience is an important part of the training program for respected membership in society. Unnecessary delay in making that experience available, particularly if the justification for delay is palpably false, contributes to frustration, and promotes neuroses, psychoses, delinquency, and crime. If Americans are victims of a cultural delusion, elaborating a customary practice, education, to the point of absurdity because a little

250

of it has made the society distinctively great, they are in the same fix as the sorcerer's apprentice in the folktale, who learned a magic formula for drawing water and sweeping floors but did not learn how to say "enough!"

The National Commission on Technology, Automation, and Economic Progress, in its first report to the President and Congress of the United States, January, 1966, concurred in the opinion that a job shortage is developing and that more education does not overcome it. The report questions whether the often-cited swing from blue-collar to white-collar jobs is clear evidence of the need for more education and training. Many highly skilled mechanics, classified as blue-collar, who are being replaced by machines, required more training than the large number of clerks and salespeople classified as white-collar, who encounter less competition from the machine. Japan and European countries operate sophisticated industrial economies on educational profiles far beneath that which Americans are trying to raise still higher. The report concludes that a highly automated economy can function on a variety of educational profiles.[6]

The report also confirms several other of my conclusions when it emphasizes the possibility of making education open-ended, through coordinated effort by schools at all levels and by employers. Most important, school systems must convince young people that they need to assume responsibility for continuing self-education in order to adapt to a changing environment.[7]

It is important to repeat that the existing educational system is a result of historical accidents which have been elaborated by the minds of various leaders who enjoyed the elaboration, and were rewarded by public acceptance of it. During America's early years, business and industry were luke-warm about free public education. Newly established factories needed manual labor which children could supply without

251

education. Such trained skills as were needed could be obtained from immigrants who came ready-prepared. About 30 percent of immigrants between 1841 and 1930 had had occupational training before leaving their native countries. One cannot blame entrepreneurs for concluding that they did not need to bother about education or training in skills. The exceptions to this attitude were in the minority. Then public-spirited reformers moved in, alarmed by the frequently indefensible exploitation of child labor and by the barrier that it imposed on the basic education of future citizens for rational participation in self-government. The reformers did a praiseworthy job, but they have continued to elaborate upon it to the absurd end of condemning all labor for pay, even on family-owned farms, before the age of eighteen, and preferably twenty-one. They have been matched by business and industrial managements, which tend to take it for granted that somebody else should train the employees they hire, except where particular company procedures and policies are concerned.

Consequently, cooperative effort in education and training by business, industry, and schools has never been regarded as important. Organized labor, naturally enough, has tacitly endorsed these historical accidents. Unions, as a matter of policy, have long favored public, tax-supported education for all children and at all levels. They also wanted to move child labor out of the arena of labor disputes and to strengthen their demands for minimum wage laws. Labor leaders have tended to elaborate the union position chiefly by getting their members tangible rewards: higher wage rates, shorter hours, and fringe benefits. With some noteworthy exceptions, union leaders avoid a broad view of their interest in a strong economy and their proper role in out-of-school training programs.

To a limited extent, the dissatisfied high school pupil may aspire to apprenticeship in a skilled trade, but the number of apprentices is usually limited by unions in order to protect the market for their journeyman members. As a result of their caution and the reluctance of management to make an issue of it, apprenticeships have declined as the economy has grown. The Bureau of the Census reported 116,789 apprentices in the experienced labor force in 1950, and only 85,282 in 1960.[8] From my viewpoint, this shows a decline in the most meaningful educational program while millions of dollars are being spent to produce a substitute in high school and junior college trade programs. The tendency of both management and labor to bypass responsibility for education through on-the-job training is dramatically illustrated by the California example: the largest state in the nation, with an average of 5,586,600 non-agricultural wage and salary workers in the labor force during 1964, issued a total of 4,371 apprenticeship certificates.[9] Further, confirmation of uninspired labor leadership's taking a chance on cutting off somebody else's nose rather than risking its members' faces is its apparent indifference to the National Alliance of Businessmen's program to reach the hard-core unemployed.

A good example of the way cultures tend to integrate their customs so that one supports another and the whole complex takes on a monolithic character, is to be found in the array of laws which make it difficult to arrange job experience for older adolescents. Employers holding government contracts can use minors in only limited ways; the goods which the labor of minors has helped to produce may not be shipped in interstate commerce. Both laws were intended to prevent exploitation of children and to promote school attendance, but they do not sufficiently appreciate the potential educational value of part-time job experience. Similarly, minimum wage laws, unemployment insurance, social security, and other highly commendable pieces of legislation ignore how they simultaneously discourage the opening of job opportunities for inexperienced young people. Management finds that the legal red tape and costs involved in hiring a minor frequently make employment of those under twenty-one impractical, even when jobs could be made available, and satisfactory applicants are clamoring at the door.

The school's exclusive responsibility for education in programs not directed toward preparing for college should end about the age of sixteen. Beyond that point, cooperation between local government, industry, business, and the technician-employing professions is essential for adequate job training and, incidentally, for the maximum efficiency of secondary schools as college preparatory institutions. There is no magic in the chronological age sixteen, of course; the person's degree of development as well as his talents and interests must be taken into consideration. But states generally permit the issuing of special work permits at about sixteen or seventeen; they authorize limited licenses to drive an automobile. The childhood privilege of fishing without a license ends then; apprenticeship indentures may be entered into; life insurance companies accept policies; the army accepts enlistments, persons convicted of a felony may be sentenced to adult prisons; marriage licenses may be issued with the consent of parents, and the individual exhausts his unqualified legal claim on his parents for food and clothing (if parents fail to keep him adequately supplied after this age, he cannot later disown them for the negligence).

Even the most conscientious and optimistic educators cannot hope to sustain the myth that the school is a "house of magic," capable of overcoming the reluctance of young people to take a vicarious classroom approach to specifically oriented job training. As of March, 1964, fewer than one of three males and one of five females were employed in professional, technical, managerial, or proprietary positions for which secondary or higher education could be considered essential.[10] This does not imply that more education would be undesirable, but simply that it is trying the patience of juvenile Jobs to insist that they forego the experience that comes with jobs.

The really important, still inadequately exploited type of

254

education is continuing part-time study, whether it be called *adult education, life-long learning,* or the like. This offers the most practical approach to continually changing demands on our "space-age" civilization. Even by this means it is doubtful whether society can cope with accelerating change, deliberately promoted by excessive subsidy of research and development, under the apparent conviction that speed of change is the key to world leadership. But continuing part-time study is the best approach to education for changing job profiles as well as improvement of leisure along culturally acceptable lines. The strongest incentive for learning, whether one is in high school or wears a doctor's hood, is always a clearly seen and immediately interesting problem. Furthermore, nothing would stimulate general interest in school more than young people's belief that school is a pursuit which has adult status.

Certainly the need for something more than tinkering with the "educational establishment" is reflected by many students of the situation. Sympathetic discontent is summed up in the observation that, although American schools have achieved a wide range of objectives for a large portion of the population, there is a growing realization that no existing school system meets the educational needs of contemporary man.[11]

If job experience is to be brought into the educational program and made effective there, the jobs should be in business, industry, or as professional assistants—where the young person feels that he, or she, has a toehold on a ladder reaching some realistic future goal—in public enterprises, community, state, or national, which, if they have not been attempted before, clearly need doing; and in private service, when the job has obvious importance to the employer and, hopefully, offers some satisfaction to the youthful employee.

Bantu boys in Africa took over the task of keeping goats out of gardens, digging drainage ditches, and cultivating unplanted fields, because these jobs had to be done, and they were ways of demonstrating readiness for membership in a status-conferring herding gang. Among the Ramkokamekra of South America, whose age-grading system has been described, boys working in age-grade groups built houses, cleared land, opened up roads and paths to new agricultural land, and even took over harvesting—normally a woman's work which they would individually not deign to touch—provided that death or sickness had created an emergency that had to be met, and the whole group participated in meeting it.

Those who doubt that American youth will respond to a challenging job which has meaning to the world as well as to itself, might find an object lesson in the success of the Peace Corps. The idea of traveling to the far corners of the world to help people who needed help, even for a pittance in the way of salary, was so attractive to young people that all connected with the enterprise were startled. The Corps was organized in 1962; by 1964 it had 10,000 volunteers at work, and by 1965 there were 15,000. Members were recruited by simply offering hard work at low pay, in a challenging program. Stimulated by this phenomenal success, a second program was organized for service within the United States. VISTA was not nearly so successful as the Peace Corps. One may guess that self-confidence, challenge, and a sense of accomplishment were all more difficult to find in prosaic cities at home than in the faraway, infinitely more backward communities which the Peace Corps singled out for aid.

Space does not permit further elaboration of the applications of anthropology to contemporary problems, but this book will have achieved its purpose if it has broadened understanding of *Homo sapiens* as a biological, evolutionary phenomenon and shown the importance of meeting demonstrable psychological as well as physical needs within the expanding pattern of culture. This is not easy, because the fall of a culture is the most probable outcome of its success. A well-adapted culture has a design which has been refined in a special direction; hence, the better adapted it is, the less adaptable it may be. Specialization makes it less capable of responding in alternate ways and less tolerant of change in the world.[12]

There is a further difficulty. That remarkable organ, the human brain, tends to explore whatever interests it, with no practical end in view. Society tends to accept the results of those explorations only as they seem to contribute to ends already established by the culture pattern. The common good is not always served by either endeavor. That common good is the interest which can justify itself as public on terms of equity that apply to all. At a certain level of human behavior, men ask for justifying reasons, and only a reason can be an answer to the questions they ask. In putting such questions and replying to them, men sometimes achieve an understanding that makes moral sense of their social relations.[13]

Trying for a better definition of the meaning of human endeavor, and particularly the endeavor of youthful humans, may lead contemporary Americans to include in their concept of the common good a little more of what a juvenile struggling out of the Stone Age would consider the common good. Rebelliousness appeals to today's young people because they cannot find their place in the world. Contemporary American culture may give them privileges, but it has no function for them to fill.[14] And those who see small reason for their own existence will be the readier to trouble that of others.

Reference Notes
Selected Bibliography
Index

REFERENCE NOTES

Foreword

1. See, for example, DAVID RIESMAN, *The Lonely Crowd* (New Haven: Yale University Press, 1950); ERICH FROMM, *Escape from Freedom* (New York: Rinehart and Company, 1941); GEOFFREY GORER, *The American People* (New York: W. W. Norton, 1964); J. F. GUBER and R. A. HARPER, *Problems of American Society* (New York: Holt, 1951); GUNNAR MYRDAL, *An American Dilemma* (New York: Harper & Row, 1962); KAREN HORNEY, *The Neurotic Personality of Our Time* (New York: W. W. Norton, 1937); JAMES A. TUFTS, *America's Social Morality* (New York: Holt, 1933).

Chapter 1. MAN IN PERSPECTIVE

1. WOLFGANG KÖHLER, *The Mentality of Apes,* translated by Ella Winter (New York: Harcourt, Brace and Company, Inc., 1925); JANE VAN LAWICK-GOODALL, "My Life Among Wild Chimpanzees," *National Geographic Magazine*, Vol. CXXIV, No. 2 (1963), 272–308; SHERWOOD L. WASHBURN and IRVEN B. DEVORE, "Social Behavior of Baboons and Early Man," in Sherwood L. Washburn (ed.), *Social Life of Early Man* (Viking Fund Publications in Anthropology, No. 31; New York: The Viking Fund, Inc., 1961).

2. WILSON M. KROGMAN, "The Scars of Human Evolution," in Noel Korn and H. R. Smith (eds.), *Human Evolution* (New York: Henry Holt & Company, Inc., 1959), p. 185.

3. ADOLPH H. SCHULTZ, "Some Factors Influencing the Social Life of Primates in General and of Early Man in Particular," in Sherwood L. Washburn (ed.), *Social Life of Early Man, op. cit.,* p. 81.

4. JAMES McCONNELL, "Conditioning of Flatworms" (paper read at International Symposium on Drugs and Human Behavior, April 28, 1962, University of California); "Cannibalism and Memory in Flatworms," *New Scientist,* Vol. 21, pp. 365–367, 1964.

5. FRANK R. BABICH *et al.,* "Transfer of a Response to Naïve Rats by Injection of Ribonucleic Acid Extracted from Trained Rats," *Science,* Vol. 149, pp. 656–657.

6. W. H. THORPE, *Learning and Instinct in Animals* (Cambridge, Mass.: Harvard University Press, 1956); GARDNER MURPHY, *Human Potentialities* (New York: Basic Books, Inc., 1959).

7. VAN LAWICK-GOODALL, *op. cit.*

8. KONRAD Z. LORENZ, *King Solomon's Ring* (New York: Thomas Y. Crowell Company, 1952).

9. MARTIN LINDAUER, *Communication among Social Bees* (Cambridge, Mass.: Harvard University Press, 1961); KONRAD VON FRISCH, *The Dancing Bees* (New York: Harcourt, Brace and Company, Inc., 1955).

10. WILHELM GOETSCH, *The Ants* (Ann Arbor, Mich.: University of Michigan Press, 1964).

11. THEODOSIUS DOBZHANSKY, *Mankind Evolving* (New Haven, Conn.: Yale University Press, 1962); NIKOLAAS TINBERGEN, *Social Behavior in Animals* (New York: John Wiley & Sons, Inc., 1953).

12. SAMUEL JACKSON HOLMES, *The Evolution of Animal Intelligence* (New York: Henry Holt & Company, Inc., 1923), p. 257.

13. FRANK A. BEACH, "Current Concepts of Play in Animals," *The American Naturalist,* Vol. LXXIX, No. 11–12 (1945), pp. 523–41.

14. JAN HUIZINGA, *Homo Ludens: A Study of the Play Element in Culture* (London: Routledge & Kegan Paul, Ltd., 1949).

15. ROGER CAILLOIS, *Man, Play, and Games,* translated by Meyer Barash (New York: The Free Press of Glencoe, 1961).

16. F. FRASER DARLING, *A Herd of Red Deer* (London: Oxford University Press, 1956).

17. JOHN PAUL SCOTT, *Aggression* (Chicago: University of Chicago Press, 1958).

18. ANTHONY F. C. WALLACE, *Culture and Personality* (New York: Random House, Inc., 1961).

Chapter 2. CULTURE IN PERSPECTIVE

1. FRANZ WEIDENREICH, *Anthropological Papers of Franz Weidenreich: A Memorial Volume*, S. L. Washburn and Davida Wolffson, eds. (Viking Fund Publications in Anthropology; New York: The Viking Fund, Inc., 1949), pp. 194–204.

2. B. DANKS, "New Britain and Its People," *Proceedings of the Australian Association for the Advancement of Science* (1892); E. TORDAY and T. A. JOYCE, "Notes on the Ethnography of the Ba-Huana," *Journal of the Royal Anthropological Institute*, Vol. xxxv (1905).

3. J. L. KAVANAU, "Compulsory Regime and Control of Environment," *Behavior* (Spring, 1963).

4. HARRY F. HARLOW *et al.*, "Learning Motivated by a Manipulative Drive," *Journal of Experimental Psychology*, Vol. 40, No. 2, 228–43; WOLFGANG KÖHLER, *The Mentality of Apes*, translated by Ella Winter (New York: Harcourt, Brace and Company, Inc., 1925), p. 324.

5. MARCELLIN BOULE and HENRY V. VALLOIS, *Fossil Men* (London: Thames and Hudson, 1957).

6. ALBERTO C. BLANC, "Some Evidence for the Ideologies of Early Man," in Sherwood L. Washburn (ed.), *Social Life of Early Man* (Viking Fund Publications in Anthropology, No. 31; New York: The Viking Fund, Inc., 1961), pp. 124–29.

7. R. P. BERGOUNIOUX, *La Préhistorie et Ses Problèmes* (Paris: Librairies Arthème Fayard, 1958), p. 244.

8. BOHUSLAV KLÍMA, "The First Ground-plan of an Upper Paleolithic Loess Settlement in Middle Europe and Its Meaning," in R. J. Braidwood and G. R. Willey (eds.), *Courses Toward Urban Life* (Viking Fund Publications in Anthropology, No. 32; New York: The Viking Fund, Inc., 1962), pp. 201–203.

9. BALDWIN SPENCER and F. J. GILLEN, *The Arunta: A Study of a Stone Age People* (2 vols., London: Macmillan and Company, Ltd., 1927).

10. ALFRED MÉTRAUX, "Ethnography of the Chaco," in Julian H. Steward (ed.), *Handbook of South American Indians* (7 vols.; Bureau of American Ethnology *Bulletin* 143), Vol. I (1950), p. 250.

11. RALPH S. SOLECKI, "Prehistory in Shanidar Valley, Northern Iraq," in Joseph R. Caldwell (ed.), *New Roads to Yesterday* (New York: Basic Books, Inc., 1966), p. 98.

12. R. J. BRAIDWOOD and BRUCE HOWE, "Southwestern Asia beyond the

Lands of the Mediterranean Littoral," in R. J. Braidwood and G. R. Willey (eds.), *Courses Toward Urban Life, op. cit.,* p. 137; Franz Schwanitz, *The Origin of Cultivated Plants* (Cambridge, Mass.: Harvard University Press, 1966), p. 121.

Chapter 3. THE SEXUAL DIALECTIC

1. George P. Murdock, "The Common Denominator of Culture," in Ralph Linton (ed.), *Science of Man in the World Crisis* (New York: Columbia University Press, 1945), pp. 123–25.
2. Ludwik Krzywicki, *Primitive Society and Its Vital Statistics* (Warsaw: University of Warsaw Press, 1934), p. 159; Aleš Hrdlička, *Physiological and Medical Observations among the Indians of the Southwestern United States and Northern Mexico,* Bureau of American Ethnology, *Bulletin* No. 34, 1908), pp. 163–65.
3. Herbert Aptekar, *Anjea: Infanticide, Abortion and Contraception in Savage Society* (New York: W. Godwin, Inc., 1931), p. 40.
4. Clyde Kluckhohn, "Variations in the Human Family," in Guy Emerson (ed.), *The Family in a Democratic Society* (New York: Columbia University Press, 1949).
5. Wilder Penfield and Lamar Roberts, *Speech and Brain Mechanisms* (Princeton, N.J.: Princeton University Press, 1959).
6. Margaret Mead, *Sex and Temperament in Three Primitive Societies* (New York: Mentor Books, 1952).
7. Marian Kreiselman Slater, "Ecological Factors in the Origin of Incest," *American Anthropologist,* Vol. LXI, No. 6, pp. 1042–59.
8. Brenda Z. Seligman, "Incest and Exogamy: A Restatement," *American Anthropologist,* Vol. LII, No. 3, pp. 305–316.
9. Sherwood L. Washburn and B. Irven DeVore, "Social Behavior of Baboons and Early Man," in Sherwood L. Washburn (ed.), *Social Life of Early Man* (Viking Fund Publications in Anthropology, No. 31; New York: The Viking Fund, Inc., 1961).
10. Bruno Bettelheim, *Symbolic Wounds* (Glencoe, Ill.: The Free Press, 1954).

Chapter 4. THE GUINEA-PIG GENERATION

1. Alice Balint, *The Early Years of Life* (New York: Basic Books, Inc., 1954), pp. 131–32.
2. George A. Pettitt, *Primitive Education in North America,* University of California Publications in American Archaeology and Ethnology, Vol. 43, No. 1, 1946.

3. JAMES A. TEIT, *The Thompson Indians of British Columbia,* American Museum of Natural History, *Memoir* 2, Part IV, 1900.
4. CURT NIMUENDAJU, *The Eastern Timbera,* University of California Publications in American Archaeology and Ethnology, Vol. 41, 1946.
5. SISTER M. INEZ HILGER, *Arapaho Child Life and Its Cultural Background,* Bureau of American Ethnology *Bulletin* 148, 1952.
6. O. F. RAUM, "Some Aspects of Indigenous Education Among the Chaga," *Journal of the Royal Anthropological Institute of Great Britain and Ireland,* Vol. LXVIII (1938), pp. 209–221.
7. HENRI A. JUNOD, *The Life of a South African Tribe* (2 vols.; The Macmillan Co., 1913), Vol. I, pp. 61 ff.
8. MARGARET READ, *Children of Their Fathers: Growing Up Among the Ngoni of Nyasaland* (London: Methuen & Co., Ltd., 1959), pp. 93, 130.
9. MONICA WILSON, *Good Company: A Study of Nyakusa Age-Villages* (Oxford: International African Institute, 1951).
10. JOHN J. HONIGMAN, *Culture and Personality* (New York: Harper and Brothers, 1954), p. 302.
11. EDWARD SAPIR, "Culture, Genuine and Spurious," *American Journal of Sociology,* Vol. XXIX (1924), pp. 401–429.
12. MAX GLUCKMAN, "The Logic of African Science and Witchcraft," *Rhodes-Livingstone Institute Journal,* June, 1944, pp. 61–71.
13. STUART PIGGOTT, *The Prehistoric People of Scotland* (London: Routledge & Kegan Paul, Ltd., 1962).
14. J. C. CAROTHERS, *The African Mind in Health and Disease,* World Health Organization *Monograph* No. 17, 1953.
15. PAUL A. WITTY and HARVEY C. LEHMAN, "Racial Differences: The Dogma of Superiority," *Journal of Social Psychology,* Vol. I, No. 3 (1953), p. 405.
16. HAROLD E. JONES and MARY C. JONES, *Growth and Behavior in Adolescence* (Berkeley, Calif.: University of California Press, 1957).
17. J. JASTAK, "A Rigorous Criterion of Feeblemindedness," *Journal of Abnormal and Social Psychology,* Vol. XLIV (1949), pp. 367–68.

Chapter 5. *THE HURDLES OF CIVILIZATION*

1. MARGARET RIBBLE, *Personality and Behavioral Disorders* (New York: Ronald Press, 1944).
2. RENÉ SPITZ, "The Influence of the Mother-Child Relationship and Its Disturbance," in Kenneth Soddy (ed.), *Mental Health and Infant*

Development (2 vols. New York: Basic Books, Inc., 1956), Vol. 1, pp. 105 ff.

3. ANNA FREUD, "Special Experiences of Young Children," in Kenneth Soddy (ed.), *Mental Health and Infant Development, op. cit.,* pp. 143–44; W. GOLDFARB, "Emotional and Intellectual Consequences of Psychologic Deprivation in Infancy," in P. H. Hoch and J. Zubin (eds.), *Psychopathology of Childhood* (New York: G. Z. Stratton, 1955), pp. 105–119.

4. HARRY F. HARLOW, "The Basic Social Capacity of Primates," in J. N. Spuhler (ed.), *The Evolution of Man's Capacity for Culture* (Detroit: Wayne University Press, 1959).

5. HOWARD S. LIDDELL, "The Biology of Individual and Group Prejudice," *Lectures on Current Issues in Medicine,* New York Academy of Medicine, March 1, 1961, p. 26.

6. ERIK H. ERIKSON, *Childhood and Society* (New York: W. W. Norton & Company, Inc., 1950), pp. 219 ff.

7. ERICH FROMM, *Escape from Freedom* (New York: Rinehart and Co., 1941), p. 19.

8. LEONARD W. DOOB, *Social Psychology* (New York: Henry Holt and Company, Inc., 1952), pp. 235, 256.

9. JEAN PIAGET, *The Moral Judgment of the Child* (Glencoe, Ill.: The Free Press, 1954), pp. 115 ff.

10. WILLIAM WELLS NEWELL, *Games and Songs of American Children* (New York: Harper and Brothers, 1884), Introduction; p. 1.

11. F. S. KRAUSS, "Geheime Sprachweisen," *Am Ur-Quell, Monatsschrift für Völkskunde,* Heft I, Band II, 1891.

12. OSCAR CHRISMAN, "Secret Language of Children," *Science,* Dec. 1, 1893, 303–305; *Century Magazine,* Vol. LVI, No. 1 (1898), 54–58.

13. BRUNO BETTELHEIM, *Symbolic Wounds* (Glencoe, Ill.: The Free Press, 1954).

14. RICHARD DEWEY and W. J. HUMBER, *The Development of Human Behavior* (New York: The Macmillan Company, 1961), pp. 324–25.

15. HOMER G. BARNETT, "Being a Palauan," in George and Louise Spindler (eds.), *Case Studies in Cultural Anthropology* (New York: Henry Holt & Company, Inc., 1960).

16. EDWARD G. NORBECK, "Age-Grading in Japan," *American Anthropologist,* Vol. 55, No. 3 (August, 1953), pp. 373–84.

17. TSUNG-YI LIN, "Two Types of Delinquent Youth in Chinese Society," in Mervin K. Opler (ed.), *Culture and Mental Health* (New York: The Macmillan Company, 1959).

18. ELIZABETH ANNE WEBER, *The Duk-Duks* (Chicago: University of Chicago Press, 1929).

19. ALICE BALINT, *The Early Years of Life* (New York: Basic Books, Inc., 1954), pp. 131–232.

20. JAMES S. COLEMAN, "Social Climates in High Schools," United States Department of Health, Education and Welfare, *Cooperative Research Monograph* No. 4, 1961, pp. 1, 7.

21. ERNEST A. SMITH, *American Youth Culture: Group Life in Teen-age Society* (New York: The Free Press of Glencoe, 1962), p. 214.

22. CHARLES SINGER *et al.*, *A History of Technology*, Vol. IV, *The Industrial Revolution* (London: Oxford University Press, 1954–58).

Chapter 6. *TOIL AND PLEASURE*

1. SIR BALDWIN SPENCER and F. J. GILLEN, *The Arunta: A Study of a Stone Age People* (2 vols., London: Macmillan & Company, Ltd., 1927).

2. GEORGES FRIEDMANN, *The Anatomy of Work: Labor, Leisure and the Implications of Automation*, translated by Wyatt Rawson (New York: The Free Press of Glencoe, 1961).

3. FREDERICK WINSLOW TAYLOR, *The Principles of Scientific Management* (1911).

4. W. WILLARD WIRTZ, "Education, Answer to Unemployment," *The Rotarian*, Vol. 105, No. 6, 1963.

5. JEANNETTE H. SOFOKIDES and EUGENIA SULLIVAN, "A New Look at School Dropouts," *Indicators* (U.S. Department of Education, April, 1964).

6. GRANT VENN, *Man, Education and Work* (Washington, D.C.: American Council on Education, 1964), p. 12.

7. ROBERT BLAUNER, "Work Satisfaction and Industrial Trends in Modern Society," in Walter Galenson and Seymour Lipset (eds.), *Labor and Trade Unionism* (New York: John Wiley & Sons, Inc., 1960), pp. 339–60, and HAROLD L. WILENSKI, "Varieties of Work Experience," in Henry Borow (ed.), *Man in a World at Work* (Boston: Houghton Mifflin Co., 1964), pp. 125–154.

8. WOODBURN HERON, "The Pathology of Boredom," *Scientific American*, Vol. CXCVI (January, 1957), 52–56.

9. SOLOMON FABRICANT, "Productivity and Economic Growth," in Eli Ginzberg (ed.), *Technology and Social Change* (New York: Columbia University Press, 1964), pp. 110–15, 125, 129.

10. JOHN J. HONIGMAN, "As the Twig Is Bent," in J. J. Honigman (ed.), *Culture and Personality* (New York: Harper and Brothers, 1954).

11. FRIEDMANN, *op. cit.*, p. 142.

12. *Ibid.*, pp. 104, 105.

13. ERIC LARRABEE and ROLF MEYERSOHN (eds.), *Mass Leisure* (Glencoe, Ill.: The Free Press, 1958), pp. 39, 119, 145–53.

14. HARVEY SWADOS, "Less Work—Less Leisure," *The Nation*, Vol. 186, No. 8 (Feb. 22, 1958), 153–58.

15. R. CLYDE WHITE, "Social Class Differences in the Use of Leisure," *American Journal of Sociology*, Vol. 61, No. 2 (September, 1955), 145–50.

16. ALFRED C. CLARKE, "Leisure and Occupational Prestige," *American Sociological Review*, Vol. 21, No. 3 (June, 1956), 301–307.

17. CLIVE BELL, *Civilization* (London: Chatto & Windus, 1928).

18. BERNARD ROSENBERG and DAVID MANNING WHITE, *Mass Culture* (Glencoe, Ill.: The Free Press, 1957).

19. WILLIAM D. CAREY, Address, Seventeenth National Conference on Administration of Research, Estes Park, Colorado, September 11, 1963.

20. Committee on Science in the Promotion of Human Welfare, "The Integrity of Science," *American Scientist*, Vol. 53, No. 2 (1965), 174–98.

21. CLARK KERR, FREDERICK A. HARBISON, JOHN T. DUNLOP, and CHARLES A. MYERS, "Industrialism and Industrial Man," *International Labour Review*, Vol. LXXXII, No. 3 (1960), 1–15.

Chapter 7. DROPPING OUT

1. HOWARD S. LIDDELL, "The Biology of Individual and Group Prejudice," New York Academy of Medicine, *Lectures on Current Issues in Medicine*, March 1, 1961, p. 5.

2. LIDDELL, "Contributions of Conditioning in the Sheep and Goat to an Understanding of Stress, Anxiety, and Illness," *Lectures in Experimental Psychiatry* (Pittsburgh, Pa.: University of Pittsburgh Press, 1961), p. 233.

3. W. HORSLEY GANTT, *Experimental Basis for Neurotic Behavior* (New York: Paul B. Hoeber, 1944).

4. HORATIO M. POLLOCK and BENJAMIN MALZBERG, "Institutional Population in the U.S.," *Annals of the American Academy of Political and Social Science*, Vol. 188 (November, 1936), p. 149.

5. Louis I. Dublin, *Suicide, A Sociological and Statistical Study* (New York: The Ronald Press, Inc., 1963).

6. Jesse R. Pitts, Introduction, Part Three, Vol. II, Talcott Parsons *et al* (eds.), *Theories of Society* (Glencoe, Ill.: The Free Press, 1961).

7. Melford E. Spiro, "Ghosts, Ifalik and Teleological Functionalism," *American Anthropologist,* Vol. LIV, No. 4 (October–December, 1952), pp. 497–503.

8. Anthony F. C. Wallace, *Culture and Personality* (New York: Random House, Inc., 1961), p. 190.

9. Philip L. Newman, " 'Wild Man' Behavior in a New Guinea Highlands Community," *American Anthropologist,* Vol. LXVI, No. 1 (February, 1964), pp. 1–19.

10. B. Danks, "New Britain and Its People," *Proceedings of the Australian Association for the Advancement of Science,* Fourth Meeting, 1892, p. 618; E. Torday and T. A. Joyce, "Notes on the Ethnography of the Ba-Huana," *Journal of the Royal Anthropological Institute,* Vol. XXXV (1905); Julian H. Steward (ed.), *Handbook of South American Indians* (7 vols.; Bureau of American Ethnology *Bulletin* 143), Vol. 6 (1946–52).

11. Morton I. Teicher, "Windigo Psychosis," *Proceedings of the 1960 Spring Meeting, American Ethnological Society,* 1960.

12. A. H. Maslow, *Motivation and Personality* (New York: Harper and Brothers, 1954), p. 39.

13. Joseph W. Eaton, with Robert J. Weil, *Culture and Mental Disorders* (Glencoe, Ill.: The Free Press, 1955).

14. John Grayson, *Nerves, Brain and Man* (London: Phoenix House, Ltd., 1961), p. 185.

15. Wallace, *op. cit.*, p. 184.

16. Eaton, *op. cit.*

17. Seymour B. Sarason and Thomas Gladwin, "Psychological and Cultural Problems in Mental Subnormality: A Review of Research," *Genetic Psychology Monographs,* Vol. 58 (February, 1958), p. 151.

18. Marvin K. Opler (ed.), *Culture and Mental Health* (New York: The Macmillan Company, Inc., 1959); Ralph Linton, *Culture and Mental Disorders* (Springfield, Ill.: Charles C Thomas, 1956).

19. Harry Stackpole Sullivan, *Schizophrenia as a Human Process* (New York: W. W. Norton & Co., Inc., 1962), p. 252.

20. G. M. Carstairs, "The Social Limits of Eccentricity: An English Study," in Opler, *op. cit.*

21. William Caudill, "Observations on the Cultural Context of Japanese Psychiatry," in Opler, *op. cit.*

22. ALEXANDER H. LEIGHTON, *My Name Is Legion* (New York: Basic Books, Inc., 1959), pp. 146, 148; LEIGHTON *et al.*, *Psychiatric Disorder among the Yoruba* (Ithaca, N.Y.: Cornell University Press, 1963), pp. 126, 273, 279.

23. WILLIAM N. DEMBER, "The New Look in Motivation," *American Scientist,* Vol. 53, No. 4 (1965), pp. 409–427.

24. ÉMILE DURKHEIM, *Le Suicide,* translated by J. A. Spaulding and G. Simpson (Glencoe, Ill.: The Free Press of Glencoe, 1951).

25. BEULAH C. BOSSELMAN, *Self-Destruction: A Study of the Suicidal Impulse* (Springfield, Ill.: Charles C Thomas, 1958), p. 69.

26. DUBLIN, *op. cit.,* pp. 61–67.

27. KARL MENNINGER, *The Human Mind* (New York: Alfred A. Knopf, Inc., 1940), p. 111.

28. WESTON LaBARRE, *The Human Animal* (Chicago: University of Chicago Press, 1954), pp. 246–47.

29. PETER L. BROADHURST, *The Science of Animal Behavior* (Baltimore, Md.: Penguin Books, 1963).

30. K. W. KAPP, *Toward a Science of Man in Society* (The Hague: Martinus Nijhoff, 1961), pp. 177–78.

Chapter 8. ROUTES TO REBELLION

1. ERIK H. ERIKSON, *Childhood and Society* (New York: W. W. Norton & Company, Inc., 1958), p. 209.

2. WILLIAM C. KVARACEUS, *Juvenile Delinquency,* National Education Association, Research Series, *Bulletin* No. 15 [n.d.].

3. A. H. MASLOW, *Motivation and Personality* (New York: Harper and Brothers, 1954), p. 338.

4. FRANK TANNENBAUM, *Crime and the Community* (New York: Columbia University Press, 1938), p. 17.

5. RICHARD A. CLOWARD and LLOYD E. OHLING, *Delinquency and Opportunity* (Glencoe, Ill.: The Free Press, 1960).

6. GRESHAM M. SYKES, *The Society of Captives: A Study of a Maximum Security Prison* (Princeton, N.J.: Princeton University Press, 1958), p. xvi.

7. R. E. THOMAS, "The Relation of Child Labor to Juvenile Delinquency" (unpublished master's thesis, Department of Economics, University of California, 1935).

8. SHELDON GLUECK and ELEANOR T. GLUECK, *Unraveling Juvenile Delinquency* (New York: Commonwealth Fund, Inc., 1950), p. 281.

9. CLIFFORD SHAW and HENRY McKAY, "Social Factors in Juvenile Delinquency," Report of the *National Commission on Law Observance and Enforcement* (Publication 13, Vol. II, Washington, D.C., 1931).

10. WILLIAM McCORD and JOAN McCORD, with IRVING K. ZOLA, *Origins of Crime* (New York: Columbia University Press, 1959).

11. FREDERIC M. THRASHER, *The Gang* (2nd rev. ed.; Chicago: University of Chicago Press, 1927), p. 412.

12. ROBERT C. ANGELL, *Free Society and Moral Crisis* (Ann Arbor, Mich.: University of Michigan Press, 1958), p. 113.

13. HARRY S. SULLIVAN, in Helen S. Perry (ed.), *Schizophrenia as a Human Process* (New York: William Alanson White Psychiatric Foundation, 1962), p. 248.

14. ERIK H. ERIKSON, *op. cit.*, pp. 219 ff.

15. GERHART PIERS and MILTON B. SINGER, "Shame and Guilt" (American Lectures in Psychiatry, Monograph No. 171; Springfield, Ill.: Charles C Thomas, 1953), p. 16.

16. HELEN M. LYND, *On Shame and the Search for Identity* (New York: Harcourt, Brace & Company, Inc., 1958), p. 34.

17. PIERS and SINGER, *op. cit.*, p. 5.

18. DANIEL BELL, "Crime as an American Way of Life" (Bobbs-Merrill "Reprint Series in the Social Sciences," No. 12, 1953); *End of Ideology* (Glencoe, Ill.: The Free Press, 1959).

19. MORRIS ROSENBERG, *Society and the Adolescent Self-Image* (Princeton, N.J.: Princeton University Press, 1965), p. 144.

20. WALTER B. MILLER, "Lower-Class Culture as a Generating Milieu of Gang Delinquency," *Journal of Social Issues,* Vol. XIV (1958), 5–19.

Chapter 9. EDUCATION AS A CULTURAL COMPULSION

1. S. H. HOOKE, "Recording and Writing," in Charles Singer *et al.* (eds.), *A History of Technology,* 5 vols. (New York: Oxford University Press, 1954).

2. SIR LEONARD WOOLLEY, *The Beginnings of Civilization* (A History of Mankind; New York: New American Library, and Harper & Row, Inc., 1965), pp. 393–96.

3. KENNETH J. FREEMAN, *The Schools of Hellas* (3d ed.; London: Macmillan and Company, Ltd., 1922), pp. 50–52.

4. URBAN TIGER HOLMES, *Daily Living in the Twelfth Century* (Madison, Wis.: University of Wisconsin Press, 1952), p. 36.

5. FOREST C. ENSIGN, *Compulsory School Attendance and Child Labor* (Iowa City, Iowa: The Athens Press, 1921).

6. SAMUEL CHESTER PARKER, *A Textbook in the History of Elementary Education* (New York: Ginn and Company, 1912), p. 48.

7. EDGAR W. KNIGHT and CLIFTON L. HALL, *Readings in American Educational History* (New York: Appleton-Century-Crofts, Inc., 1951).

8. *Ibid.,* pp. 146–48.

9. RAYMOND G. FULLER, *Child Labor and the Constitution* (New York: Thomas Y. Crowell Company, 1923).

10. LUCY MANNING, "Why Child Labor Laws?" U.S. Department of Labor, Division of Labor Standards, *Child Labor Series,* No. 1.

11. J. A. LIVINGSTON, "What Price a College Degree?" *American Alumni Council News,* April, 1960.

12. National Science Foundation, *Scientific and Technical Manpower Resources* (Washington, D.C.: 1964), p. 112.

13. SOLOMON O. LICHTER *et al., The Drop-outs* (New York: The Free Press of Glencoe, 1962).

14. R. A. GORDON, "Has Structural Unemployment Worsened?" *Industrial Relations,* Vol. 3, No. 3 (May, 1964).

15. Committee for Economic Development, *Raising Low Incomes Through Improved Education,* Research and Policy Committee, September, 1965.

16. R. A. GORDON, "Twenty Years of Economic and Industrial Change," *Proceedings, Conference on Space, Science and Urban Life* (Washington, D.C.: National Aeronautics and Space Administration, 1963).

17. J. H. SOFOKIDES and EUGENIA SULLIVAN, "A New Look at School Drop-outs," U.S. Department of Health, Education and Welfare, *Indicators,* April, 1964.

18. R. J. HAVIGHURST, "Research on the School Work-Study Program in the Prevention of Juvenile Delinquency," in W. R. Carriker, *Role of the School in Prevention of Juvenile Delinquency* (U.S. Office of Education, Cooperative Research Monograph No. 10, 1963), p. 31.

19. New York City Board of Education, "600 Schools Yesterday, Today, and Tomorrow," *Study,* 1964–65.

20. SEYMOUR B. SARASON and THOMAS GLADWIN, "Psychological and Cultural Problems in Mental Subnormality: A Review of Research," *Genetic Psychological Monographs,* Vol. 57 (1958), p. 170 ff.

21. W. LLOYD WARNER, ROBERT J. HAVIGHURST, and MARTIN LOEB, *Who Shall Be Educated?* (New York: Harper and Brothers, 1944).

22. SEYMOUR M. LIPSET and REINHARD BENDIX, *Social Mobility in Industrial Society* (Berkeley, Calif.: University of California Press, 1960).

23. ARTHUR M. ROSS, "Toward Better Utilization of Scientific and Engineering Talent," National Academy of Sciences *Publication* 1191, 1964.

24. LEWIS CARROLL, *Through the Looking Glass* (New York: Random House, Inc., 1946), p. 32.

Chapter 10. THE FUTURE OF YOUTH

1. RALPH LINTON (ed.), *Acculturation in Seven American Indian Tribes* (New York: Appleton-Century Company, 1940).

2. MARVIN OPLER, "The Southern Ute of Colorado," in Linton, *op. cit.*

3. ARNOLD J. TOYNBEE, *A Study of History*, abridged by D. C. Somervell (New York: Oxford University Press, 1947), p. 276.

4. RENÉ DUBOS, *Man Adapting* (New Haven, Conn.: Yale University Press, 1965), p. 28.

5. Office of Economic Opportunity, *Community Action Program Guide* (Washington, D.C.: October, 1965, Vol. 1), p. 7.

6. National Commission on Technology, Automation, and Economic Progress, "Technology and the American Economy" (Mimeographed Report to the President and the Congress of the United States, Jan. 29, 1966), p. 32.

7. *Ibid.*, p. 76.

8. U.S. Bureau of the Census, *Statistical Abstract of the United States* (Washington, D.C., 1964), Tables 149–150, p. 230.

9. *Ibid.*

10. *Ibid.*, Tables 206–307, p. 228.

11. FRANCIS S. CHASE and HAROLD A. ANDERSON (eds.), *The High School in a New Era* (Chicago: University of Chicago Press, 1963), p. viii.

12. MARSHALL D. SAHLINS, "Culture and Environment," in Sol Tax (ed.), *Horizons of Anthropology* (Chicago: Aldine Publishing Co., 1964), p. 138.

13. ARTHUR E. MURPHY, "The Common Good" in Sidney Hook (ed.), *American Philosophies at Work* (New York: Criterion Books, 1956), pp. 435–36, 438–39.

14. "Guidelines for Dealing with Youth," in *Youth Report* (New York: Grafton Publications, Inc., June, 1968).

SELECTED BIBLIOGRAPHY

EVIDENCE RELATING TO EARLY MAN

BROOM, ROBERT, and SCHEPERS, G. W. H. *The South African Fossil Ape Man* ("Transvaal Museum Memoir 2"). Pretoria, 1949.

CLARK, W. E. LeGros. *The Antecedents of Man*. Chicago: Quadrangle Books, 1960.

———. *History of the Primates: An Introduction to the Study of Fossil Man*. Chicago: University of Chicago Press, 1961.

DART, R. A., and CRAIG, DENNIS. *Adventures with the Missing Link*. New York: Harper and Brothers, 1959.

HOWELLS, WILLIAM. *Mankind in the Making: The Story of Human Evolution*. Garden City, N.Y.: Doubleday & Company, Inc., 1959.

KORN, NOEL, and SMITH, H. R. (eds.). *Human Evolution*. New York: Henry Holt & Company, Inc., 1959.

KRAUS, BERTRAM S. *The Basis of Human Evolution*. New York: Harper & Row, 1964.

LEAKEY, L. S. B. *Adam's Ancestors: The Evolution of Man and His Culture*. New York: Harper & Row, 1960.

MOORE, RUTH. *Man, Time, and Fossils*. New York: Alfred A. Knopf, Inc., 1953.

VON KOENIGSWALD, G. H. R. *The Evolution of Man*. Ann Arbor, Mich.: University of Michigan Press, 1962.

WASHBURN, S. L., ed. *Classification and Human Evolution* ("Viking Fund Publications in Anthropology, No. 37"). New York: The Viking Fund, Inc., 1963.

WEIDENREICH, FRANZ. *Anthropological Papers of Franz Weidenreich, A Memorial Volume.* New York: The Viking Fund, Inc., 1949.

EVOLUTION OF MAN AS A CULTURE-PROMOTING PRIMATE

BRODRICK, ALAN H. *Man and His Ancestry.* London: Hutchinson & Co., Ltd., 1960.

DOBZHANSKY, THEODOSIUS. *Mankind Evolving* ("Silliman Lectures," XXXVIII). New Haven, Conn.: Yale University Press, 1962.

HAWKES, JACQUETTA. *History of Mankind.* Vol. 1, Part 1. *Prehistory.* New York: New American Library, Inc., and United Nations Educational, Scientific and Cultural Organization, 1965.

LABARRE, WESTON. *The Human Animal.* Chicago: University of Chicago Press, 1954.

ROE, ANNE, and SIMPSON, GEORGE (eds.). *Behavior and Evolution.* New Haven, Conn.: Yale University Press, 1958.

SPUHLER, J. N. (ed.). *The Evolution of Man's Capacity for Culture.* Detroit, Mich.: Wayne State University Press, 1959.

WASHBURN, SHERWOOD L. (ed.). *Social Life of Early Man* ("Viking Fund Publications in Anthropology," No. 31). New York: The Viking Fund, Inc., 1961.

THE PROTO-CULTURAL BEHAVIOR
OF SUBHUMAN ANIMALS

ALPERS, ANTONY. *Dolphins: The Myth and the Mammal.* Boston: Houghton Mifflin Company, 1960.

BRELAND, KELLER, and BRELAND, MARIAN. *Animal Behavior.* New York: The Macmillan Company, 1966.

BROADHURST, PETER L. *The Science of Animal Behavior.* Baltimore, Md.: Penguin Books, 1963.

BURTON, M. *Animal Courtship.* New York: Frederick A. Praeger, 1953.

CARPENTER, C. R. *Naturalistic Behavior of Non-human Primates.* University Park, Pa.: Pennsylvania State University Press, 1964.

DARLING, F. F. *A Herd of Red Deer.* London: Oxford University Press, 1956.

276

DeVore, Irven. *Primate Behavior: Field Studies of Monkeys and Apes.* New York: Holt, Rinehart, and Winston, 1964.

Etkin, William. *Social Behavior from Fish to Man.* Chicago: University of Chicago Press, 1967.

Goetsch, Wilhelm. *The Ants.* Ann Arbor, Mich.: University of Michigan Press, 1964.

Hayes, Catherine. *The Ape in Our House.* New York: Harper and Brothers, 1951.

Heinroth, Oskar, and Heinroth, Katharina. *The Birds.* Ann Arbor, Mich.: University of Michigan Press, 1958.

Kellogg, W. N., and Kellogg, L. A. *The Ape and the Child.* New York: McGraw-Hill Book Company, Inc., 1933.

Köhler, Wolfgang. *The Mentality of Apes.* New York: Harcourt, Brace & Company, Inc., 1925.

Lilly, John C. *Man and Dolphin.* Garden City, N.Y.: Doubleday & Company, Inc., 1961.

Lindauer, M. *Communication among Social Bees.* Cambridge, Mass.: Harvard University Press, 1961.

Lorenz, K. Z. *King Solomon's Ring.* New York: Thomas Y. Crowell Company, 1952.

Schaller, George B. *The Mountain Gorilla.* Chicago: University of Chicago Press, 1963.

Schrier, A. M., and Harlow, H. F. (eds.). *Behavior of Non-human Primates.* New York: The Academic Press, 1964.

Scott, John P. *Animal Behavior.* Chicago: University of Chicago Press, 1958.

Thorpe, W. H. *Learning and Instinct in Animals.* Cambridge, Mass.: Harvard University Press, 1958.

Tinbergen, Nikolaas. *Social Behavior in Animals.* New York: John Wiley & Sons, Inc., 1953.

Van Lawick-Goodall, Baroness Jane. *My Friends the Wild Chimpanzees.* Washington, D.C.: National Geographic Society Special Publications Division, 1967.

Von Frisch, K. *The Dancing Bees.* New York: Harper and Brothers, 1944.

Yerkes, Robert M., and Yerkes, Ada W. *The Great Apes: A Study of Anthropoid Life.* New Haven, Conn.: Yale University Press, 1929.

Zuckerman, S. *The Social Life of Monkeys and Apes.* London: Kegan Paul, Trench, Trubner & Co., Ltd., 1932.

PRIMITIVE CULTURE

DRIVER, HAROLD E. *Indians of North America*. Chicago: University of Chicago Press, 1961.

HERSKOVITS, MELVILLE J. *Dahomey: An Ancient West African Kingdom*. 2 vols. New York: Augustin, 1938.

MEAD, MARGARET. *Growing Up in New Guinea: A Comparative Study of Primitive Education*. New York: New American Library, 1950.

MURDOCK, GEORGE P. *Our Primitive Contemporaries*. New York: The Macmillan Company, 1934.

PETTITT, GEORGE A. *Primitive Education in North America* ("Publications in American Archaeology and Ethnology," Vol. 43, No. 1). Berkeley, Calif.: University of California Press, 1943.

SPENCER, SIR BALDWIN, and GILLEN, F. J. *The Arunta: A Study of a Stone Age People*. 2 vols. London: The Macmillan Company, 1927.

WILSON, MONICA. *Good Company: A Study of Nyakusa Age-Villages*. London: Oxford University Press, for the International African Institute, 1951.

FACTORS IN THE DEVELOPMENT OF CIVILIZATION

BRAIDWOOD, R. J., and WILLEY, GORDON (eds.). *Courses toward Urban Life* ("Viking Fund Publications in Anthropology," No. 32). New York: The Viking Fund, Inc., 1962.

CALDWELL, J. R. *New Roads to Yesterday*. New York: Basic Books, Inc., 1966.

HONIGMAN, JOHN J. *Culture and Personality*. New York: Harper and Brothers, 1954.

LINTON, RALPH (ed.). *The Science of Man in the World Crisis*. New York: Columbia University Press, 1945.

———. *The Cultural Background of Personality*. New York: Appleton-Century-Crofts, Inc., 1945.

LOWIE, ROBERT H. *Are We Civilized?* New York: Harcourt, Brace and Company, Inc., 1929.

PIERS, GERHART, and SINGER, MILTON. *Shame and Guilt* ("American Lectures in Psychiatry," Monograph No. 171). Springfield, Ill.: Charles C Thomas, 1953.

MASLOW, A. H. *Motivation and Personality: A General Theory of Human Motivation*. New York: Harper and Brothers, 1954.

278

MOURANT, A. E., and ZEUNER, F. E. *Man and Cattle* ("Royal Anthropological Institute of Great Britain and Ireland, Occasional Papers," No. 18). London: 1963.

MURPHY, GARDNER. *Human Potentialities*. New York: Basic Books, Inc., 1958.

SCHWANITZ, FRANZ. *The Origin of Cultivated Plants*. Cambridge, Mass.: Harvard University Press, 1966.

SCOTT, J. P. *Aggression*. Chicago: University of Chicago Press, 1958.

SINGER, CHARLES, HOLMYARD, E. J., and HALL, A. R. (eds.). *A History of Technology*. Vol. I. *From Early Times to Fall of Ancient Empires*. New York and London: Oxford University Press, 1954.

WALLACE, ANTHONY F. C. *Culture and Personality*. New York: Random House, Inc., 1961.

WOOLLEY, SIR LEONARD. *A History of Mankind*. Vol. I, Part II. *The Beginnings of Civilization*. New York: New American Library, Inc., and Harper & Row, 1965.

MENTAL PLAY AS A CULTURE MOTIVATION

BEACH, FRANK A. "Current Concepts of Play in Animals," *The American Naturalist*, LXXIX (November–December, 1945), 785.

CAILLOIS, ROGER. *Man, Play and Games*. Translated by Meyer Barash. New York: The Free Press of Glencoe, 1961.

HUIZINGA, JAN. *Homo Ludens: A Study of the Play Element in Culture*. London: Routledge & Kegan Paul, Ltd., 1949.

MITCHELL, C. P. *The Childhood of Animals*. New York: Frederick A. Stokes Company, 1912.

CULTURALLY RELATED MENTAL ABERRATIONS

BOSSELMAN, BEULAH C. *Self-Destruction: A Study of the Suicide Impulse*. Springfield, Ill.: Charles C Thomas, 1958.

DeROPP, ROBERT S. *Drugs and the Mind*. New York: Grove Press, 1961.

DUBLIN, LOUIS L. *Suicide: A Sociological and Statistical Study*. New York: Ronald Press, Inc., 1963.

DURKHEIM, ÉMILE. *Le Suicide*. Translated by J. A. Spaulding and G. Simpson. New York: The Free Press of Glencoe, 1951.

EATON, JOSEPH W., and WEIL, ROBERT J. *Culture and Mental Disorders: Comparative Study of Hutterites and Other Populations*. Glencoe, Ill.: The Free Press, 1955.

GINZBERG, E., and BRAY, D. W. *The Uneducated.* New York: Columbia University Press, 1953.

GLUECK, SHELDON, and GLUECK, ELEANOR T. *Unraveling Juvenile Delinquency.* New York: Commonwealth Fund, Inc., 1950.

HENRY, A. F., and SHORT, JAMES F., JR. *Suicide and Homicide.* Glencoe, Ill.: The Free Press, 1954.

KVARACEUS, WILLIAM C. *Juvenile Delinquency* ("National Education Association, Research Series, Bulletin No. 15"). Washington, D.C.: n.d.

KLINEBERG, OTTO. *Social Psychology.* New York: Henry Holt & Company, Inc., 1940.

LEIGHTON, ALEXANDER H. *My Name Is Legion.* New York: Basic Books, Inc., 1959.

——— *et al. Psychiatric Disorder among the Yoruba.* Ithaca, N.Y.: Cornell University Press, 1963.

LINTON, RALPH. *Culture and Mental Disorders.* Springfield, Ill.: Charles C Thomas, 1956.

McCORD, WILLIAM, McCORD, JOAN, and ZOLA, IRVING K. *Origins of Crime.* New York: Columbia University Press, 1959.

OPLER, MARVIN K. *Culture and Mental Health.* New York: The Macmillan Co., 1959.

PENFIELD, WILDER, and ROBERTS, LAMAR. *Speech and Brain-Mechanisms.* Princeton, N.J.: Princeton University Press, 1959.

SODDY, KENNETH (ed.). *Mental Health and Infant Development.* New York: Basic Books, Inc., 1956.

THE SIDE EFFECTS OF CIVILIZED LIVING

BELL, CLIVE. *Civilization.* London: Chatto & Windus, 1928.

BLUM, HAROLD F. "On the Origin and Evolution of Living Machines," *American Scientist,* XLIX, No. 4, 474–501.

DUBOS, RENÉ. *Man Adapting.* New Haven, Conn.: Yale University Press, 1965.

ENSIGN, FOREST C. *Compulsory School Attendance and Child Labor.* Iowa City, Iowa.: The Athens Press, 1921.

ERIKSON, ERIK H. *Childhood and Society.* New York: W. W. Norton & Company, Inc., 1950.

FARBER, SEYMOUR M., and WILSON, R. H. L. (eds.). *Control of the Mind: A Symposium.* New York: McGraw-Hill Book Company, Inc., 1961.

FRIEDMANN, GEORGES. *The Anatomy of Work: Labor, Leisure, and the Implications of Automation.* Translated by Wyatt Rawson. New York: The Free Press of Glencoe, 1961.

GINZBERG, ELI (ed.). *Technology and Social Change.* New York: Columbia University Press, 1964.

HOLMES, URBAN TIGER. *Daily Living in the Twelfth Century.* Madison, Wis.: University of Wisconsin Press, 1952.

LARRABEE, ERIC, and MEYERSOHN, ROLF (eds.). *Mass Leisure.* Glencoe, Ill.: The Free Press, 1958.

ROSENBERG, B., and WHITE, DAVID M. (eds.). *Mass Culture.* Glencoe, Ill.: The Free Press, 1959.

SMITH, ERNEST A. *American Youth Culture: Group Life in Teen-age Society.* New York: The Free Press of Glencoe, 1962.

VENN, GRANT. *Man, Education and Work.* Washington, D.C.: American Council on Education, 1964.

WADDINGTON, C. H. *The Ethical Animal.* Chicago: University of Chicago Press, 1967.

WEBER, ELIZABETH A. *The Duk-Duks: Primitive and Historic Types of Citizens.* Chicago: University of Chicago Press, 1929.

WEIL, ERIC. "Science in Modern Culture," *Science and Culture.* Edited by Gerald Holton, Boston: Houghton Mifflin Company, and the American Academy of Arts and Sciences, 1965.

WILLIAMS, R. M., JR. *American Society.* New York: Alfred A. Knopf, Inc., 1960.

INDEX

Index

apprenticeships, 253
Arapaho age-grades, 96
Arapesh of New Guinea, 68
Arunta hunters, 48, 136
athletic teams, 184
Australopithecus, 8, 9
Azande belief in sorcery, 100

Bantu, 96–99, 255
bees, 24, 25
bipedal locomotion, 13, 15
birds, potential for intelligence in, 27
birth rate as measure of strength, 237
bone fractures in arboreal life, 14
brain
  complex
    neoplastic pathology, 78
    play potential, 31, 48
    reaction to monotony, 143
    rule-setting propensity, 135
    self-willed stubbornness, 40
  dual function, 18, 134
  evolving, 16, 18
  geared to work, 133
  primate, 15
  receptor nerves, 17, 18
  record size, 40, 41
  released from social controls, 152
  subnormal functioning, 156
  tested in contests, 39
brain potential surplus, 21
brain potential threshold, 102

Caddis fly grubs, 26
Cambridge-Somerville study, 186, 189, 190
cannibalism, 165, 166

Caribou Eskimo, 153, 154
Carroll, Lewis, 228
Chaga, 96, 118
Chamacoco, 50
child labor, 211, 213, 214
  elaborated to the absurd, 252
child training
  age-grading systems, 91–96
  American Indians, 86
  herding gangs, 97, 98
  in primitive society, 81–84, 90
  supernatural disciplinarians, 82
children
  compulsory school assembly line, 168
  lack cultural objective, 126
  lack sense of identity, 182
  own culture, 97
  secret languages, 117, 118
  underprivileged group, 241
Choukoutien caves, 35–38
citizenship, 126
civilization
  modern
    basic conflicts, 177
    child's expectancies, 105–109
    crime in, 179
    difficult for children, 127, 130
    juvenile delinquency, 179
    key achievements, 104
    neglect of personality growth, 86
  modern American
    Cro-Magnon brain, 80
    increase in goods and services, 235
    individuals with low resistance to strain, 167
    juvenile outside adult economy, 119, 125

284

288

ABOUT THE AUTHOR

George A. Pettitt was born in Oakland, California. He received his A.B. in English Literature in 1926 and his Ph.D. in Anthropology in 1940 from the Univeristy of California at Berkeley. For 28 years he served as assistant to the president of the University of California, on a statewide basis, and at present he is a member of the Department of Anthropology at Berkeley. Dr. Pettitt is a member of Phi Beta Kappa and Sigma Xi and a Fellow of the American Anthropological Association. He was co-originator of The University Explorer, a weekly radio program translating science into lay language that is carried nationwide by CBS. Dr. Pettitt is the author of several scholarly books but this is his first major work for the layman.